Challenges Beque

TRANSGRESSIONS: CULTURAL STUDIES AND EDUCATION
Volume 46

Series Editors
  Shirley Steinberg, *McGill University, Canada*
  Joe Kincheloe, *McGill University, Canada*

Editorial Board
  Heinz-Hermann Kruger, *Halle University, Germany*
  Norman Denzin, *University of Illinois, Champaign-Urbana, USA*
  Rhonda Hammer, *University of California Los Angeles, USA*
  Christine Quail, *SUNY, Oneonta*
  Ki Wan Sung, *Kyung Hee University, Seoul, Korea*

Scope
Cultural studies provides an analytical toolbox for both making sense of educational practice and extending the insights of educational professionals into their labors. In this context *Transgressions: Cultural Studies and Education* provides a collection of books in the domain that specify this assertion. Crafted for an audience of teachers, teacher educators, scholars and students of cultural studies and others interested in cultural studies and pedagogy, the series documents both the possibilities of and the controversies surrounding the intersection of cultural studies and education. The editors and the authors of this series do not assume that the interaction of cultural studies and education devalues other types of knowledge and analytical forms. Rather the intersection of these knowledge disciplines offers a rejuvenating, optimistic, and positive perspective on education and educational institutions. Some might describe its contribution as democratic, emancipatory, and transformative. The editors and authors maintain that cultural studies helps free educators from sterile, monolithic analyses that have for too long undermined efforts to think of educational practices by providing other words, new languages, and fresh metaphors. Operating in an interdisciplinary cosmos, Transgressions: Cultural Studies and Education is dedicated to exploring the ways cultural studies enhances the study and practice of education. With this in mind the series focuses in a non-exclusive way on popular culture as well as other dimensions of cultural studies including social theory, social justice and positionality, cultural dimensions of technological innovation, new media and media literacy, new forms of oppression emerging in an electronic hyperreality, and postcolonial global concerns. With these concerns in mind cultural studies scholars often argue that the realm of popular culture is the most powerful educational force in contemporary culture. Indeed, in the twenty-first century this pedagogical dynamic is sweeping through the entire world. Educators, they believe, must understand these emerging realities in order to gain an important voice in the pedagogical conversation.

Without an understanding of cultural pedagogy's (education that takes place outside of formal schooling) role in the shaping of individual identity--youth identity in particular--the role educators play in the lives of their students will continue to fade. Why do so many of our students feel that life is incomprehensible and devoid of meaning? What does it mean, teachers wonder, when young people are unable to describe their moods, their affective affiliation to the society around them. Meanings provided young people by mainstream institutions often do little to help them deal with their affective complexity, their difficulty negotiating the rift between meaning and affect. School knowledge and educational expectations seem as anachronistic as a ditto machine, not that learning ways of rational thought and making sense of the world are unimportant.

But school knowledge and educational expectations often have little to offer students about making sense of the way they feel, the way their affective lives are shaped. In no way do we argue that analysis of the production of youth in an electronic mediated world demands some "touchy-feely" educational superficiality. What is needed in this context is a rigorous analysis of the interrelationship between pedagogy, popular culture, meaning making, and youth subjectivity. In an era marked by youth depression, violence, and suicide such insights become extremely important, even life saving. Pessimism about the future is the common sense of many contemporary youth with its concomitant feeling that no one can make a difference.

If affective production can be shaped to reflect these perspectives, then it can be reshaped to lay the groundwork for optimism, passionate commitment, and transformative educational and political activity. In these ways cultural studies adds a dimension to the work of education unfilled by any other sub-discipline. This is what Transgressions: Cultural Studies and Education seeks to produce— literature on these issues that makes a difference. It seeks to publish studies that help those who work with young people, those individuals involved in the disciplines that study children and youth, and young people themselves improve their lives in these bizarre times.

Challenges Bequeathed

Taking up the challenges of Dwayne Huebner

Patrick Lewis
University of Regina, Canada

Jennifer Tupper
University of Regina, Canada

SENSE PUBLISHERS
ROTTERDAM/BOSTON /TAIPEI

A C.I.P. record for this book is available from the Library of Congress.

ISBN 978-90-8790-832-4 (paperback)
ISBN 978-90-8790-833-1 (hardback)
ISBN 978-90-8790-834-8 (e-book)

Published by: Sense Publishers,
P.O. Box 21858, 3001 AW
Rotterdam, The Netherlands
http://www.sensepublishers.com

Printed on acid-free paper

All Rights Reserved © 2009 Sense Publishers

No part of this work may be reproduced, stored in a retrieval system, or transmitted in any form or by any means, electronic, mechanical, photocopying, microfilming, recording or otherwise, without written permission from the Publisher, with the exception of any material supplied specifically for the purpose of being entered and executed on a computer system, for exclusive use by the purchaser of the work.

DEDICATION

Dwayne E. Huebner

CONTENTS

    ACKNOWLEDGEMENTS   ix

    FOREWORD   xi
    David G. Smith

    Introducing Challenges Bequeathed: Taking up the Challenges
    of Dwayne Huebner   xvii
    P. J. Lewis & Jennifer Tupper

1. Challenges Bequeathed   1
   Dwayne Huebner

2. Who in this Culture Speaks for Children and Youth?   13
   P. J. Lewis

3. Writing Lives, Writing Worlds: Literacy as Autobiographical
   and Cosmopolitan Text   25
   Erika Hasebe-Ludt

4. Imagining Otherwise: Tantalizing Tales from the Centre   39
   Karen Meyer & Carl Leggo

5. Imagination and Inner Literacies of a Teaching Consciousness   51
   Leah Fowler

6. Schooling Memories: Surpassing the Technical
   with Education Largesse   66
   James McNinch

7. Giving Voice to the Voiceless: Advocacy for Transient
   Children and Youth   82
   Barbara McNeil

8. And Carry on as Though Nothing Happened   99
   Valerie Mulholland

9. Disrupting the Discourse of Public Education:
   A Conversation with Dwayne Huebner   115
   Jennifer A. Tupper

TABLE OF CONTENTS

10. A Somewhere Middle: Undoing Illusions of the Discrete in Times
    of Curricular Contradictions   127
    Lace Marie Brogden

11. Foucault and the Lure of the Transcendent: Curriculum
    Knowledge, Schooling, and the Public World   143
    Douglas Brown

12. Encountering Hope—Ten Meditations Towards Utopia
    in a Phd Program   161
    Heather Ritenburg

13. Surpassing the Technical: A Friendlier Discourse   173
    Wendy Donawa

    NOTES ON CONTRIBUTORS   187

ACKNOWLEDGEMENTS

The editors wish to gratefully acknowledge Lawrence Erlbaum Associates Inc, a division of Taylor and Francis Group for permission to reproduce, Huebner, D. (1999). Challenges Bequeathed. In V. Hillis (Ed.), *The Lure of the transcendent, Collected Essays by Dwayne E. Huebner* (pp. 432–445). Mahwah, NJ: Lawrence Erlbaum Associates.

We would also like to thank all the contributors to this volume and David Geoffrey Smith for his very thoughtful foreword. To our families we thank you for your support and understanding. To my friend and colleague, Jennifer Tupper, I thank you for your willingness to accompany me on this adventure. And to Patrick Lewis, gratitude for conceiving of the book and inviting me to work alongside you as a friend and colleague in this worthwhile endeavour. However, most importantly we wish to thank Dwayne E. Huebner for his teachings, inspiration and his encouragement for pursuing this project.

FOREWORD

The invitation to write this *Foreword* has bestowed on me a great honour, although the task ahead is at once daunting and humbling. Dwayne Huebner's direct as well as latent legacy in the field of Curriculum Studies is immense, as the essays in this wonderful book attest.

Insofar as I have been trying in recent years to challenge the hyperverbalism of the Western tradition's rather distorted comprehension of the Word (Gk. *Logos*), (as if we can talk, read and write ourselves into existence), anything put forth here may be hypocritical. Still, to paraphrase the wisdom writer of *Ecclesiastes*, there must be a time to speak as much as a time to be silent, and even the Buddha had to verbally exhort his disciples to be quiet if they wanted to learn how to live. All this is to plunge directly into a central theme in Dwayne Huebner's work, namely a concern for language and the necessity of attending to it with utmost care for its absences as much for what is present in it – at least if we want to better understand who we are, where we have been and where we are going. I'll come back to this theme later.

Inevitably too, all real knowing is personal, another theme in Huebner's work. Knowledge, to be such, must take up habitation in persons, and participate in their embodiment. This is where my own involvement in this project comes into focus, and for me there has seemed a certain cosmic quality at play. Patrick Lewis, one of the editors, was a student in a graduate course in Curriculum Inquiry I taught at the University of Victoria in the early 1990s. It was one of those courses every instructor has occasionally. I thought things didn't go that well, and felt badly about it for years. Even more years later, I met Patrick at a conference, and by that time he had his Ph.D. When he expressed how much he'd appreciated the course, I was instantly healed, but more importantly reminded that as teachers we never know when seeds are being planted that will bear fruit far into the future, to which the response to Huebner's work also bears witness. There's a connection here too with the co-editor, Jennifer Tupper. She was one of our excellent doctoral students at the University of Alberta where in my Curriculum Foundations course she would have read at least one of Dwayne Huebner's papers. When Jennifer accepted a position at the University of Regina, she met Patrick, and this important collaboration began.

Obviously Dwayne Huebner is the lynchpin in the ever-expanding web of relations to which this book gives notice, and I need to say a few words about my own somewhat limited, yet for me very significant connections with him as a prelude to some more pointed comments later. The year was 1976 and I was rather unhappily enrolled in an M.A. program at the University of British Columbia, writhing under the burden of the positivism dominating graduate studies in education at the time. In desperation, I went to the university bookstore to see if *anyone* was taking up educational questions as questions about human living, rather than just as technical questions about how to fix this or that, including

FOREWORD

children, according to some pre-given unquestioned normative paradigm. Suddenly my eyes fell on Eisner and Vallance's *Conflicting Conceptions of Curriculum* (1975). Philip Phenix's essay, "Curriculum and Transcendence" was the first to open randomly in my hands, and reading a single paragraph was enough to convince me that this was a true path. I looked down at the shelf to determine the course instructor's name. "T. Aoki". I rushed back to the Education building to see if this person might be there, and he was, as the new Director of the Centre for the Study of Curriculum and Instruction, freshly ensconced in one of the old army huts still in use at the time. After half an hour's discussion with "Ted", he said, "Come and work with me." Then he put into my hands a book he had just received himself, William Pinar's *Curriculum Theorizing: The Reconceptualists* (1975): "Read this. It's important." I took it back to my tiny apartment where the first piece to fall open was Dwayne Huebner's 1966 essay, "Curricular Language and Classroom Meanings", which I devoured like a starving man. Within a single day, everything that would determine the next thirty years of my life fell into place.

In 1978 Ted Aoki returned to the University of Alberta as Chair of the Department of Secondary Education, and on his encouragement I went too, to become the first doctoral student of newly appointed Max Van Manen, Ted's former doctoral student, who was beginning to develop his long range project in phenomenology and pedagogy. Max knew of Dwayne Huebner's interest in phenomenology and other human sciences, so together Max and Ted invited Dwayne to the University of Alberta to give a lecture to the full faculty. I was fortunate enough to be Dwayne's chauffeur during that visit, and shared several meals and good conversation with him and others, but never saw him again afterwards.

The reference above to the 1966 essay "Curricular Language and Classroom Meanings" is pertinent to what I think may be the most important dimension of Dwayne Huebner's contribution to educational scholarship as a whole, not just curriculum scholarship, and that is his prescience, his ability to see, years in advance of everyone else, what is deeply at work in present times, where it is headed, and what needs to be done about it, especially in terms of social healing. When the essay first appeared in Pinar's book, it had already been circulating for almost ten years, its relevance only growing in stature. I still use it in my Curriculum Foundations course.

In his introduction to the collected works of Dwayne Huebner (*The Lure of Transcendence,* edited by Vicky Hillis 1999), Bill Pinar notes this distinctive prophetic quality of Huebner:

> Consider the following: a decade before political issues would consume a wing of the field, Huebner was writing about the importance of political theory to curriculum studies. Fifteen years before phenomenology would emerge as an important discourse in the field, Huebner was studying Heidegger and Jaspers. Nearly a decade before Joseph Schwab judged the field moribund, Huebner declared the field lacked vitality. And twenty years before religious and theological studies would constitute a major sector of

curriculum scholarship, Huebner was studying transcendence while teaching courses at the Union Theological Seminary in New York.... (p. xv)

In 1980 I accompanied Ted Aoki to the annual meeting of the Association for Supervision and Curriculum Development (ASCD) to give a paper there, in St. Louis, Missouri, and was introduced to Alice Miel, a generational cohort of Huebner's. While waiting together for an airport shuttle, we mentioned that Dwayne had recently been at the University of Alberta, and Alice immediately declared of him, "Dwayne Huebner is our prophet."

So far as I know, nobody has taken up for serious examination the role of prophecy in educational inquiry. Of course we have our futurologists, cheap prognosticators, armchair wand-wavers and trajectory specialists, but what Huebner represents is surely something quite different. His is the hermeneutic ability to see in the details of everyday life and practice things of much larger import, and if this ability has any value for our work as contemporary scholars, perhaps it behooves us to explore what makes it possible. Like any true poet, genuinely creative person, or indeed prophet, Huebner himself may be largely unaware of the specific processes involved, at least in a self-conscious sense, all of his writing on imagination, art and aesthetics notwithstanding.

At this point I refer to an article written by biblical scholar Walter Conrad Klein on prophecy and prophets that first appeared in James Hastings's *Dictionary of the Bible* in 1963. While Klein's study is primarily of the Hebrew prophets, he notes that "no ancient society would have done without" such a person, with many traits, habits and methods held in common. The amazing range of scholarship in *Challenges Bequeathed* bears witness to an important aspect of prophetic inspiration generally: "Prophecy has nothing to say to a merely curious humanity. Its particularities must be accepted, and when they are, it is discovered that they are susceptible of infinite engagement." (Klein, p. 809).

The first task of prophecy according to Klein is to "break the people's faith in the ritual stereotype of destiny (conquest, prosperity and honour...)" and bring them back to their most fundamental responsibility i.e. faith in the One who has created them, and to live righteously and justly. Indeed it is estrangement from God, the personal creator of human beings who desires to live personally with his creatures, that is the root cause of an "aimlessness that is worse than death." In the words of the prophet Amos, "Seek Him and live" (Amos 5:4). "Creation has a goal, and the proper role of man (sic) is to contribute to the attainment of the goal." (p. 808). Running away from that responsibility in the name of self-interest, rebellion, pride, forgetfulness, indifference, self-satisfied ignorance etc. is the nature of sin, a conscious standing over against goodness and divine intention. The essence of sin is to deliberately "miss the point" (Gk. *hamartia*) of human life.

The prophetic view is to see human beings as divinely gifted but possessed of "a fatal ability to foul the world that God has given (them)" (p. 807). In the words of the prophet Isaiah: "And he expected honesty, but beheld homicide/And righteousness, but behold wretchedness" (Isaiah. 5:7). This "fatal ability" however is never beyond redemption. Prophecy is always a summons to repentance – to return to fidelity, and forgiveness is always granted. Redemption involves a "reconstituted nature in a re-energized universe" (p. 808). This basic dialectic can be summed up in the words of two Hebrew prophets: "The person who sins shall die" (Ezekiel 18:4); and "The righteous shall live by his faithfulness (Habakkuk2: 4).

If the above briefly describes the theology that inspires prophecy, this is not to be understood abstractly. Indeed it is precisely the mark of true prophecy that it is temporally and existentially specific. That is, the true prophet identifies the specific characteristics of sin in his own specific time. As Klein suggests, "All prophetic teaching…is given under the stimulus of a situation and is meant primarily to show how corporate righteousness is to be maintained in the face of the unfamiliar difficulties of the situation" (p. 808). It is on this point that I think we come back to Dwayne Huebner. There is throughout Huebner's *oeuvre* a deeply passionate righteous indignation that the specific political, philosophical and cultural assumptions and practices of our time are too narrow and constraining, that the fuller range of human potentiality is being undercut. Huebner's later writings in particular reveal that behind this passionate concern for the human condition is a profound love of God. Reflect on the five challenges bequeathed and one finds the basic grammar of the prophetic call: "surpass" any understanding of education that is purely instrumental or technical, tied to the material realm alone; "affirm the imagination" as what can draw one out of oneself and one's circumstances, i.e. to be open to That which can lead us to new worlds; use the "world's" (Gk. *aeon*) intellectual achievements and not be stuck in parochial understandings so often tied to blind and naïve patriotism and other ills; and engage in "public" discourse about education because what goes on in education should concern us all, not just special or private interests. Interestingly, Huebner's last challenge concerning speaking out for children and youth reiterates a strong theme in classical prophecy. In the prophet Malachi's vision of redeemed community, the prophet Elijah "will turn the hearts of fathers to their children…" (Malachi 4:6) In other words, inattention to the needs of children is a mark of grave sin.

One final point about the prophetic tradition is worth mentioning. Klein emphasizes, "while…prophecy utilizes cultic facilities, it remains an essentially autonomous force, never wholly explicable in cultic terms" (p. 801). This is important because it underscores how an effective prophet must necessarily live and operate *within* the context he or she decries. Prophecy is never armchair theorizing about 'other' people; prophecy is always about 'us', and it is practiced in the veins, arteries and capillaries of institutions like schools and universities without succumbing to their idolatrous capitulations. Again, Huebner is exemplary.

To sum up here, my resounding purpose in directly linking Dwayne Huebner to the prophetic tradition is pedagogical. If as graduate students and colleagues we find Huebner's work inspiring, I think we are under some obligation to try to better understand Huebner's own inspiration. Of course this can never be a matter of pure reduction; indeed the whole prophetic tradition speaks implicitly against this, to the importance of honouring the freedom of God and persons to act freely and autonomously, not fettered by convention or context. There is a way in which the ultimate source of human inspiration cannot be named, and that any attempt to do so actually violates inspiration itself. Such is the nature of true faith, living without 'knowing'. So the Hebrews understood/understand that God actually cannot be named fully, just as LaoTzu said: "That which can be named is not the Constant

Name". The deepest Way of life defies any *a priori* reduction in language. To be human is to live ever more fully in the presence of Presence, i.e. to be ever more fully present, to be here, to attend to what needs to be done now, to take up responsibility for co-creation with the creator. How can this be done? Are there manners of preparation that can facilitate its possibility, and if so do they have pedagogical relevance?

Ironically the biggest impediment today to the kind of human maturity to which authentic prophecy calls us may in fact be the god concept itself. Generally I am sympathetic to the rants against god belief by people like Christopher Hitchins (*God is not great: How religion poisons everything*) and Richard Dawkins (*The God delusion*). This is because we live in a time when even the most radical monotheisms have been conflated with specific, narrow temporal agendas, whether they be the invisible hand of the Market, democracy, land of the free, or war against the infidel. What happens under such circumstances is a forgetfulness of the necessary dynamic between the specific and the universal, between 'this' commitment and everything that lies beyond it. Eventually 'this' becomes so full of itself that it either implodes or explodes, or, through a process William Irwin Thompson (1987) calls "enantiomorphism", turns into its opposite. The Market crashes, democracy becomes an instrument of tyranny, freedom becomes unfreedom, and fidelity against the infidel a call to suicide.

Does this mean we should give up on "God"? That will never happen, since deep within the human imagination is the realization that we are always more than 'this', this set of circumstances which are always subject to the limits of our interpretive ability of the moment. A most telling image in Al Gore's *An Inconvenient Truth* is of the planet Earth taken from millions of miles out in space. For the first time in the human story we can see ourselves for what we are, a tiny dot within the infinite expanse of all there is. Perhaps it's time to shift from our petty theories of difference to a new understanding of our commonality, our human unity, with an ancillary effort required to re-imagine and re-articulate what "God" might mean and be for us. Actually such a task turns us backward as much as forward, to the ancient wisdom of prophets and mystics. The prophets, we have heard from here already, with Dwayne Huebner a contemporary witness. W. H. Auden, another more contemporary prophet, and poet, once remarked, "If there is to be a twenty-first century, it will be mystical."

Below I cite a sixteenth century poem from one of the Western tradition's greatest mystics, Juan de Yepes, better known as John of the Cross (1987), author of the term "the God beyond all knowing":

> *To come to the pleasure you have not*
>   *you must go by the way you enjoy not*
> *To come to the knowledge you have not*
>   *you must go by a way in which you know not*
> *To come to the possession you have not*
>   *you must go by a way in which you possess not*
> *To come to be which you are not*
>   *you must go by a way in which you are not.*

FOREWORD

Those familiar with Eastern wisdom traditions will recognize in John's words what has long been recognized, that 'this' and 'not this' always exist in an organic unity. In today's world, which as I write seems to be at the end of something as much as at a beginning, this call to recover the 'negative' constitutes a call not just for a new way of knowing and being; it articulates the basis of ethics. Reach out to the stranger; investigate what you think you hate for it may bear the news of how to love; lasting pleasure cannot be found in trying to secure what gives you pleasure now; do not cling to your possessions or they will possess you; be open to what you are yet to become.

Can these words be translated into the work of curriculum, teaching/pedagogy and scholarship today? I think the essays in this book, each in its own way, serves in affirmation.

David Geoffrey Smith
University of Alberta

REFERENCES

Dawkins, R. (2008). *The God delusion*. London: Mariner Books.
Eisner, E., & Vallance, E. (Eds.). (1974). *Conflicting conceptions of curriculum*. Berkeley, CA: McCutcheon.
Hitchins, C. (2007). *God is not great*. London: Twelve Books, Hachette Book Group.
John of the Cross. (1987). *Selected writings* (K. Kavanaugh, Ed.). New York: Paulist Press.
Klein, W. (1963). Prophecy, prophets. In J. Hastings (Ed.), *Dictionary of the Bible* (pp. 800–809). New York: Scribners.
Pinar, W. (1975). *Curriculum theorists: The reconceptualists*. Berkeley, CA: McCutcheon.
Thompson, W. (1987). The cultural implications of the new biology. In W. Thompson (Ed.), *GAIA: A way of knowing*. Great Barrington, MA: Lindisfarne Press.

P. J. LEWIS & JENNIFER TUPPER

INTRODUCING CHALLENGES BEQUEATHED: TAKING UP THE CHALLENGES OF DWAYNE HUEBNER

In 1999 a book entitled, *The Lure of the Transcendent: Collected Essays by Dwayne E. Huebner*, was published. It was to be the last piece of work by Dwayne Huebner from his 40 plus years in educational research and teaching. The final chapter in that book, "Challenges Bequeathed" was written in 1996. In that essay Professor Huebner put forward five challenges to educators and then discussed each of them in turn. The five challenges are:
– Surpass the technical foundations of education
– Affirm the significance of the imagination
– Use the world's intellectual traditions and achievements
– Engage in public discourse about education.
– Speak out for children and youth.

In this book we invited a group of scholars to each take up one of the educational challenges bequeathed by Dwayne Huebner. Contributors from a variety of backgrounds and interests have extended, and in some ways transcended, the discussion of these five challenges. The first chapter is that of the title by Dwayne Huebner wherein he delineates the challenges for educators, as he perceived them. We invite readers to begin with this chapter. However, after taking in Professor Huebner's "prescience, his ability to see, years in advance of everyone else, what is deeply at work in present times, where it is headed, and what needs to be done about it..." (Smith, this volume) we encourage readers to dip into this volume randomly rather than in sequential order. While doing so, it is important to be mindful that "these challenges do not exist in isolation of each other; rather they are inextricably linked in myriad ways. Each one of these challenges requires consideration of classroom spaces, the individuals who occupy these spaces, and how these spaces are influenced by external forces" (Tupper this volume).

Leah Fowler takes up the challenge to "affirm the significance of the imagination" both demonstratively and rhetorically as we join in with select dinner guests from across human memory to unravel the "meaning" and import of imagination; a task tantamount to unraveling the Gordian Knot. It is the story, the stories of self and Other, intricately woven together that must be thoughtfully listened to and reflected upon in those inner spaces where we might "imagine if it could be otherwise". The world is imagined and this is what we have imagined; can we transcend this through the lure of the transcendent? In her own words she declares,

> I want to hear and tell both autobiographical and theoretical discourse, to hear and tell both the Grand Narratives and the petit récits. I want to engage memory, perception, and imagination so that the everyday world as problematic is opened, questioned, and re-understood – to enlarge both the boundaries of discourses, and the meaning and quality of our lives. (this volume)

And in that reciprocal process of listening and telling, she sees that the, "narrative line of each discipline is an invitation to the young to participate in the great chain of being, to find a generative place for contributing to the actual and possible world."

Drawing on her lived experiences as a teacher and teacher educator, as a person dwelling between worlds and always in the midst of shifting locations, Erika Hasebe-Ludt eloquently and thoughtfully responds to Huebner's challenges through her exploration of the importance of life writing and the necessary tensions that emerge in and through this practice. She engages autobiographical writing in an effort to be wide awake in the world, to make sense of its messiness, complexities and 'great untruths'. With the teacher education students she works with, Hasebe-Ludt illuminates how we may author new pedagogical texts as a continual process of (re)creating self and other. She takes seriously the process of pedagogical becoming, of mapping ourselves, of attending to the "vulnerable, fluid place between knowing and being" (Hasebe-Ludt, this volume) reminding us of the importance of learning to see with our hearts so that we may be and become in the midst of difference.

Karen Meyer and Carl Leggo take up the challenge "affirm the significance of the imagination" through the story of their lived experience of maneouvring in and through "the centre" of a large Faculty of Education; a *Centre for the Study of Curriculum and Instruction*. It is a journey that is sometimes reminiscent of Derrida's (1972) notion, in that the centre is both within and without so it is neither. It is elsewhere (p. 248), where we are not. And yet, in that realization they come to know the fragility of our world and the imaginative possibilities of building community at the centre. The centre, it would seem, is at the heart; it is at the heart of relationship, of listening the story of others into being and the requital gesture from the storyteller. So, they ask of themselves and the academy, how might we re-imagine ourselves?

Throughout his chapter, Patrick Lewis speaks out for and with children and youth as he critiques policy and legislation that fails to consider the "local needs of children" (Lewis, this volume); educational policy that renders children powerless and voiceless in a system where care and hope are so often elusive. He issues an eloquent cry for children and teachers to journey together in reciprocity, to participate collaboratively in surpassing the technical foundations of education that continue to inform the ways in which education is conceived and delivered in school systems across North America. "It is through the act of being present in our living and teaching with children that we may *do* the most", writes Lewis, as he challenges us to step outside of officially sanctioned curriculum ever mindful of our relational, storied and fluid being. In his acknowledgment of the profound role of story(ies) in who we are as learners and teachers and who we might become as human beings, Lewis reminds us of the epistemological and ontological significance of narrative imagining for curriculum and education. Teachers must become storytellers and story listeners, always considering their own stories, the stories of the institutions in which they work, and the stories of their students, if they hope to surpass the traditions, the technical foundations of education that render the lives of students meaningless in current curricular spaces.

Douglas Brown, in taking up the challenge to "surpass the technical foundations of education", reminds us of the difficult ground work carried out by Dwayne Huebner in his questioning and critiquing of the legacy of Bobbit, Charters, and the Tylerian rationale which influenced what became known as the reconceptualization movement. In so doing, he (re)calls the concomitant struggles and challenges inherent in the public institution called school and the possibilities of what that might be, juxtaposed with what was and what is. In delineating Huebner's critical view of school/curriculum, Brown weaves us through the machinations of the political and its inherent power by drawing on the post-structural notions of Foucault in order to brush the critique across the canvas of the critiquer. The result is a dynamic theoretical under-painting of Huebner's theoretical works that calls for "a more critical educational path" with Focauldian post-structural intrigues. As Brown suggests, "Huebner is searching", searching through "a power that moves beyond traditional hierarchies of interpretation moving towards a more circular and capillary presence"; it is a search for a more humane, democratic and emancipatory place that we imagine as school.

Through a series of ten meditations, Heather Ritenburg invites us to heed Huebner's call to affirm the significance of the imagination. First into spaces of exile, next into spaces of dreams and imaginings, and then into spaces of hope, we dance through the words, thoughts, and poetics offered in this chapter. Grounded in her own experiences as a doctoral student occupying theoretical and pedagogical spaces of tension, Ritenburg offers a creative and critical representation of her own curricular process. She grapples with the possibilities of education when we step outside of tradition in our journey toward hope, in our journey toward utopia. In both words and form, this chapter takes seriously the significance of the imagination as integral to thinking anew our relationships to curriculum, teaching and learning.

James McNinch autobiographically demonstrates the importance of trying to "surpass the technical foundations of education". He reminds teachers, nay everyone, that words, a phrase, comment or quip may have an unimaginable affect upon the being who is in receipt of them. Words and the stories we create from them can have a profound, sometimes life-forming influence upon us. It is not that Mr. C. our grade 5 teacher taught us how to do long division nor the concept of the planetary waltz of our solar system; he was in relationship with us for some 197 days that year and we made memories—stories of self and the other that are part of the narrative process of our becoming in a place called school.

In her chapter, Lace Marie Brogden asks "how might we, as curriculum theorists, adopt critical and imaginative intellectual positions as we conceive the work we have yet to do?" (Brogden, this volume) as she responds to Huebner's challenge to use the world's intellectual traditions and achievements. Drawing on myriad theoretical approaches and theorists, her writing challenges the dominance of technicality, of Tylerian sensibilities which are ubiquitous in curricular spaces of learning and being. She offers altered readings of curricular art/if/acts through a series of juxtapositions in which she re:reads curriculum objectives and re:writes the lesson plan. It is with/in these juxtapositions that Brogden creates a 'somewhere middle' for her reader where spaces of uncertainty lead to possibility which lead to curriculum.

Barbara McNeil takes up the challenge of "speaking out for children and youth"; however, she speaks out for a particular group of children and youth—the transient child. She asks, who advocates for accommodating, no, for pedagogical sensitivity to the lived-experience of this significant group of children and youth whose circumstances propel them from school to school multiple times from September to June each year? Their stories loiter around the periphery of the dominant narrative that is promulgated as a year in school. Schools, and all those who live and work there with transient children need to "adopt approaches to curriculum that will consider and respond to the totality of the students as persons experiencing systemic hardships that arise from the social and political context of their schooling" (McNeil, this volume) and in so doing they might listen the child into being. And in that listening, teachers need to *be with* transient children and youth in the language of school so that they might negotiate and manoeuvre successfully through a world that is often strange, unfamiliar, perhaps, even dangerous, to them.

In Wendy Donawa's chapter, friendship and the simultaneous notions of empathy and trust are at the heart of her inquiry of surpassing the technical. Through the mindfulness that is attendant in friendship, we may find a path that transcends the seductive and alluring promise of the technical not only in teaching but as it pervades the quotidian. Everyday life in North America is infused with the technical; if Huxley were alive he most certainly would see the manifestation of his *Brave New World* and how it has affected human beings in ways not even he imagined. However, she reminds us that "attunement-based relationships (parental, pedagogical) have always structured human experience" (Donawa, this volume) and it is through such relationships that we may find a path to surpass the technical. She delineates a theory and practice of friendship as a template for self understanding and inquiry that requires the integration of four qualities: imaginative empathy, trust, reflexivity, and narrative connection.

Valerie Mulholland takes up Huebner's challenge to engage in public discourse about education as she interrogates the officially sanctioned story of school and community revealed in and through the imagery of art displayed in common public spaces. She invites the reader into her gallery of words and images as she draws on post-colonial theory to examine and critique the landscape created in and through art, museums and monuments in Saskatchewan. She sees this art as representative of the discourse system at work in schools, a system which privileges white-settler identity and history. A similar critique is levied at the English Language Arts curriculum in Saskatchewan as students are invited to read particular texts demonstrative of particular ideology. If art in public spaces is revealing of the white-settler narrative that permeates the stories students learn in Saskatchewan schools, it is also revealing of a curriculum "of amnesia" (Mulholland, this volume) that renders absent and/or voiceless the historical and contemporary experiences of First Nations peoples. Mulholland implores us as educators to engage in public discourse about the on-going process of colonization inherent in the visual landscapes of curriculum, schools, and society.

Jennifer Tupper engages in a conversation with Huebner's writings and in so doing she disrupts the discourse of public education. Public discourse can and does affect educational practices, but more importantly we must recall that those practices and the institutions that house them are inherently political and ideological, enacted and/or disrupted by those who live there—children, youth, parents and teachers. However, the official story told of school is often in juxtaposition to how the story of school is lived by children and youth. The sanctioned curriculum enjoys a hegemonic privilege so pervasive that it allows little space for students or teachers to manoeuvre imaginatively in the creation of their own stories. The discourse of accountability has become the aegis under which public education hones standards into standardization. Tupper, through a series of narratives "attempts to complicate, disrupt, interrupt, rupture the discourse of accountability", in order to lay bare how such a discourse "effects classroom acts in real and often political ways" (Tupper, this volume).

REFERENCES

Derrida, J. (1972). Structure, sign, and play in the discourse of the human sciences. In R. Macksey & E. Donato (Eds.), *The structuralist controversy* (pp. 247–272). Baltimore: The John Hopkins Press.

DWAYNE HUEBNER

CHALLENGES BEQUEATHED[1]

The story line of how my thinking developed over nearly fifty years seems much less important than my current awareness of the challenges faced by educators. I do not seek to explain the pathways that led me to recognize and articulate these challenges, although a perusal of the previous chapters may provide clues to those pathways. Nor will I endeavor to convince others that I see truly. In as much as I no longer gain much pleasure from reading current curriculum literature, I plead ignorance about whether these challenges are being worked on or even sensed by others. My intent is merely to bequeath five challenges to those interested in my earlier work. They are to:
– Surpass the technical foundations of education,
– Affirm the significance of the imagination,
– Use the world's intellectual traditions and achievements
– Engage in public discourse about education.
– Speak out for children and youth.

SURPASS THE TECHNICAL FOUNDATIONS OF EDUCATION

The positivistic and technical aspects of education have been frequently criticized by me and a host of others. Testing, textbooks programmed material, media, competency based teaching, as well as the undergirding intellectual structures such as learning theory and some developmental theories, have all been grist for the mills of criticism. Some of the criticism has been unwarranted, and suggests mere frustration or irresponsibility. Much has been well deserved. To attend to the appropriateness or inappropriateness of criticism, however, hides the more significant factor—that criticism is an important aspect of our work. Marcuse calls attention to this by his valuing of negation. Tillich argues that protest against form is necessary for the continual creation of the human world. But Hegel is the primary source with his articulation of the dialectic of thesis, antithesis, and synthesis. To surpass does not mean to discard, but to identify significant achievements and their accompanying new problems, and to move to a different level of human life. In education this means recognizing achievements and losses that accompany the research of the past seven decades, acknowledging new problems and identifying their possible resolutions. It means being about the next stage in the history of intentional education. To participate responsibly in history one must criticize *and* create. To surpass the technical foundations of education,

then, requires historical awareness of where we once were, sensitivity to present problems, resistances and binds, and openness to future possibilities. To label any particular development a "movement" is to hide the historical continuity and the dialectical processes which led to that development, a substitute for hard historical work. Labeling undermines awareness of the historical relationships among thesis, antithesis, and synthesis. We need to better understand such things as the following:
- How testing became such a significant influence in educational decisions, practices and thought, and the reasons for the overwhelming acceptance of the work of Thorndike and his followers.
- Why William Torrey Harris made more of an impact on schooling and its administration than Dewey,
- How the work of Bobbitt, Charters, and Tyler and their lineage became so instrumental in curriculum.
- How the growth of AERA from about a thousand or so in the early nineteen fifties to about twenty-three thousand now has influenced educational thought and practice.

Specifically, what is to be surpassed with respect to the use of the technical achievements of the past fifty years and the positivistic modes of reflection accompanying them? First, as many have pointed out, these practices and modes of thought do not depict the complexity, or even begin to approach the mystery, of the human condition. The beauty and tragedy of the new human being's journey with others and their prejudices, cultural accouterments, and power is glossed over. Technical views of persons need to be surpassed. Progress has been and continues to be made on this problem. The educational process (an aspect of that mystery) and educational institutions (manifestations of the prejudices, cultural accouterments, and power) can never be encompassed by a single intellectual form or structural arrangement.

Next, the technical fall out from the scientific movements of the past seven decades has contributed significantly to the creation of educational environments, which Dewey[2] identified in 1916 as central to education. We surpass that achievement when the power to build environments is gratefully acknowledged and its various ramifications explored. To compare the classrooms of today with those of the first thirty years of this century, or the wealth of educational resources today with the limited resources that accompanied the McGuffey readers, is to glimpse and appreciate that power. Learning theories have reshaped educational materials and teacher behaviors. Cognitive theories and the explorations of knowledge structures have sharpened educational purposes, improved the sequencing of educational materials and led to the construction of diagnostic instruments. Information processing knowledge and its instruments, (computers and communication tools) have altered the relationships among people and their use of language and symbols. The power to fabricate educational environments has increased many fold in the past fifty years. This is a wonderful and significant achievement.

However, the technical must become a subsidiary language for educators, a tool that helps build educational environments. A more inclusive language net is required if more consequential questions and problems are to be entertained. It should call attention to the variety of fabricated environments available in this culture and ask about their relative worth and larger social function. The environments available for children and youth should be contrasted with other environments in a culture. In the large cities of Chicago, New York and Washington, D.C., and elsewhere, run down schools come to mind. Parks, alleys, rooftops, crowded one room apartments, stoops and streets, and perhaps playgrounds are other spaces used by children and youth. The environments built for or available to children and youth illustrate the poverty of our culture. Schools are often in poor physical shape. They often lack aesthetic qualities. But more significantly they lack the qualities that permit morally gratifying relationships among people. Compare the environments created for children and youth with the environments created for the corporate elite. Today's corporate headquarters are some of the most exquisite architectural spaces created in this country-spaces designed with sensitivity to the work needs and ease of social relationships of the people they house, and enhanced with works of art. They illustrate the wealth of our culture. Schools are usually designed for functional efficiency, without much sensitivity to the work needs or social relationships of teachers and students and without aesthetic qualities. Corporate headquarters are often designed as symbols-representative of the values of the corporation and the culture. Who asks about the symbolic function or the aesthetic quality of the buildings known as schools? The architectural creativity financed by corporations is a business expense, using pre-taxed dollars of the corporations (although the resulting building and facilities are taxed per the local property tax codes with tax abatement to entice them to build one place rather than another). Imagine what could be achieved if the expenses of building new corporate headquarters were taxed to help finance the creation of spaces for children and youth. A small percentage of the wealth used to build symbolic and beautiful structures for the corporate elites could be used to provide beauty and morally redeeming space for the young of this society, the future corporate leaders and the producers and consumers of their products and services.

Another contrast is of the poverty of the symbolic world of the schools with the wealth (not necessarily the beauty) of the symbolic worlds of the mass media. Businesses spend millions of dollars educating consumers to purchase their goods and services, via the media, a pre-tax expenditure. This educational form is known as advertising. Advertising attempts to shape desire and value. So do schools, usually with meager resources. What would happen if all advertising was taxed to provide new educational resources for children and youth? If but a portion of the money spent to educate people via media was spent for the cultural social and moral education of children and youth the schools would be vastly different cultural spaces.

Third, these technical developments have led to significant shifts in power, both within the educational establishment and in the relationship between the educational establishment and the larger social order. The technologies of textbook making and test construction have resulted in powerful new industries that influence local decision makers and school teachers. The information processing industries have become another powerful group in the political mix, as TV, computer and information highway people seek income and influence by educating children and youth. The rhetoric associated with these industries shapes public discourse and influences public thinking about education. For instance the rhetoric of tests and test scores has become an extremely powerful vehicle for talking about schools, hiding or covering other markers that also depict school quality. Talk about linking every classroom to the information highway displaces other kinds of talk about schools- school libraries, the quality of educational materials, the moral qualities of classroom action. Rhetoric shaped by technical interests rather than educational interests influences public perception about the nature of education and thus grants undue power to people with technical interests who sway the minds and affections of young people. To truly surpass the technical foundations of education demands that these shifts in power be understood and confronted.

These are the kinds of questions that result from the efforts to surpass the present technical modes of thought and practice that now dominate education. Other questions can be asked if the technical is seen as auxiliary, rather than primary, and if other phenomena of the social world are juxtaposed against the formal and informal structures that educate children and youth.

AFFIRM THE SIGNIFICANCE OF THE IMAGINATION

The need to surpass the technical foundations points to the undervaluing of imagination in the educational enterprise. A causal relationship may exist between the educators dependency upon the technical and the undervaluing of the imagination. Mary Warnock suggests as much when she states that *"The greatest enemy of the imagination is to be locked in the present,"*[3] It is to the present that the technical calls attention. The technical foundation of education tends to emphasize the need for clarity about what is to be achieved, or next steps, as if the future can be known and controlled by human reason. Shaping educational processes around the known diminishes the need for the imagination, for then the future is no longer a field of imagined possibilities. The imagination makes connections between present and future, present and past, and future and past. With connections already known and no need to imagine those connections, the imagination takes on a minor role. It merely serves to shape emotional expression and stimulates the expressive arts.

Imagination plays a much more significant role in human life. It is central to all aspects of human life and is at the core of educational phenomena. It is not an add on to the educational project. It undergirds everything that the educator thinks and does.

Imagination is a manifestation of human freedom-a cultural birthright. Persons participate in the necessities passed on down through cultural forms and social relationships, but they also participate in a freedom that transcends these necessities. Of course, the imagination can also be hooked into those necessities-distorted, turned into mere fancy, or an instrument of escapism from the necessities in which we dwell- Imagination is the storehouse of human possibility- ethical, intellectual, political. It shapes the possibilities from which the choices for perceiving, knowing and acting are selected, Perceiving, knowing and acting not grounded in the imagination reek of pride and incline toward idolatry. To focus only on the formation of the young person's intellect, values, and actions diminishes freedom. By encouraging the imagination, freedom is affirmed. It is protected by disciplining that imagination with the outpourings of the imagination throughout human history of East and West, North and South.

Mary Warnock states that *"imagination... should be central in any curriculum decision"*[4] and it has not been ignored by educators. It has been an off and on concern for years. Rugg's interests in the imagination took published form in 1963.[5] During the 1960s that interest was manifested in frequent writings about creativity. Today the work of Sloan,[6] Eisner,[7] and Egan[8] are probably only the tip of an iceberg, the whole of which is more clearly seen by those swimming in the icy waters of the curriculum field. But it deserves even more careful and sustained attention, and significant intellectual effort. Warnock warns that "In addressing the topic of Imagination, (one enters) . . . a field that is not only very ancient, but increasingly well trodden."[9] Kearney, much concerned about the potential decline of the imagination today, states that "The story of imagination needs to be told. Like all species under threat of extinction, the imagination requires to be recorded in terms of its genealogy: its conceptual genesis and mutations."[10] For the next two decades or so imagination should receive the volume and quality of attention that learning received during the fast half of this century.

Increased attention to the role of imagination in the life of the young and in education needs to be paralleled by increased attention to how the imagination is being shaped, perverted, and diminished by the easy commerce in symbols and images of the mass media. This is also an arena receiving considerable attention, but with few consequences within the educational enterprises. The problems of reading achievement are still seen by the public as a problem of reading scores in the third and sixth grades, not as a problem of the distribution of and access to word images and visual and sound images. Appropriate concern is still being given to the skills of writing, but too little given to the skills of other tools of the imagination. The cultural dominance of media experts cannot be confronted by people who remain unaware of how their imagination- the foundation of their knowing, acting, valuing, and freedom-has been and is being shaped or formed.

USE THE WORLD'S INTELLECTUAL TRADITIONS AND ACHIEVEMENTS

A major achievement within the curriculum field over the past forty years has been its emerging openness to a host of intellectual enterprises. Pinar's[11] most recent volume is a witness to that achievement. The isolation of educational thought from the wealth of the intellectual life of the world no longer exists. The monopoly of certain discourse systems has been broken. But warranted depictions of how those monopolies became established, and broken, do not yet exist. How did psychological thought become so powerful? Why did it take so long for the exciting post World War II developments in European philosophy to make an impact on the study and practice of education?[12]

One reason for the failure to embrace a wide variety of intellectual systems earlier was the early separation of the study of education from the main centers of intellectual life-the universities. A case in point was the establishment of two year teacher training schools. Many of these eventually became four year teachers colleges, then liberal arts colleges, and finally universities as the need for universal higher education became greater. However, even in universities where the study of education was legitimated by the establishment of departments or schools of education, the separation continued. University schools of education developed their own mini-university, with departments in which the faculty of education taught educational psychology, educational philosophy, educational sociology, educational history. The history of Teachers College, Columbia University, is an illustration of that unfolding story. It established its own departments of educational foundations. Not until after the mid-twentieth century did it establish substantial working relationships with the academic departments at Columbia University and some joint appointments. The historical and structural reasons for the separation of the study and practice of education from the centers of intellectual vitality deserve to be exhumed. Pinar's volume celebrates these achievements of increased openness, but it does not explore the conditions that brought about the intellectual monopolies. The volume is not to be faulted for that, however, for his basic intent-to picture the variety of current approaches to the study of education-was achieved.

He argued, correctly, that a separation between practice and reflection about practice is needed if important intellectual work is to be achieved. Ortega y Gasset[13] and Macmurray[14] both refer to the importance of the rhythm of withdrawal from and return to action. The university is the premier place for withdrawal for developing the critical and imaginative resources needed by society. To be completely tied to and responsible for practice decreases the quality of the critical and imaginative work required for the renewal and continued development of cultural forms and social institutions. Pinar forcefully acknowledges this.

Once the monopoly of educational thought was broken, a few educators engaged in a virtual orgy with other university based disciplines and fields of inquiry. The educational tower of Babel was destroyed, and as Pinar has suggested, people in the "field" now find it difficult to communicate with each other. The "scattered people of curriculum" are now brought into a new tent where the various discourse systems and texts can be acknowledged and where people can be helped with the difficult task of interpretation. However, he points to, or suggests, a potential new monopoly: "The next stage will involve a relative movement away from sources, although historically informed students will not forget them, and the establishment of a conceptually autonomous discipline of curriculum theory."[15] The prediction seems unwise and unwarranted. Pinar's philosophical idealism or foundationalism breaks through his own commitments to post modernism and the significance of university dialogue. The significant development has been the commerce with other departments of the university. Better historical and analytic studies should temper any hope for a new monopoly, even if theoretical, and reinforce the importance of dialogue within the university.

But this privileged status of the university, as a location of criticism and imagination, is a fragile social arrangement, and cannot be guaranteed by a mere commitment to "truth." It is guaranteed by wealth, by the commitment of some members of society to make provisions for those who would critique and imagine. There is no reason to believe that such freedom will continue in universities supported by public funds, unless the redeeming social value of critique and imagination are demonstrated over a period of years. Pinar is correct, at this moment in time, that

> . . . curriculum theorists must still offer friendship and colleagueship to teachers; we must offer teachers our expertise as they request . . . . We can offer politicians and policy makers that expertise but we ought not be surprised, and certainly not deflated, when they decline to employ it. After all, their interests in the schools are not necessarily educational, rather political and economic. We curriculum theorists must be firm that we are not responsible for the ills of the public schools, especially given that our advice ... has been and is so consistently ignored.[16]

> . . . Like physics or art, curriculum as a field cannot progress unless some segment of the field explores phenomena and ideas that perhaps few will comprehend and appreciate, certainty not at first and perhaps never.[17]

However, it needs to be pointed out that much of this theoretical activity is taking place in state supported universities, and that few well endowed universities have supported such educational activity. Yale abolished a department of education in the 1950s, and there has been no effort to re-instate it. This is only to suggest that imagination and critique must be seen as having redeeming social value by other than the theorists themselves. And as the struggle at the University of Minnesota between the faculty and the trustees indicate, tenure is no longer an assured status. Therefore, questions remain about how the recent intellectual excitement about education relates to current educational structures and problems.

The opening to other discourse systems, important as it is, does not clarify how these different discourse systems can be related to educators and educational structures. The university is the locus of social/cultural critique and imagination. The whole university is the source of potential discourse about education, not just a department or school of education. The problem is how these different voices within the university reflect on educational matters. The establishment of a "conceptually autonomous discipline of curriculum theory" co-ops the rest of the university. Looked at another way, the educational experience and the institutions and arrangements that influence it partake of the profundity and mystery of the human condition. To think, even for an instant, that there will be a time when that profundity and mystery can be contained by any single discourse system reflects that quality that shapes so much human tragedy and comedy-hubris.

We are left with the task of asking how the great diversity of intellectual systems of critique and imagination can be related to the human enterprise of education. The self-contained departments of educational psychology, philosophy, history, sociology, were a solution of the forties through the seventies. Pinar's focus on curriculum discourses and texts is a solution for the nineties. What historical patterns will next come into being as current intellectual sorties are replaced by new explorations of education? The need is great for significant historical studies of this problem and its solution over the years.

One way to begin to sort some of this out is to look at different aspects of the educational process, rather than lumping everything under the label "curriculum." For instance, understandings of the journey of individuals as they pass through their allotted time are needed. Learning theories, developmental theories, therapeutic theories, autobiography, narrative, currere- these are different ways of speaking about that process or aspects of that process, each shaped by the intellectual milieu and fashion of the times. Where in the university is this phenomena addressed? Where should it be addressed? Will there ever be a time when the educator has something unique to say to which the philosopher or psychologist will have to listen? A history of the structures of those conversations between the educators and others in these privileged social locations of imagination and critique might uncover patterns of conversations that need to continue, perhaps with some modification.[18] Other illustrations would be to consider how the school as a structured place of education has changed over the years, how reflection about teachers has changed, or as I pleaded earlier, to limit the study of curriculum to the study of content[19]-the factors that influence its selection and structure. Attention to educational domains or phenomena, acknowledging that they too will change with different intellectual fashions, might make it easier to see how the forms of critique and imagination in the universities have influenced educational thought and practice. The next stage in the work before us is again historical, exploring how the problems and domains of education have been identified, critiqued, and imaginatively confronted.

ENGAGE IN PUBLIC DISCOURSE ABOUT EDUCATION

Other discourse systems, not part of the university, are equally important in education and to the educator. These are the "text" of public discourse about education: the texts in various media-TV, newspapers and journals, and books for the non-specialist; the talk of parents; and of course, the talk of young people. Each significantly influences the practices of and thinking about education. Typically, the educator does not participate in these public discourses. They are not usually considered "texts" that must be consulted, studied, interpreted or mastered by the educator.

But the phenomena of education is not esoteric, in spite of the educator's professional language. Education "happens" to everyone through informal and formal activity. Some try to articulate that experience, but find professional language a barrier. It tends to mask the educational experience rather than open it up. Hence, the conditions which foster education cannot be clearly perceived, understood, and critiqued by those who are being educated. The problem probably originated in the first half of this century, although few (or no) studies exist that chart or depict the changing patterns of every day talk about educational experience. Educational language became increasingly distant from the experience of people as the study of education became a scholarly activity. Eager to better understand and control educational activity, educators developed or took on a specialized language, forsaking the language of those who endure the educational process. Perhaps the problem emerged as educators became more dependent on psychological language, or as the language became more technical and farther removed from the everyday speech of children, parents, and teachers. This problem also deserves significant historical attention.

Three problems are created by the separation of educational language from public discourse. First, those who use current intellectual fashions to understand educational phenomena need to understand the changing fashions of everyday discourse about education. What has influenced the evolving forms of public discourse about education in various media? How have the various media influenced the way that parents and community members talk about education? How did the fashion of using test scores become so firmly embedded in public parlance about education? Are there studies of how people, in various contexts, use different idioms to talk and write about education?

Next, the university educator needs to participate in that larger discourse.

Educators tend to write for and to each other. Writing for public consumption is usually done by professional journalists, or by individuals with an ideological axe to grind, with specific suggestions for schools (e.g., Sizer, Bennett), or with trenchant criticisms of the lives of children in schools (e.g., Kozol). Educators either lack interest or know-how to participate in the dialogue. Both are unfortunate and unnecessary. The professional educator needs to master and participate in the public discourse about education, and not be content to merely engage colleagues. Such activity could easily be a project for teacher education and the advanced study of education.

Third, educators have given insufficient attention to the educational discourse of students and parents. Students are often at a loss to describe their own education and how it has happened. The language of educators is not descriptive of their own educational experiences, in or out of school. Young people either lack words to describe these experiences or lapse into school language-covering texts, passing tests, getting grades, passing the grade or course, graduating, or being prepared for work. The educational language of the university classrooms is not a language they can use. Technical and psychological language, and the language of tests and grades, mystifies their educational experience, fails to correspond to their feelings, and displaces their talk. Reflective and critical thought about their own experiences is difficult or impossible. Consequently, when they become parents they have difficulty talking about education with their children. They lack the ability to reflect in their own language on their experiences of education, and are often rooted in the outdated school language of their own school days. The need is for the educator to talk about educational experience in such a way that those outside the professional community can gain personal insight into how education is happening to them. This means that teachers, and other educators, need the ability to converse with them about education, without imposing the mystifying language of educators.

Educators must forsake their imperialistic language and enter into public discourse, the discourse of young people, and the discourse of parents. As the language of these three publics critique the language of educators, so must the language of educators critique theirs. Ways of talking about education must be found and fostered that resonate with the experience of young people and their parents, that can be used in the mass media without being captured by ideological positions, and that can displace or replace the slogans used to shape political judgments about education.

SPEAK OUT FOR CHILDREN AND YOUTH

Tyler, in his significant contribution to the curriculum field,[20] suggested three sources for objectives: studies of the learners, studies of contemporary life, and suggestions from subject specialists. For years arguments raged about the appropriate focus of the school. Should it be the student? The social order? Or subject matter? Dewey, of course, offered a profound philosophical resolution to that problem, showing how the three were connected. Tyler removed the ground for argument. He claimed that all three should be sources of objectives, and that final objectives would be identified by screening them through a philosophy of education and a psychology of learning. The attention to the focus of the school gave way to objectives of the school. The great debate gave way to a concern for identifying objectives within a prescribed methodology. Philosophy became another tool in the calculus of defining objectives. One of the unacknowledged consequences of that great synthesis was to dampen major arguments or ideological positions.

Lost in this methodological synthesis was concern for the student. Knowledge of the student, as a source of objectives, replaced concern for the student as a person. Of course, Tyler's synthesis didn't end interest in the student His framework merely fed into the cultural stream that saw the school as only a place where children and young people learn, not as a place where they also live a good share of their young life. Another negative influence was the establishment of the guidance counselor, first in secondary schools, and then in elementary schools. Teachers should teach. The personal life of the student would be the guidance person's concern. But this specialization of interest also gave way as the guidance person increasingly served the school; or served the larger educational complex by helping students think about the next stages in their journey through educational institutions, rather than their journey through life.

Teachers have become increasingly removed from concern for the uniqueness and individuality of the student qua person. The educational task has been so strongly focused by the need for the teacher to teach and the student to learn, that neither has time to think about how that which is taught influences the life of the student-his own unfolding journey through a difficult time in history. Educators no longer speak for the students they educate. That is a task left to someone else, and consequently to no one else. This development feeds the current interest in parental rights and the "hands off" values concern that is part of current popular educational rhetoric. The concern has sufficient truth to warrant it, yet given the complexity of this particular epoch, a non-family friendly voice might be of help to the student, and to the parent. But the current rhetoric encourages the separation of this work from acts of teaching.

Who in this culture speaks for children and youth? For the most part, they remain essentially voiceless. A few find their voices in the counter-cultural activities of youth. More find them in the great cultural chorus, which celebrates this era without reflection or criticism.

The school is the only institution in this culture built specifically for children and youth to live in. The old argument about the role of the school-for children, for society, for content-need to be exhumed from its burial by the grand synthesis that saw all as sources of objectives. The argument needs to be kept alive. The competing interests among these three should not be permitted to be folded into any technical or other grand synthesis. The vitality of the argument can feed the lives of teachers and students if the tension is lived in productively. The three foci should critique each other. Today, the social critique of both subject matter and the student seems uppermost. The critique of society seems beyond the pale, as major social and economic forces tend to silence most criticism. But the student, inherently the element of newness required for social renewal, also brings under criticism content and the social order. Students are graded against the backdrop of content and society, but the reverse is not true.

The significant need today is to include the interest of the young person in the ongoing and needed debate about the place of children and young people, not only in the school but in the society. Who is more able to do that than the educators? Who know the hurts, pains, pressure points of children and young people as well as teachers and educators. By becoming captive of a particular educational ideology, the educator cannot voice the irritations produced by the friction between the society (as it is embodied in the school) and the student. The irritations can not, indeed, should not be removed. They can be a pearl producing irritant for individual and social creativity. Nor does speaking for children and youth turn the school into the old child centered school of the twenties through the fifties. The competition of voices should never be silenced by any group in a position of dominance. Educators too busy trying to understand the educational process may fail to hear and respond to the muffled sounds of those caught in the system. Please, please speak for the children and youth, those persons who give meaning to all educational endeavor and thought.

NOTES

[1] The editors wish to acknowledge the permission of Taylor and Francis for the use of this chapter.
[2] John Dewey, " ... the only way in which adults consciously control the kind of education which the immature get is by controlling the environment in which they act . . . We never educate directly, but indirectly by means of the environment" *Democracy and Education* (New York: The Macmillan Company, 1961, first published in 1916). 19.

[3] 'Warnock, *Imagination & Time* (Oxford: Blackwell, 1994), 174.
[4] Ibid., 173.
[5] Harold Rugg, *Imagination* (New York: Harper & Row, 1963).
[6] Douglas Sloan, *Insight-Imagination: The Emancipation of Thought and the Modern World* (Westport, CT: Greenwood Press, 1983).
[7] Elliot Eisner, The Educational Imagination: On the Design and Evaluation of School Programs (New York: Macmillan, 1979. 1985).
[8] Kieran Egan, *Imagination in Teaching and Learning* (Chicago: University of Chicago Press, *1992*).
[9] Warnock, *Imagination and Time*, 1.
[10] Richard Kearney, *The Wake of Imagination: Ideas of Creativity in Western Culture* (London: Hutchinson, 1988).
[11] William F. Pinar, William M. Reynolds, Patrick Slattery and Peter M. Taubman, *Understanding Curriculum: An Introduction to the Study of Historical and Contemporary Curriculum Discourses* (New York; Peter Lang, 1995).
[12] Obviously the commitment to Dewey's pragmatism was one factor.
[13] Jose Ortega y Gasset, "The Self and the Other," In *The Dehumanization of Art; and* Other *Writings on Art, Culture and Literature* (Garden City, NY: Doubleday & Company, 1956),152.
[14] John Macmurray, *The Self as Agent* (New York: Harper and Brothers, 1957), 181.
[15] Pinar et al., *Understanding Curriculum*, xvii.
[16] Ibid., 851.
[17] Ibid., 852.
[18] For an example in another field see Brooks Holifield, *A History of Pastoral Care in America: From Salvation to Self Realization* (Nashville: Abingdon Press, 1983).
[19] Dwayne Huebner, "The Moribund Curriculum Field: Its Wake and Our Work," *Curriculum Inquiry* 6, no. 2 (1976): 153-167; Chapter 20.
[20] Ralph Tyler, *Basic Principles of Curriculum and Instruction* (Chicago: The University of Chicago Press, 1949).

P. J. LEWIS

WHO IN THIS CULTURE SPEAKS FOR CHILDREN AND YOUTH?[1]

Since in order to speak, one must first listen, learn to speak by listening.
Rumi

The curriculum wars have ebbed and flowed with a regularity reminiscent of the tides; hence we see periods when one group or another rises up and purports to represent what is best for the education of children and youth until, of course, the tide turns. A survey of the past century would suggest there are, and have been, many people, often called experts or stakeholders, who claim to speak out for children and youth in deciding what is best or most beneficial for them in the realm of education. However, more recently, there are many others who not so much speak out for children and youth, but rather influence their consumer consciousness and consequently their thinking. That is, the media also speak out for children and youth in another way, by teaching a set of values and beliefs (Huebner, 1999, p. 435) with multi-billion dollar a year budgets and an almost pervasive access to children and youth; what some suggest is a major mechanism of imperialistic domination in manufacturing accepted ways of viewing and interpreting the world (Cannella & Viruru, 2004). "Patterns of consumption shaped by corporate advertising empower commercial institutions as the teachers of the new millennium. Corporate cultural pedagogy has 'done its homework'—it has produced educational forms that are wildly successful" (Kincheloe, 2002, p. 84).

Add to this, recent legislation in America such as NCLB (No Child Left Behind) and Good Start, Grow Smart, or the mandated standardized testing in several provinces of Canada, which also claim to speak out for children and youth. One of the most significant results of the NCLB and other similar legislation is that it has facilitated an already growing influence of another group claiming to have children's and youth's interest at heart; the publishing houses of standardized tests and scripted curriculum programs which generate annual profits in the hundreds of millions of dollars. And now the OECD (Organization for Economic Cooperation and Development) claims to speak out for children and youth through such international endeavours as PISA (Programme for International Student Assessment) or the Review of Early Childhood Education and Care policies and organizations of participating countries; all of which draws attention to public policy in education in many countries and then arms centralized government policymakers with "data" to support significant educational decisions that fail to consider the regional and/or local needs of children across the sociopolitical landscape. "Globalization is remaking societies" (Law & Urry, 2004, p. 402), consequently, that means it is remaking education and schooling in its own image. Yes, who indeed speaks for children and youth?

Dwayne Huebner (1999, p. 444) suggested that teachers, because of their living together with children in the place called school, might be best positioned to speak out for children and youth; however, their voices, but more importantly the voices of children and youth themselves, seem lost in the din of others who claim to speak out for children and youth. It may seem that if teachers speak out for children and youth they, too, will be perpetuating the powerlessness and voicelessness children and youth currently experience. However, speaking out *for* must become speaking out *with,* so that teachers, children and youth face the educational journey together supporting and understanding each other in a culture of *care* and *hope*. Education must transcend the technical focus on efficient literacy and numeracy learning to prepare children and youth to join the global mobility of economies. One way this may happen is by remaking education as a reciprocal journey with teacher and child as partners, collaborators removed from the present hierarchy of school and learning; similar to Paulo Freire's (1970, 1994) desire to cultivate a deep reciprocity between teacher and child/youth. It would see a flattening of the hierarchal structure of school and learning so that teachers, children, youth and parents *care for* and have *hope with* each other.

But in order to speak with children and youth we must first surpass the technical foundation of education and schooling as influenced and shaped by the notions and discourses of human developmental psychology, learning theory, and the legacy *and* evolution of scientific curriculum, objectives and taxonomies. "The bewitching language of psychology and the behavioral sciences has skewed our view of education" (Huebner, 1999, p. 404). Over time the idea of developmental norms have shifted from "description to prescription: from a mythic norm (mythic because no one actually 'fits' it) to statements of how people should be" (Dahlberg & Moss, 2005, p. 7). When we can stand outside the very discourse(s) that have (in)formed us as students and as teachers marching toward a prescribed future based upon "secur[ing] both social order and economic success" (p. 5), perhaps then we can begin to speak more clearly and loudly *with* children and youth and live, not "objectives", "learning outcomes" and a place in a prescribed future, but the wonder and uncertainty of life's journey together.

In such a living together, teachers and children might listen and tell their stories into being. The pedagogical project becomes a "journey into story" (Huebner, 1999, pp. 381–382) where the newness and wonder that children bring to their engagement with the quotidian reminds us, parents and teachers, of the incongruencies, the entanglements and the rhizomatic renderings of being. The curriculum becomes the "journey through life" (p. 443) traveled together in a partnership of reciprocity; facing the challenges, difficulties and joys of being. However, this living together requires the teacher to transcend current notions of teaching; to move outside of the current technical approach to literacy and numeracy teaching beyond the increasingly discrete "learning outcomes" to a space/place that resurrects the question; what is the aim of education or rather what is the spirit of education? To ask this suggests that education can be "more than the forms in which it is currently lived" (p. 343). However, in order to enact this it requires an integration of passion and intelligence, care and hope, empathy and trust with each other on a journey into an uncertain future.

Dwayne Huebner (1999) was not the first person to speak of teaching as a vocation, however, his was a clearer articulation of teaching as dwelling authentically in the risk and vulnerability that is a teacher's life; a life lived with children and youth in a relationship of care and hope. But it is not care in the easy currency of the sociopolitical language we hear today; rather it is a care reminiscent of Max van Manen's (1991) notion that a teacher or a parent may alleviate a young person's cares or worries engendered through "pedagogical love" where a teacher is attentive to the child, present in the moment in such a way that the child is liberated from concern or worry when facing life and its concomitant challenges. Accompanying this care is a hope that transcends a wish or optimism for something else; hope becomes a way of being present with the child, a mode of being rather than doing (p. 67). It is through the act of being present in our living and teaching with children that we may *do* the most.

Of course, there is a long history of curriculum development and theory, which has both influenced and shaped current and earlier policy and practices in education. One need only look to the past century to see some of the more prominent figures of the 20th century who have not so much spoken for children and youth, but have certainly helped determine their educational experiences and helped lay the ground work for the aforementioned recent legislation and expanding use of standardized testing. Informed by the dominant cognitive models of the times (such as scientific management, social efficiency movement and developmental psychology), schooling was influenced by individuals such as W.W. Charters whose activity-analysis approach to curriculum construction influenced George Counts and Ralph Tyler; Tyler's transformation of measurement to the grander idea of evaluation enshrined in learning objectives in turn influenced Benjamin Bloom and his taxonomy and learning for mastery; both their works were instrumental in shaping education through the 1950s to the present. However, it was the work of Franklin Bobbitt, through his scientific approach to curriculum making that set the course for Counts, Tyler, Bloom and numerous other educators in the evolution of the technical approach to teaching. Bobbitt's curriculum making method has had a profound and lasting influence upon teaching, schooling, and the curriculum; and still lies at the core of curriculum development.[2]

As Lauren Sosniak (1997) reminded us, Benjamin Bloom's taxonomy permeates the language of curriculum theory and practice and is referenced in almost all texts on curriculum. She suggested, circa 1995, that there was a return to objectives "that resemble more closely Tyler's view", however, at the time of this writing most curriculum guides consist of a plethora of increasingly discrete learning outcomes with direct links to assessment and evaluation. Tyler's objectives remain as the extension of Bobbitt's foundation and the evolution of the use of Bloom's taxonomy have ensured the technical turn in teaching despite more than three decades of critique, reform and deconstruction.[3]

HOW CAN TEACHERS SURPASS THE TECHNICAL FOUNDATIONS OF EDUCATION AND SPEAK OUT WITH CHILDREN AND YOUTH? WHAT MIGHT THAT STORY OF TEACHING BE?

The story(ies) that is teaching is never a single thread rather it is but one of a multiplicity of stories that are woven through the larger more intricate tapestry of public schooling. The sanctioned curriculum is another story that seems to enjoy a privileged pervasiveness within current school policy and practice. Through prescribed learning outcomes and the barrage of required objectives teachers face, the story of school that students encounter mostly ignores their lived experiences - those stories of self that each individual brings to the classroom, enriching rather than fragmenting learning. Instead, the curriculum weaves a story that many students find themselves absent from (Chambers, 1999). It is an incomplete story that privileges a dominant narrative masquerading as common sense curriculum. We teach what we teach the way we teach because it just makes sense (Tupper & Cappello, 2008).

The curriculum, and by consequence teaching practice, tends to focus on what needs to be learned next rather than focus on the curriculum of now. The Euro-American concept of time as linear and universal, forever pushing forward in a straight line (i.e. historical time lines in schools) is fundamental to curriculum planning and teaching. However, in this process "the concern for the student has been lost" (Huebner, 1999, p. 443) replaced by concern for the next stages, objectives or outcomes in the young person's manoeuvring through educational planning; what Kieran Egan has called the "expanding horizons curriculum" – where students trudge through one developmental labour only to come face-to-face with another in a long seemingly endless list. But what this "leaves out is the feeling for life and history, which is such an essential part of human existence" (Cannella & Viruru, 2004, p. 44). The child, the young person, like all of us, is a narrated self who should be accompanied in that temporal journey through life and not marched through one learning objective on to the next, but be situated in her subjectivity where time is a fluid movement of past, present and future in any given moment. In this approach to learning, there is little room for the student's own stories to inform the ways in which curriculum is conceived, enacted and lived. The student lives outside officially sanctioned curriculum, and while she may find ways into this curriculum, she is dependent upon the teacher to mediate and negotiate with that curriculum, so she may create meaning. A great disappointment of schooling is that the learning is neither relevant nor meaningful for most students. We cannot redeem our existing curriculum by simply adding missing content. Instead, we must step out from under it in a relational, storied, fluid way.

Our relationship with time is, as Merleau-Ponty (1962) remarked, "intimate… by virtue of an inner necessity" we are temporal so that time emerges from a person's relationship with things and others so that "what is past or future for [a person] is present in the world" (p. 412). A child, a youth, an adult, we all experience the self as multidimensional, augmented through the situated awareness of human being. Each of us "without even wanting to know it, is aware of being a *narratable self*—immersed in the spontaneous auto-narration of memory" (Cavarero, 2000, p. 33). The curriculum then becomes a child's "journey into story" and the teacher lives with the child through that unfolding story. "There is an abiding recognition that existence is inherently storied. Life is pregnant with stories" (Kearney, 2002, p. 130). Ours is a story shaped world, being human is to live in narrative; story is one of our fundamental ways of making meaning; narrative imagining has both epistemological and ontological import in all that we do and become.

Consequently, teaching must be seen as vocation, engendered with the care and hope mentioned earlier so that teaching "is to find one's life and work participating in the formation of another's story, and vice-versa" (Huebner, 1999, p. 382). But how do we hear "curriculum in a new key" (Aoki, 2004). The official curriculum story, in which learner is a 'technical term' and the language of instruction negates the "complexity and mystery of a fellow human being" (Huebner, 1966, p. 102) leaves little room for care and hope. Instead, this curriculum offers narrative 'truth' masked as objective knowledge. Curriculum as ideological text privileges certain stories, ways of knowing, narratives of self, common sense understandings of language, place, and identity. Through this curriculum, students are encouraged, perhaps even required, to step outside of their storied beings, particularly when these storied selves are incompatible with the curricular story. What then are we offering students when we take hours of their freedom away as they sit in traditional classrooms, consuming content that is in tension with their storied selves? Officially sanctioned curriculum is limited and limiting in this respect. It separates "place from language from pedagogy" (Hurren & Hasebe-Ludt, 2003, xx) creating a strange and unnatural disconnection for students. We must awaken to classrooms in many forms, always asking ourselves what is learning? What is it to learn as storied beings? Too often, curriculum as plan usurps curricula as lived, with the discipline oriented discourses of literacy and numeracy playing leading roles in public discourses of education.

Literacy and numeracy learning become more than an educational end in themselves to serve prescribed objectives of functional efficiency "mainly concerned with the future development, educational attainment and employability of the child, in a context of increasing competition and change, as well as with the prevention or amelioration of a range of social ills among children, families and communities" (Dahlberg & Moss, 2005, p. 4). Literacy and numeracy become one of the *means* by which a child may augment her lived-experience, the journey into life, the story of the self and other together. But, in order for this to happen we must bear in mind and be cautious because the teaching of literacy "is always first and foremost a social practice, one that is constrained and enabled by the changing economics and politics of schools and communities" (Luke, 1998, pp. 305–306).

However, to speak out with children and youth requires teachers to know the story of the institutions in which teachers live with children and to know the story of ideas that have shaped and (in)formed our notions of education and teaching and all that entails. Without knowing those stories we cannot understand our own personal story in our calling to teach, but more importantly without those stories we cannot "listen" the child's story into being. These four stories; the teacher's personal story or autobiography, the story of the institution, the story of ideas and the story of the student/child (D. Huebner, personal communication, June 10, 2007) are inextricably entwined in the complexity and messiness that is the life of teaching. Teachers, if we are to live and speak out with children and youth, must negotiate and hold the tension amongst these competing stories. It is important to acknowledge that there may be fear in these spaces of tension as they cause us to see anew. Such fear may in turn bring about the desire to return to safe, familiar, tidy spaces of curriculum as planned. Our stories become predictable. How may we come to see that transformation is made possible through the experience of tension? How might we live into a new story if we are unable or unwilling to recognize the story that we are situated in?

As a teacher my personal story, that is my "narratable self" (Cavarero, 2000) "describes or narrates where I have been, where I am and where I might be going and how all of these shape how I understand the present moment" (D. Huebner, personal communication, June 10, 2007). But if I am a captive of my own history without awareness, without being cognizant of that very captivity, I am unable to narrate my own story; I am merely a character utilized in the story of the institution and the story of ideas, a functionary of the other. Until I am unfettered from that captivity and begin to author my lived story through my own agency, I am unable to listen authentically to those persons I live with in the classroom everyday—children and youth.

The story of school, like all institutions, is steeped in a history of traditions, norms, customs, procedures and many other practices that regulate and/or "manage" life in the institution. As a teacher in the institution I am simultaneously caught in that story and possessed with the possibility to act to alter or change the story of the institution. However, I am only able to do that if I am aware of my own story and cognizant of the story of the institution that will act upon me and in which I will act. How I read that story and my "life in it also then adds to or modifies my own personal story—a real and difficult task of integration" (D. Huebner, personal communication, June 10, 2007).

The story of the world of ideas, in particular the ideas with which we as teachers have contact, can be both pervasive and seductive. It is in this realm, which the story of the self; the child's story and the teacher's story, is eclipsed because in the world of ideas the idea is often put forth "as truth—the way, a timeless solution to complexity". However, as a teacher I need to navigate the plethora of idea systems rather than seek some truth about schooling or education so that I draw "upon those ideas that seem to open up my own story, or the story of the institutions within which I work or will work. The world of ideas is the world of imagination–the neglected dimension of most people's autobiography" (D. Huebner, personal communication, June 10, 2007). It is to see myself, and the institution from multiple perspectives, which then may inform or shift my standpoint so that I have a new telling, iteration of my story and/or the story of the institution. When this complexity is denied in my teaching, my teaching becomes routine, mechanistic, reductionistic, behavioral, a scripted practice and there is a dearth of creativity and an unwillingness or perhaps even fear, to imagine other possibilities or realities—I become a functionary of the realm. But most important, it prevents me from recognizing and living with the fourth story; the story children and youth bring to the classroom each new school year and every new school day. However, by being aware and present I may see that it is the story of "the newness of the young people who call us farther into our journey of selfhood" (Huebner, 1999, p. 384) which then may enable me to understand that in order to "participate in a young person's emerging or unfolding story, [I] must be an able listener, one who 'listens' the young person into an articulate consciousness, and a narrator who has the necessary language to fit an episode into the young person's story line" (p. 383).

I must become a storyteller and a story listener; mediate, translate and recast the language of school (the stories of the institution and of ideas) for children and youth, so that their story of school and education makes sense beyond common sense, has meaning in their lived experience of the journey into life. In turn this becomes an integral part of my story, the teacher's story of holding the tension of these competing stories in order to create the space for the stories of children and youth. However, I cannot do this alone. I need colleagues, peers, friends; "a community of care and support, one in which members take time for telling and listening to the stories of each other's journeys" (Huebner, 1999, p. 385). In such a community teachers, children, youth and parents may hold the story space together and draw strength from that place so that in community, they may try and live well with "the ontology of the human existential situation with all of its pain, suffering, joy and desire" (Kincheloe, 2005, p. 318). We teachers, similar to parents, have to participate in children's "journeys, open up futures for them, reconcile their past and presents, participate in the narration of their lives [because] they [are] tied closely to our story and our own search for what is of value and has meaning" (Huebner, 1999, p. 386). This may seem daunting work, fearful work, but it is necessary if we are to be awake in education.

HOW CAN TEACHERS DO THIS AND SPEAK OUT WITH CHILDREN AND YOUTH?

What happens when our stories bump up against the stories of our students; the stories of the institution? This is not a bad thing for it offers us opportunities to dwell in the in-between where seeing anew is made possible, where living pedagogy is located (Aoki, 2003). Understanding our own stories in tension with those of our students and/or the institution may compel us to speak and act with greater care and hope. But we cannot speak out for children if we cannot speak out for ourselves. This requires that we know our own story and the story of the institution. We must listen the story into being. However, the question that invariably emerges from all sides when suggesting change is: What would replace it? And if we get past that the second question is usually: How? I'm not certain these are useful questions in that they perpetuate the binary hierarchical thinking that seems to have characterized our journey to the current circumstances experienced in public education. Perhaps what is needed is to think about more and/or other questions that transcend the habit of binary thought and move through a rhizomatic wondering that contemplates, horizontally, the connectivity, heterogeneity and multiplicity of thought and being without controlling desire (see Gilles Deleuze & Félix Guattari, 1988). "In the rhizomatic view, knowledge can only be negotiated, and the contextual, collaborative learning experience shared by constructivist and connectivist pedagogies is a social as well as a personal knowledge-creation process with mutable goals and constantly negotiated premises" (Cormier, 2008).

We might borrow from the praxis of the Zen teacher and rather than providing correct answers, which only serve to end the student's thinking upon other possible or better questions, we could take up a "curriculum of questioning since through questions children could more deeply understand their situation and Being" (Blades, 2003, p. 220). This might move us to a space that Ted Aoki (2003) called *Yu-mu*, which is "non-essentialist, denying the privileging of either 'presence' or 'absence'" (p. 3) in between the sanctioned curricula and no curricula. It is the place where child and teacher might engender the live(d) curriculum through a living pedagogy (pp. 1–10). A curriculum of questioning would not only allow, but would augment children and youths' journey into life in order, "to discover the value, characteristics, and depth of humanity" (Blades, 2003, p. 218).

Stories engender this kind of questioning, even though most stories end or are possessed with a sense of an ending with a possible answer, for the moment, however, there are always more questions with the answer that generates endless imagined possibilities. When a young person asks to hear a story there is always a question implicit in the request and it is the oldest question of all—why? Through stories we come to meaning: of experience, of the world we have been born/e, and the story we are living. It is the stories of family, culture, and community that (in)form each one of us; individually and together these stories can be adopted, emulated, reworked, integrated, re-created, endured, rejected, transformed or transcended. The ontological and epistemological nature of story is an implicit condition of communal life. And in that life "identity is a matter of telling stories – hence *narrative* identity" consequently, "the construction of narrative identity is a collective act, involving tellers and listeners" (Whitebrook, 2001, p. 4). Furthermore, "a system of education must help those growing up in a culture find an identity within that culture. Without it they stumble in their effort after meaning" (Bruner, 1996, p. 42). Stories cultivate and enrich the imagination in its creative endeavor for identity, meaning and possibility. "We come to know ourselves through the world and its stories. We come to know the world through our experiences and our stories" (Lewis, 2007, p. 11). We narrate as a way of knowing and being and children and youth must have their story listened into existence so that they do not "stumble" in their journey into life.

However, story exists nowhere, it has no place, yet story is pervasive in that it creates place through the telling and listening. Michel de Certeau (1984) reminds us that story "constantly transforms places into spaces or spaces into places" (p. 118) so that stories are places of possible resistance, resistance to the narratives of instituted power. In this way "stories offer their audience a repertory of tactics for future use" (p. 23) and teachers, children and parents can draw from those stories, tactics in telling and listening their stories of school, education into being. Certainly, there are increasingly technically dominated curriculum guides and a plethora of discrete learning outcomes housed in every subject area curriculum document with direct links to assessment and evaluation all under the aegis of government mandated testing and measuring standards. But, we can teach through that in such a way that our stories, the children's, parents' and teachers' are not overwhelmed and lost in the ascendancy of the stories of the institution, ideas and the current testing mania.

I am not suggesting the role of saboteur rather the role of storyteller/listener. Story has its etymological roots in Old French, *estorie,* which comes from the Latin *historia,* which in turn comes form the Greek *idein*, "to see" and *eidenai,* "to know" (Harper, 2001). In oral cultures story and the storyteller are integral to the education of children and youth and today in North American schools I would suggest it is teachers who are the storytellers/listeners; however, only if they are cognizant of the four stories outlined earlier. Teachers need to remember that the documents or online versions called the curriculum are guides and overviews that have evolved toward prescribed learning outcomes, but they are still just guides. Yes, we should be familiar with them, but rather than following the suggested or prescribed technical delivery of the lesson, why not invert the process and begin with the children through an emergent or negotiated curriculum of questioning, the rhizome, that sees an engaged process of exploration horizontally, of the connectivity, heterogeneity and multiplicity of thought and being that would not only "cover the learning outcomes" but transcend and bring into question those outcomes and ask: why, why stop there? How are our stories connected, interconnected as we strive to make meaning, to make sense beyond common sense?

Pedagogical transformation requires that we live into something, including the fear we teachers may encounter as we venture out from prescribed learning objectives and technical approaches to teaching and learning. We can neither predict the future nor anticipate the skills, attributes or knowledges that may be needed. However, we can see, know that humans will continue to need to be adaptive, flexible and imaginative in thought and actions in order to engage with the challenges, desires and pain of every day life and all that that may entail. Does our current curriculum and approach to schooling and education cultivate that?

Ours is a period of great change, often characterized by notions of fear and uncertainty. We no longer look to or talk about the possibility of Utopian futures in education or the lived world. Gunilla Dahlberg and Peter Moss (2005) drawing on the work of Boaventura de Sousa Santos, Frederick Jameson and Emanuel Levinas suggest the dominant worldview tells us, "the future, in short is unimaginable or catastrophic or just plain depressing promising only more of the same" (p. 177). However, they do not accept this view, in fact they are "unapologetically Utopian" arguing for a return or a reawakening of Utopian thinking to confront such a flat and uninspired view of the future. Story provides us with the means to transform spaces into places; that is, to narratively imagine something more, something other, something Utopian. But it does more than that, story enables us to act, to do something to engender some change; things do not have to remain the same. Schools can be sites of resistance to trends that are not in the best interests of all children and youth. Teachers, children and youth can transform school into " a hermeneutical site, that is, a place where meaning is made, where understanding and interpretation are engendered" (Kincheloe, 2002, p. 83). By looking to story, the four stories that teachers live in/with, they will find "the possibility of thinking and practicing differently, of getting beyond technical practice and creating a space for ethics and politics" (Dahlberg & Moss, 2005, p. 16) to try and live well with the children and youth who gather to them every day in their process of becoming.

We need to engage our thoughts and actions with imagined futures rather than prescribed futures where we ask what kind of community do we want to create? What kind of world do we want to envision beyond this current experience? We need to remember, to be mindful that "while the real is indeed real, it is also made" (Law & Urry, 2004, p. 395) and that stories are not the other's perspective, but rather other realities, both real and possible. Stories "do not simply describe the world as it is, but also enact it" (p.391). Consequently, we need to "think about the worlds [we] want to *help* to make" (p. 391) and the possibility of teachers speaking out with children and youth to create communities where "curriculum is not driven by predefined inputs from experts; it is constructed and negotiated in real time by the contributions of those engaged in the learning process" (Cormier, 2008) and the stories engendered through those interactions and relationships.

Heidegger said that "language is the house of being" (1993) and in that house, that home we have everything we need to enact our relationship with the world—language is the memory of all Being—our stories. We have a residence, a home in language prior to everything else in the world (Heidegger, 1971, 1993). Narrative imagining, story, shapes our aesthetic understanding of reality because it is a generative and creative process, which renders life meaningful. As Merleau-Ponty said "to know the world is to sing of it in a melody of words" (as cited in Huebner, 1999, p. 37) and we do that as we live in the telling of stories. "Our experiences of human affairs come to take the form of the narrative we use for telling about them" (Bruner, 1996, p. 132). We use the story form and the story forms us. Through story we must come to see notions of curriculum as fluid, dynamic and most important, *lived*; we are the curriculum, we create it, we enact it and like story we listen it into being through the ontological and epistemological recursiveness of narrative being. It is from that place that teachers may speak out with children and youth.

Listen; what will our story be?

NOTES

[1] Dwayne Huebner asks this question in Challenges Bequeathed pointing out children and youth remain essentially voiceless because the task of speaking out for them is "left to someone else, and consequently to no one else"(p. 443).

[2] See Herbert M. Kliebard (1975), The rise of scientific curriculum making and its aftermath in *The curriculum studies reader 2nd Edition*/edited by David J. Flinders and Stephen J. Thornton. New York: Routledge, 2004 for a discussion of Franklin Bobbit's influence.

[3] This is only a very partial list of the writings that have been produced over the last half century:
Apple, M. W. (1979/2004). *Ideology and curriculum.* New York : RoutledgeFalmer
Eisner, E. (1964). *Instruction, teaching, and learning : an attempt at differentiation.* Columbus, Ohio: Merrill.
Eisner, E. (1994). *The educational imagination: on the design and evaluation of school programs.* New York: Macmillan.
Freire, P. (1970). *Pedagogy of the oppressed.* (Trans. Myra Bergman Ramos) New York: Seabury Press.
Freire, P. (1994). *Pedagogy of hope: reliving Pedagogy of the oppressed.* (Trans. Robert R. Barr). New York: Continuum.
Giroux, H. A. (1981). *Ideology, culture & the process of schooling.* Philadelphia: Temple University Press.
Giroux, H. A. (1997). *Pedagogy and the politics of hope: theory, culture, and schooling: a critical reader.* Boulder, CO: Westview Press.
Giroux, H. A. (2005). *Schooling and the struggle for public life: democracy's promise and education's challenge.* Boulder, CO: Paradigm Publishers.
Goodlad, J. I. (1966). *The changing school curriculum.* New York: Fund for the Advancement of Education.
Goodlad, J. I. (1997). *In praise of education.* New York: Teachers College Press.
Greene, M. (1973). *Teacher as stranger; educational philosophy for the modern age.* Belmont, CA: Wadsworth Pub. Co.
Greene, M. (1967). *Existential encounters for teachers.* New York : Random House.
Greene, M. (1995). *Releasing the imagination: essays on education, the arts, and social change.* San Francisco: Jossey-Bass.
Grumet, M. R. (1979). *A Methodology for the Reconstruction of Educational Experience.*
Grumet, M. (1981). Restitution and reconstruction of educational experience: An autobiographical method for curriculum theory. In M. Lawn & L. Barton (Eds.), *Rethinking curriculum studies: A radical approach* (pp. 115-130). London: Croom Helm.
Grumet, M. R. (1988). *Bitter milk : women and teaching.* Amherst, MA: University of Massachusetts Press.
Huebner, D. (1999). V. Hillis & W. Pinar (Eds) *The lure of the transcendent: Collected essays by Dwayne E. Huebner.* Mahwah: Lawrence Erlbaum Associates.
Jackson, P. W. (1968/1990). *Life in classrooms.* New York: Teachers College Press.
McLaren, P. (1989*). Life in schools: introduction to critical pedagogy in the foundations of education.* New York: Longman.
Noddings, N. (1984). *Caring, a feminine approach to ethics & moral education.* Berkeley, CA: University of California Press.
Noddings, N. (1992). *The challenge to care in schools: an alternative approach to education.* New York : Teachers College Press.
Noddings, N. (2003). *Happiness and education.* New York: Cambridge University Press.
Pinar, W. and Grumet, M. (1976). Toward a poor curriculum. Dubuque, IA: Kendall/Hunt.
Schwab, J. J. (1969). *College Curriculum and Student Protest.* Chicago: University of Chicago Press.
Schwab, J. J. (1983). The Practical 4: Something for Curriculum Professors to Do. *Curriculum Inquiry, 13*(3): 239–265.

REFERENCES

Aoki, T. (2004). In W. Pinar & R. Irwin (Eds.), *Curriculum in a new key: The collected works of Ted T. Aoki.* New York: Routledge.
Aoki, T. (2003). Locating living pedagogy in teacher "research": Five metonymic moments. In E. Hasebe-Ludt & W. Hurren (Eds.), *Curriculum intertext: Place/language/pedagogy* (pp. 1–10). New York: Peter Lang.
Blades, D. (2003). The pedagogy of technological replacement. In E. Hasebe-Ludt & W. Hurren (Eds.), *Curriculum intertext: Place/language/pedagogy* (pp. 205-226). New York: Peter Lang.
Bruner, J. (1996). *The culture of education.* Cambridge, MA: Harvard University Press.

Cannella, G. S., & Viruru, R. (2004). *Childhood and postcolonization: Power, education, and contemporary practice* (pp. 205–226). New York: RoutledgeFalmer.
Cavarero, A. (2000). *Relating narratives: Storytelling and selfhood*. New York: Routledge.
Certeau de, M. (1984). *The practice of everyday life*. Los Angeles: University of California Press.
Chambers, C. (1999). A topography of Canadian curriculum theory. *Canadian Journal of Education, 22*, 137–150.
Cormier, D. (2008). Rhizomatic education: Community as curriculum. *Innovate, 4*(5). Retrieved July 3, 2008, from http://www.innovateonline.info/index.php?view=article&id=550
Dahlberg, G., & Moss, P. (2005). *Ethics and politics in early childhood education*. London: Routledge/Falmer.
Deleuze, G., & Guattari, F. (1988). *A thousand plateaus: Capitalism and schizophrenia* (B. Massumi, Trans.). London: Athlone Press.
Harper, D. (2001). *Online etymology dictionary*. Retrieved March 31, 2008, from www.etymonline.com
Hasebe-Ludt, E., & Hurren, W. (Eds.). (2003). *Curriculum intertext: Place/language/pedagogy*. New York: Peter Lang.
Heidegger, M. (1971). *Poetry, language, thought* (A. Hofstadter, Trans.). New York: Harper & Row.
Heidegger, M. (1993). The way to language. In D. F. Krell (Ed.), *Basic writings from being and time (1927) to the task of thinking (1964)* (pp. 397–426). London: Routledge.
Huebner, D. (1999). Challenges bequeathed (1996). In V. Hillis (Ed.), *The lure of the transcendent, collected essays by Dwayne E. Huebner* (pp. 432–445). Mahwah, NJ: Lawrence Erlbaum Associates.
Huebner, D. (1999). Teaching as a vocation (1987). In V. Hillis (Ed.), *The lure of the transcendent, collected essays by Dwayne E. Huebner* (pp. 379–387). Mahwah, NJ: Lawrence Erlbaum Associates.
Huebner, D. (1999). Spirituality and knowing (1985). In V. Hillis (Ed.), *The lure of the transcendent, collected essays by Dwayne E. Huebner* (pp. 340–352). Mahwah, NJ: Lawrence Erlbaum Associates.
Huebner, D. (1999). Knowledge: An instrument of man (1962). In V. Hillis (Ed.), *The lure of the transcendent, collected essays by Dwayne E. Huebner* (pp. 36–43). Mahwah, NJ: Lawrence Erlbaum Associates.
Kearney, R. (2002). *On stories: Thinking in action*. New York: Routledge.
Kincheloe, J. (2005). On to the next level: Continuing the conceptualization of the bricolage. *Qualitative Inquiry, 11*(3), 323–350.
Kincheloe, J. (2002). The complex politics of McDonald's and the new childhood: Colonizing kidworld. In G. S. Cannella & J. L. Kincheloe (Eds.), *Kidworld: Childhood studies, global perspectives, and education* (pp. 75–121). New York: P. Lang.
Law, J., & Urry, J. (2004). Enacting the social. *Economy and Society, 33*(3), 390–410.
Lewis, P. J. (2007). *How we think but not in school*. Rotterdam, NL: Sense Publishers.
Luke, A. (1998). Getting over method: Literacy teaching as work in "new times". *Language Arts, 75*, 305–313.
Merleau-Ponty, M. (1962). *Phenomenology of perception* (C. Smith, Trans.). London: Routledge & Kegan Paul.
Sosniak, L. (1997). The taxonomy, curriculum, and their relations. In D. J. Flinders & S. J. Thornton (Eds.), *The curriculum studies reader* (pp. 76–91). New York: Routledge.
Tupper, J., & Cappello, M. (2008). Teaching treaties as (un)usual narratives: Disrupting the curricular commonsense. *Curriculum Inquiry, 38*(5), 560–578.
Van Manen, M. (1991). *The tact of teaching: The meaning of pedagogical thoughtfulness*. London: Althouse Press.
Whitebrook, M. (2001). *Identity, narrative and politics*. New York: Routledge.

ERIKA HASEBE-LUDT

WRITING LIVES, WRITING WORLDS: LITERACY AS AUTOBIOGRAPHICAL AND COSMOPOLITAN TEXT

A call for transformation always originates from specific geographic locations and their unique mixed inter/national narratives. But these stories reach out to a larger cosmos through their power to question dominant borders and discourses....They remind the world about its responsibility to critique ideologies of indifference and homogeneity and to confirm the ethical value of heterogeneity and difference.

—Giovanna Borradori, *Philosophy in a Time of Terror*

INTRODUCTION

In this essay, I explore the multi-textured tensions inherent in entering relationships that require pedagogical responsiveness and responsibility towards others. In order to better understand these tensions in "the living that teaching is" (Huebner, 1999c, p. 397), I examine the personal and professional, local and global, planned and lived curriculum worlds (Aoki, 2005) which teachers create together with their students. Against the background of my experiences as a teacher researcher in cosmopolitan classrooms and an educator in different Western Canadian teacher education programs in transnational/multicultural and language/literacy education, I illuminate dialogues woven together by threads of creative nonfiction, narrative, poetic, and mixed-genre texts. I reflect and ruminate on questions and quandaries borne out of being situated in between curricular and epistemological frameworks, and belonging to different worlds in and outside the classroom. This writing constitutes a theoretical trope as well as a praxis that aims at accentuating rather than essentializing difference while simultaneously seeking a rapprochement between conflicting discourses. By reimagining and rewriting curriculum and literacy as auto/biographical and cosmopolitan texts and acts, students and teachers may be able to respond to Dwayne Huebner's (1999b) call for a renewed spiritual and intellectual consciousness in teaching and learning. I argue that this new ethical turn, one that is appropriate and necessary for our precarious times, can lead to new vibrant and visceral knowledge and vital

P. Lewis and J. Tupper (eds.), *Challenges Bequeathed: Taking up the Challenges of Dwayne Huebner*, 25–37.
© 2009 sense publishers. All rights reserved.

literacies. Following Huebner, this turn can also give us insight into "where we have been, where we are, and where we are going" (1999c, p. 382), allow us to reimagine schools as places of "enlivened" knowledge, and create a more open, loving educational and social reality for us all in our mixed (up) worlds.

LIFE WRITING AS AN ETHOS FOR OUR COSMOPOLITAN TIMES

There is no easy exit from the quandary.

—Zygmunt Bauman, *Postmodern Ethics*

For a number of years, I have been teaching and researching with different groups of undergraduate and graduate students in Canadian cosmopolitan sites such as Vancouver, Calgary and Lethbridge and their surrounding Southern Alberta and West Coast communities, and in transnational locations in Europe, Asia, and the Caribbean. With students and colleagues in and from these locations, I use auto/biographical writing in a variety of life writing genres (journals, poetry, letters, personal essays, and other, mixed genres), as a way to make sense of our professional and personal lives in and outside K-12 and post-secondary classrooms (Chambers & Hasebe-Ludt, 2008; Hasebe-Ludt, Chambers, & Leggo, 2009).

As a teacher, writer and researcher, I advocate and use auto/biographical writing as a way to better understand selves and others in the world and as a means to implement meaningful literacy and social practices. In my classroom, students write regularly about their life experiences in and outside of school. This kind of "memory work" (Mitchell & Weber, 1999) encourages writing as thinking and learning in relation to others who have significantly influenced one's life, and in relation to one's place in the cosmos. Students generate writing individually and collaboratively, often through free flow timed writing exercises (Goldberg, 1986, 2000) on themes and topics such as names, place, identity, migration, and home (Bly, 2001). They then read aloud from their writing and enter into conversations about the resonances and resistances the writing created, thus finding starting points for negotiating their identities as learners and teachers in relation to others (Hasebe-Ludt, Bright, Chambers, Fowler, Pollard, & Winsor, 2003).

This life writing is accompanied by reading widely and deeply about issues of global and local cultures, languages, pedagogy, and curriculum in the context of classroom research (Carson & Sumara, 1997). Students sample texts from contemporary Canadian and North American curriculum scholars (Hasebe-Ludt & Hurren, 2003) and read exemplars of creative nonfiction, fiction, poetry and prose from world literature. While students remember and articulate their day-to-day lived worlds, I respond to their writing and write along with them, read aloud my own writing and other life writing texts. Thus we create a dialogical exchange, an intertext between self and world, a braided tapestry, or *métissage*, of creative reading and writing composed of the fabric of our own and others' words (Hasebe-Ludt, 2004; Chambers, Hasebe-Ludt, Leggo, & Oberg, 2008). This new pedagogical text is, in Huebner's (1999) words, also part of "the continual creation of the universe—of one's self, of others, of the dwelling places of the world" (p. 350).

Reflecting on these experiences, I trace our travels to cosmopolitan landscapes where students and teachers do the work of the world, in hermeneutical acts of becoming, through language. I illuminate parts of the geo-cultural landscapes we enter and through this writing come to know ourselves and the universe in a different way. Through threads of prose and poetic texts, I aim to document a movement towards a *currere* where students and teachers can find vital and vibrant interpretive and imaginative spaces for (re)reading and (re)writing the word and the world auto/biographically (Freire & Macedo, 1987; Pinar, 1994a). Through this movement, in turn, life writing,, "may get us a heart of wisdom" (Myerhoff, as cited in Kadar, 1993, p. ix), one that is urgently needed at this time, "in the midst of turmoil and unsettledness" (Huebner, 1999b, p. 350).

THE HEART OF PEDAGOGICAL REALTIONSHIPS

"Adieu," dit le renard. "Voici mon secret. Il est très simple: on ne voit bien qu'avec le coeur. L'essentiel est invisible pour les yeux."...."C'est le temps que tu as perdu pour ta rose qui fait ta rose si importante. "Tu deviens responsable pour toujours de ce que tu as apprivoisé. Tu es responsable de ta rose...." "Je suis responsable de ma rose..." répéta le petit prince, afin de se souvenir.

—Antoine de Saint-Exupéry, *Le Petit Prince*

In this epigraph from a classic story, a fox reminds a boy of two truths that the child should never forget: that the important things can only be seen with the heart, and that he is responsible for what he has cultivated. The animal also teaches the boy to remember that it is the time "lost" for taking care of his rose that matters. This story illustrates the conflict that still resides in our world today, and particularly in the teaching world: children's playful and cognizant voices are drowned by the dominating noise of powerful adults (Huebner, 1999c, p. 381).

David Jardine (1994), in quoting the philosopher Hannah Arendt (1958), urges teachers to remember that the heart of pedagogy remains with the fact that children are *borne* into the world and brought up—taken care of, cultivated—in relation to others in the world. The generativity and generosity of the idea of students or the young being in the world as gifts we must (at)tend to holds both promise and difficulty for those responsible for them "in loco parentis," responding to their pedagogical needs. Dwayne Huebner (1999c) reminds us that as teachers we need to respond to students' calls and be an active part in the formation of their life stories. "Responsibility is to keep the ability to respond," the poet Robert Duncan (1960, n.p.) proclaimed. Hannah Arendt believed that to truly live responsibly in a "common world shared by others" (Varner Gunn, 1982), we must think and lead an active life, a "vita activa," in relation to those others, tell our stories and listen to each others' stories in order to learn from our respective lives (Arendt, 1958; Neumann & Peterson, 1997). Through this, according to Dwayne Huebner (1999b), we can also access the myths, stories, and poetry of others that are part of our spiritual, social and historical fabric of life. In that vulnerable, fluid place between knowing and being, we go back and forth negotiating those conditions for both preserving and generating life and pedagogical becoming between the old and new, between memories and imaginings. And it is there where, as teachers, we open ourselves up to the questioning of *pre-scribed* notions of existing frameworks and, together with our students, create vibrant possibilities for new understandings of curriculum and for engaging in border crossings between different existing and imagined worlds. This movement towards embracing difference surpassesmodernist, neo-liberalist, and neo-conservative projections of otherness that do not consider marginality. Rather, this new imagining seeks out a *third space* beyond dualist and universalist notions of pluralism that merely hide or erase difference (Aoki, 1999/2003; Bhabha, 1990; Smith, 2006). Huebner connects this openness and sensitivity to the "otherness of the world" (1999b, p. 345) with a vulnerability that includes hope, patience, and love.

When crossing the threshold into the newness of experiences, of emerging personal and pedagogical meanings, identities shift in the transgressive spaces of *currere* between the historical past and the present reality of our lives (Pinar, 1994a). To describe the experience of living in those spaces, in the context of her own work as a literary scholar and ethnographer moving between two cultural geographies—Germany and the California Coast—and attempting to translate her work into a new language, Gabrielle Schwab (1994) uses the German term *Entgrenzung*:

> *Entgrenzung* is a word whose connections run from the action of the lifting of boundaries—their transgression, transformation, or expansion—to the syncretistic experience in which details and structures are grasped holistically. Moreover, *Entgrenzung* also recalls the fragmentations and dissolutions of form and structure prominent in modernism and post-modernism. It is a word that calls up such different realms of discourse as geography and geopolitics, morphology, psychoanalysis and aesthetics. (p. vii)

This experience of being "an ethnographer in two foreign cultures" resonates with me, having lived in transcultural contact zones (Pratt, 1992) between different languages, cultures and discourses throughout much of my life. In these zones, I remember my once familiar German birth place and original home, and I juxtapose it with my seemingly familiar present Canadian home. As an immigrant, this challenges me to rethink my identity in relation to what constitutes home and not-home, as I continually negotiate self and other in a transcontinental dialogue about the stranger within myself (Wang, 2004). As a teacher and a learner, I am immersed in a similar dialogue between different curriculum fields, that of the mandated *curriculum-as-plan* of teacher education institutions and public schools and that of the *curriculum-as-lived* (Aoki, 1986/2005) where students and teachers try to make sense of their own daily worlds and the larger world they live in. Where we are from, geographically and historically, and where we place ourselves in the present landscapes of cultural and linguistic mixed identities—these shifting locations are part of a continuous process of mapping "our mongrel selves" (Rushdie, 1991; Sandercock, 2003) in order to discover what matters in our lives and work. The connotations and resonances that emerge can become generative acts of traveling, visiting and living with/in the "many faces of cosmo-polis" comprised of different peoples, places, cultures, and histories (Mignolo, 2000) and cosmopolitan and particular identities (Pinar, 2008).

In this process, memory plays the part of the shifter, or the trickster, taking on an ambiguous role of both here *and* there, this *and* that, then *and* now, not only/but also—illuminating a metonymic as well as metaphoric space of partial truths, joyful and painful at the same time. Carl Jung, in his essay *On the Psychology of the Trickster Figure* (Jung, 1956/1972), uses the analogy of the medieval carnival with its reversal of the hierarchical order and "contradictoriness" to illuminate the trickster as the shadow figure that reminds us of "the memory image of things as they were" (p. 200), pointing back to an earlier stage of consciousness and the psyche's meaning making. Standing behind the shadow trickster figure is the *anima* (relationship). The encounter between shadow and *anima* affects our inside and outside worlds by integrating the shadow "on the plane of the *anima*…through relatedness" (p. 211). We carry the shadow parts of self, the personal memories that are also connected with collective myths and stories (Huebner, 1999b) into our present and strive to integrate them into our literary and literacy endeavours, much like the visual and visceral images of a *scene* that leave a lasting impression. We aim for a holistic, imaginative integration of these memories that are connected to Jung's "archetypes" of powerful ideas and inspirations of history. Huebner (1999b) sees these spiritual experiences as part of a people's "tradition," expressed through stories, histories, myths, and poems. We begin with fragments, memories of moments, or *scenes.* Referring to Goethe's epistolary autobiographical novel *Die Leiden des Jungen Werther/The Sorrows of Young Werther*, Roland Barthes (1978) illuminates this inspired imagination:

> Stepping out of the carriage, Werther sees Charlotte for the first time (and falls in love with her), framed by the door of her house (cutting bread-and-butter for the children: a famous scene, often discussed): the first thing we fall in love with is a *scene*. Is the scene always visual? It can be aural, the frame can be linguistic: I can fall in love with a *sentence spoken to me:* and not only because it says something which manages to touch my desire, but because of its syntactical turn (framing), which will inhabit me *like a memory.* (p. 192)

Through language and storied memories that illuminate those sometimes shining, sometimes sad, often angry, but also healing moments, understandings of what matters in our lives are forged. Elizabeth Ellsworth (1997) reminds us that pedagogy is an embodied relationship that

> …gets right in there—in your brain, your body, your heart, in your sense of self, of the world, of others, and of possibilities and impossibilities in all those realms. A pedagogical mode of address is where the social construction of knowledge and learning gets deeply personal. It's a relationship whose subtleties can shape and misshape lives, passions for learning, and broader social dynamics. (p. 6)

Teachers' knowledge about teaching derives from their own lives and in relationship with the world (Neumann & Peterson, 1997, p. 1). Conversely, how teachers work with students and respond to their call/ing influences their lives (Huebner, 1999c). These reciprocal processes constitute autobiographical as well as cosmopolitan pedagogical acts. Through life writing, students' and teachers' memories of pedagogical and personal relationships come alive as part of their curriculum in the cosmos of pedagogical responsibility.

In addition to writing, when students respond to readings and to conversations with invited guests—visiting scholars, artists, authors, and others whose life work focuses on issues of identity, difference, culture, and community—students enter new layered dialogues about living with others in the ambiguous metonymic spaces in between different worlds. Examining specific memories of experiences, such as being in the majority or minority, feeling excluded or included, working through im/migration and diaspora and other experiences that "evict us from ourselves" (Cixous, 1997)—these movements often illuminate the vulnerability and risk-taking that makes learning as a transformative process possible (Huebner, 199b). Experiencing oneself as other, such as in the case of a Chinese student who grew up in a small coastal town in Western Canada as the only Asian student and then moved to Vancouver where he was one among many Chinese students in his elementary classroom, has a profound effect on one's shifting identity in different geo-cultural landscapes.

The complexities of relating to others and their lives in the context of reading and writing the word and the world often involve a doubling or layering of an individual's voice and a reversal of roles of teacher and student, writer and reader. This also involves the responsibility of putting one's self in the other's heart and mind, the other's text. The ability to enter into a reciprocal relationship and "take both sides" (Garrison, 1996), the deliberate attempt to discover one's self in the other, and to care for the other and the self—often constitutes a paradoxical challenge. There is no comfortable closure that presents itself (Bauman, 1993). There is, instead, an "unending dialogue" (Gadamer, 1975) with self and other that opens up in the responsibility toward the other and that is, paradoxically, grounded in local, individual truths (Levinas, 1985). In pedagogical terms,

> this requires a fidelity to that which calls out to us from within the heart of what we do not understand and for which we may not at present have words. Pedagogy then becomes a vocation to live and act within the difference between what we know and what we do not know and what calls us from within and beyond ourselves. (Smith, 1997, p. 276)

In addressing this alterity or open-endedness, the poet Kenneth Rexroth, in his commentary on Robert Duncan's *The opening of the field* (1960)asserts: "The use of language may have changed or developed, but the theme is consistently the mind and body of love" (n.p.). Duncan, like Dante, was often called a poet of cosmic imagination, intensely aware of language's role in the ever-expanding and recurrent creation of new worlds (Bertholf, 1993). Similarly, in his book *Waiting for the Earth to Turn Over*, which links identity, landscape and belonging, Philip

Garrison (1996) describes the notion of memory as clinging like an asterisk to one's thinking, saturating the present by internalizing past events, a private chronology of thoughts "floating along on nudges and tugs of associations" (p. 77). He retells the mythical association of landscape with memory and identity by Indigenous peoples of the American North- and Southwest, illuminating the complex relationship between place, storied identity, and pedagogical and moral knowing. Similarly, Cynthia Chambers traces Canadian Indigenous peoples'—the Blackfoot of Southern Alberta and the *Kangiryuarmuit* of the Northwest Territories—situated dwelling on the land and their "education of attention" through their stories (Chambers, 2006, 2008). Dwayne Huebner sees this vulnerability and receptivity towards living in relationship with others and with other-ness as a condition for experiencing the spiritual as part of pedagogical calling—and of new knowledge (Huebner, 1999c, p. 385). We journey through the landscapes of learning and teaching in both intimate and worldly ways, poetically, narratively, through words and the movements between words, building on the lessons of the shadow, the trickster, and on the dreams of the past. We write the texts of pedagogical relationships in new and unpredictable ways, resonating with the memory of storied living with others, through communicative and performative acts, by "dancing with desire" (Leggo, 1996) among the community of treasured relations, be it through writing, reading, listening, speaking or creative movements of other kinds. The *care-full* cultivation of relationships is at once inevitable and necessary while we struggle and soar to perform the complex steps of teaching/learning in order to find "new ways to make sense of the sense children are making" (Gallas, 1994, p. 161). In order for this to happen, we must talk together and listen to each other, exchange and express the stories of our lives together. Decades after her influential writing in *Landscapes of Learning* (Greene, 1978), Maxine Greene reaffirmed the need to "think together" and learn from our lives together, urging us to shape our lives through stories, and to remember "how much that enables us to begin to understand...and to discover our moral purpose" (Greene, 1997, p. 34). Thus, our common task remains that of composing and texturing our lives to discover our selves in others while reaching out for community and affinity in our work. In these acts, it is crucial for us to imagine, as Adrienne Rich reminds us, "whom we envision as our hearers, our co-creators, our challengers; who will urge us to take our work further, more seriously, than we had dared; on whose work we can build" (Rich, 1979, p. 214).

IMAGINING A NEW COSMOS

You can only understand what you love.

—Johann Wolfgang von Goethe, *West-East Divan*

When working with life writing, I continue to invite teachers to ask questions about "what matters," what it means to live in the face of others—supervisors, colleagues, peers, elders, and the young people in their charge--through the task of pedagogical care. It is the open-endedness, the "indeterminability" of that task which inevitably gets in the way for those who see teaching predominantly as a set of techniques, as perfecting the mechanics and delivering the content of the curriculum, and as controlling life inside the classroom. The difficulties involved in facing one's own evolving identity in relation to that of others, continue to challenge me in relation to my students as a necessary and inevitable pedagogical act. Robert Kroetsch (1989) reminds me that we must confront our locations and dislocations, and in doing so, confront our traditions, our memories, our identity construction from those (dis)locations. Similarly, Dwayne Huebner (1999c) reaffirms that, as teachers, we need to listen to others and be the narrators of their stories, just as much as they listen to and narrate our stories as part of dialogical pedagogical action. I also recallTed Aoki, who speaks and writes about identity not so much as something already present but as being constituted as we live in the messy spaces and imperfect places of difference, so that our identities as teachers can be understood as ongoing effects of our imagining and becoming in difference (Aoki, 2003; Low & Palulis, 2004).

Ted Aoki and Dwayne Huebner, both eminent curriculum scholars, pay attention to the ways teachers are subjected to prescribed notions of curriculum and identities, especially beginning teachers. I remember how whenever Ted Aoki met with my undergraduate and graduate students, he stimulated muchthinking about what qualities an educator should embody. A Zen Buddhist saying, "The greatest human delusion is that I am here and you are there," stirred a great deal of discussion about the interconnectedness between self and other, about how being/becoming in the midst of difference affects teachers' relationships with students.

In our precarious lives and times (Butler, 2006; Chambers, 2006), tainted with tales of terror (Borradori, 2003) and great untruths (Smith, 2006), pedagogical action requires a new ethical foundation for social, cultural and pedagogical relations, so that the interdependency that is at the heart of these actions does not produce, as David G. Smith (1997) warns, "a certain hypocrisy in human relations, insofar as ultimate self-interest inevitably overshadows any genuine interest-free concern for another's welfare, or love of another purely for their own sake" (p. 269). It is not enough, Smith asserts, for others "to simply provide the backdrop for that autobiography in which inevitably I am the hero" (p. 270). In considering what truly sustains us in the world pedagogically, lovingly, in the sense of the Taoist notion of *The Way* as a path to wisdom (Smith, 1997, 2008), in the Eastern tradition, or in the Western tradition in the notion of *wide-awakeness* (Greene, 1978), we can move beyond seeing self and other as separate entities. Instead we can turn towards acceptingwhat we already are and what is while imagining what we are not yet.

In our lifewriting, identity remains a recurring theme, interwoven into textual layers of cosmos, community, neighbourhood, school, and classroom, reflected in the folds and fissures created by the contact of different textual, geographical, cultural, and human relations. We start with the tangible, the geographical *where*, to trace our place. We follow the *curriculum-as-plan* only to discover much more than a map of topographical and curricular variables. Inevitably, we discover the *curriculum-as-lived*, the geo-cultural human relationships, mappings of the human heart that are deeply personal and at the same time transcend local and individual places of learning.

Unvermeidlich

Wer will mir wehren zu singen
Nach Lust zum Himmel hinan,
Den Wolken zu vertrauen
Wie lieb sie mir's angetan?

Inevitable

Who can prevent me from singing
my desire to the heavens,
to entrust to the clouds
the measure of my love?
(Goethe, 1819/1977, p. 314)

In the German language, the verb "vertrauen," a key word in Goethe's poem from his *Buch der Liebe [Book of Love]*, bears the double meaning of (en)trusting/ confiding in another person and of joining two people in matrimony. By adding the reflexive pronoun "*sich*" to the verb "trauen," the semantic field expands to the notion of risk taking: it becomes the act of "daring to do something." In this doubling and mixing of semantic properties, love becomes an expression of intellect, wisdom and spirituality in the relations of self to other, to the world, so that love of another is always also a love of the world. These tropes are reflected in many of Goethe's poems, and the poet and philosopher intended them to express the "double drama" of desire and intellect, of heart and soul, of earthly pleasure and heavenly spirit, of west and east, young and old, male and female (Goethe, 1819/1977, pp. 765–766). Goethe wrote these poems close to the end of his life. They resonate with the unbridled passion and wisdom of a philosopher whose never-ending love of the world and hope for dialogue and freedom were expressed through both his senses and his intellect and illuminated by the mirroring of the other within the self. Goethe, through the poetic voice of Suleika, who represents his female other, rejoices in the double nature of the self and the representation of the inner world in/to the outside world through the poetry of the female *anima*.

Similarly, world-renowned curriculum scholar William F. Pinar, in his essay on *currere* as an autobiographical force, expresses the doubling action constituted by life writing through the metaphor of matrimony:

> ...autobiographical studies are windows which permit us to see again that which we loved before, and in so doing, see more clearly what and whom we love in the present. The regressive phase of *currere* asks us to speak again...,to see again what was outside our windows, and to become married—that is, in unison—with ourselves and with those around us, by renewing our vows to those who are past, exchanging vows with those who are present, and dancing our way until the morning dawns. (Pinar, 1994b, p. 267)

In the domain of writing, Jacques Derrida invokes the notion of intertextuality (Bennington & Derrida, 1991) to describe how an outside layer repeats or folds itself back on itself in an inside layer and becomes a multi-layeredness that invites us to probe for meaning in the folds and fissures. Similarly, the "faults" in Paul Ricoeur's notion of openness to other-ness and newness in the world (Huebner, 1999c) invite us to read lives as texts that reverberate with the lived experiences of students and teachers dwelling together in inspirited relationships. These dialogical processes of reading and writing, and of teaching and learning, require a shifting of perspective by reader and writer, teacher and student, blurring the boundaries between where one starts and the other ends. The notion and motion of "en glissade" (Taylor, 1991) captures the vital and vibrant action of reconceptualizing and reimagining curriculum as an artistic and aesthetic sliding into a third space of meaning making in between self and other (Bhabha, 1990).

This new imagining is a space of possibility that sees teaching as indeterminable, curriculum and the construction of self as an intertwined infinite process, much like Gadamer's (1987) never-ending dialogues that constitute inaugural performative acts, resonant of Bakhtin's (1986/1979) understanding of the end of one narrative as the beginning of a new one. We do not know where our stories of teaching and learning are going and where teaching and for that matter "good" teaching happens. Elizabeth Ellsworth (1997) acknowledges that all thoughts are afterthoughts and that "the good teacher is the one who gives what s/he doesn't have: the future as undecidable, possibility as indeterminable" (p. 173). Thus, we live with the paradoxes of the recurrence of memory and the invention of new autobiographical acts, charged with the responsibility to produce "partial texts that reconfigure what counts as the world, and by doing so, what counts as valued and valuable bodies and lives in that world" (p. 164).

Teaching, as a relational and transformational act, constitutes and requires a loving disposition for both teachers and students. Nel Noddings (1997), in an autobiographical essay on her own acts of love as a teacher and philosopher, reminds us that "kids will do things for people they like and trust. They are inspired by a form of love" (p. 180). David G. Smith (1997) equates this act with "accepting all others in the way a very young child does, trusting the world as being the only world there is, engaging in it without fear" (p. 278). Teachers' lives are composed out of the contradictory loves for their students and their subjects. As a teacher of teachers, of language and literacy, I must face that to write about love is to confront the chaos of language, to move into "that panic-stricken region where language is both too much and too little" (Barthes, 1978, p. 328). My own love of language resonates with the paradoxical and exhilarating act of what Karen Gallas (1992) has called "nurturing our ability to speak in tongues" (p. 160). Through "unending dialogues" (Gadamer, 1987) infused with the texts of others we write and rewrite the lived world of curriculum and the lived curriculum of the world. We enter into the transgressive spaces that emerge in between mixed geographical and cultural identities—graphing, (re)writing the cosmo-polis we live in, thus, ultimately taking writing to the state of a non-personal power (Deleuze & Parnet, 1986).

And so I linger, together with my co-writers, in the difficult pleasure of our shared texts and our teachings, as we create a new intertextual cosmos of worldly complicated conversations and sometimes shining moments, immediate and imagined , engaged in communal pedagogical wondering and wandering. Pulled by Huebner's "lure of the transcendent," we write daringly, lovingly, and hopefully, scripting scenes of poetic radiance on the edge of a future memory.

REFERENCES

Aoki, T. T. (1986/2005). Teaching as in-dwelling between two curriculum worlds. In W. F. Pinar & R. L. Irwin (Eds.), *Curriculum in a new key: The collected works of Ted T. Aoki* (pp. 159–165). Mahwah, NJ: Lawrence Erlbaum.
Aoki, T. T. (1992). Layered voices of teaching: The uncannily correct and the elusively true. In W. F. Pinar & W. M. Reynolds (Eds.), *Understanding curriculum as phenomenological and deconstructed text* (pp. 17–27). New York: Teachers College Press.
Aoki, T. T. (2003). Locating living pedagogy in teacher "research": Five metonymic moments. In E. Hasebe-Ludt & W. Hurren (Eds.), *Curriculum intertext: Place/language/pedagogy* (pp. 1–9). New York: Peter Lang Publishing.
Arendt, H. (1958). *The human condition.* Chicago: University of Chicago Press.
Bakhtin, M. M. (1986). *Speech genres and other late essays* (C. Emerson & M. Holquist, Eds.; V. W. McGee, Trans.). Austin, TX: University of Texas Press.
Barthes, R. (1978). *A lover's discourse: Fragments* (R. Howard, Trans.). New York: Hill and Wang.
Bauman, Z. (1993). *Postmodern ethics.* Oxford, UK & Cambridge, USA: Blackwell.
Bennington, G., & Derrida, J. (1991). *Jacques Derrida.* Paris: Seuil.
Bertholf, R. J. (Ed.). (1993). *Robert Duncan: Selected poems.* New York: New Directions Publishing.
Bhabha, H. K. (Ed.). (1990). *Nation and narration.* New York: Routledge and Keegan Paul.
Bly, C. (2001). *Beyond the writers' workshop: New ways to write creative nonfiction.* New York: Anchor Books.
Borradori, G. (2003). *Philosophy in a time of terror: Dialogues with Jürgen Habermas and Jacques Derrida.* Chicago: University of Chicago Press.
Bruner, J. (1996). *The culture of education.* Cambridge, MA: Harvard University Press.
Butler, J. (2006). *Precarious life: The power of mourning and violence.* London: Verso.
Carson, T. R., & Sumara, D. (Eds.). (1997). *Action research as a living practice.* New York: Peter Lang Publishing.
Chambers, C. (2006, Fall). "The land is the best teacher I ever had": Places as pedagogy for precarious times. *Journal of Curriculum Theorizing, 22*(3), 27–37.
Chambers, C. (2008). Where are we? Finding common ground in a curriculum of place. *Journal of the Canadian Association for Curriculum Studies, 6*(2), 113-128.
Chambers, C., & Hasebe-Ludt, E., with Donald, D., Hurren, W., Leggo, C., & Oberg, A. (2008). Métissage: A research praxis. In J. K. Knowles & A. L. Cole (Eds.), *Handbook of the arts in qualitative research: Perspectives, methodologies, examples, and issues* (pp. 141–153). Los Angeles: Sage Publications.
Deleuze, G., & Parnet, C. (1986). *Dialogues* (H. Tomlinson & B. Habberjam, Trans.). New York: Columbia University Press.
Duncan, R. (1960). *The opening of the field.* New York: Grover Press.
Ellsworth, E. (1997). *Teaching positions: Difference, pedagogy, and the power of address.* New York: Teachers College Press.
Freire, P., & Macedo, D. (1987). *Literacy: Reading the word and the world.* South Hadley, MA: Bergin & Garvey.
Gadamer, H.-G. (1975). *Truth and method* (J. Weinsheimer & D. G. Marshall, Trans.). New York: Continuum.
Gadamer, H.-G. (1987). *Gesammelte Werke (Band 4). Neuere philosophie II: Probleme, gestalten [Collected works (Vol. 4). Newer philosophy II: Problems, contours].* Tübingen: J. C. B. Mohr.

Gallas, K. (1994). *The languages of learning: How children talk, write, dance, draw, and sing their understanding of the world.* New York: Teachers College Press.

Garrison, P. (1996). *Waiting for the earth to turn over: Identity and the late twentieth-century American West.* Salt Lake City, UT: University of Utah Press.

Goethe, J. W. (1819/1977). West-östlicher Divan [West-east divan]. In *Johann Wolfgang Goethe: Sämtliche Werke, Band 3 [Johann Wolfgang von Goethe: Collected works, Volume 3].* Zürich: Artemis-Verlags-AG.

Goldberg, N. (1986). *Writing down the bones: Freeing the writer within.* Boston: Shambhala Publications.

Goldberg, N. (2000). *Thunder and lightning: Cracking open the writer's craft.* New York: Bantam Books.

Greene, M. (1978). *Landscapes of learning.* New York: Teachers College Press.

Greene, M. (1997). Exclusions and awakenings. In A. Neumann & P. L. Peterson (Eds.), *Learning from our lives: Women, research and autobiography in education* (pp. 18–36). New York: Teachers College Press.

Hasebe-Ludt, E. (2004). "We talked freely of many things": Writing home/away from home. In A. L. Cole, L. Neilsen, J. G. Knowles, & T. C. Luciani (Eds.), *Provoked by art: Theorizing arts-informed research* (pp. 203–213). Halifax, NS: Backalong Books.

Hasebe-Ludt, E., Bright, R., Chambers, C., Fowler, L., Pollard, M., & Winsor, P. (2003). What are the new literacies? Writing and teaching and living with the questions. In G. Erickson & A. Clarke (Eds.), *Teacher inquiry: Living the research in everyday practice* (pp. 103–114). RoutledgeFalmer.

Hasebe-Ludt, E., Chambers, C., & Leggo, C. (2009). *Life writing and literary métissage as an ethos for our times.* New York: Peter Lang.Hasebe-Ludt, E., Chambers, C., Leggo, C., & Oberg, A. (2008). Embracing the world, with all our relations: Métissage as an artful braiding. In S. Springgay, R. L. Irwin, C. Leggo, & P. Gouzouasis (Eds.), *Being with a/r/tography* (pp. 57–68). Rotterdam/Taipei: Sense Publishers.

Hasebe-Ludt, E., & Hurren, W. (Eds.). (2003). *Curriculum intertext: Language/place/pedagogy.* New York: Peter Lang Publishing.

Huebner, D. (1999a). Challenges bequeathed (1996). In V. Hillis (Ed.), *The lure of the transcendent: Collected essays by Dwayne E. Huebner* (pp. 432–445). Mahwah, NJ: Lawrence Erlbaum Associates.

Huebner, D. (1999b). Spirituality and knowing (1985). In V. Hillis (Ed.), *The lure of the transcendent: Collected essays by Dwayne E. Huebner* (pp. 340–352). Mahwah, NJ: Lawrence Erlbaum Associates.

Huebner, D. (1999c). Teaching as a vocation (1987). In V. Hillis (Ed.), *The lure of the transcendent: Collected essays by Dwayne E. Huebner* (pp. 379–387). Mahwah, NJ: Lawrence Erlbaum Associates.

Jardine, D. W. (1994). *Speaking with a boneless tongue.* Bragg Creek, AB: Makyo Press.

Jung, C. G. (1956/1972). On the psychology of the trickster figure (R. F. C. Hull, Trans.). In P. Radin (Ed.), *The trickster: A study in American Indian mythology* (pp. 195–211). New York: Schocken Books.

Kadar, M. (1993). *Reading life writing.* Toronto, ON: Oxford University Press.

Kroetsch, R. (1989). *The lovely treachery of words: Essays selected and new.* Toronto, ON: Oxford University Press.

Leggo, C. (1996). Dancing with desire: A meditation on psychoanalysis, politics, and pedagogy. *Teachers and Teaching: Theory and Practice, 2*(2), 233–242.

Levinas, E. (1985). Responsibility for the other. In *Ethics and infinity: Conversations with Phillipe Nemo* (R. A. Cohen, Trans., pp. 93–101). Pittsburgh: Duquesne University Press.

Low, M., & Palulis, P. (2004). Laboured breathing: Running with and against internationalizing texts of currere. *Transnational Curriculum Inquiry, 1*(1). Retrieved from http://www.deakin.edu.au/tci

Mignolo, W. D. (2000). The many face of cosmo-polis. *Public Culture, 12*(3), 721–748.

Mitchell, C., & Weber, S. (1999). *Reinventing ourselves as teachers: Beyond nostalgia.* London: Falmer Press.

Noddings, N. (1997). Accident, awareness, and actualization. In A. Neumann & P. Peterson (Eds.), *Learning from our lives: Women, research and autobiography in education* (pp. 166–182). New York: Teachers College Press.

Neumann, A., & Peterson, P. (Eds.). (1997). *Learning from our lives: Women, research and autobiography in education*. New York: Teachers College Press.

Pinar. W. F. (1994a). *Autobiography, politics, and sexuality: Essays in curriculum theory 1972-1992*. New York: Peter Lang.

Pinar, W. F. (1994b). The lost language of cranes: Windows and mirrors in the regressive phase of currere. In *Autobiography, politics and sexuality: Essays in curriculum theory 1972–1992* (pp. 253–268). New York: Peter Lang.

Pinar, W. F. (2008). *On the agony and ecstasy of the particular: Identity politics, autobiography, cosmopolitanism*. Centre for the Study of Internationalization of Curriculum Studies, Faculty of Education, University of British Columbia. Retrieved from http://csics.educ.ubc.ca/projects.html

Pratt, M. L. (1992). *Travel writing and transculturation*. London: Routledge.

Rich, A. (1979). *On lies, secrets, and silence: Selected prose 1966–1978*. New York: Norton.

Rushdie, S. (1991). *Imaginary homelands: Essays and criticism 1981–1991*. London: Granta Books.

Saint-Exupéry, A. (1946). *Le petit prince*. Paris: Gallimard.

Sandercock, L. (2003). *Cosmopolis II: Mongrel cities of the 21st century*. New York: Continuum.

Schwab, G. (1994). *Subjects without selves: Transitional texts in modern fiction*. Cambridge, MA: Harvard University Press.

Smith, D. G. (1997). Identity, self, and other in the conduct of pedagogical action: An east/west inquiry. In T. R. Carson & D. J. Sumara (Eds.), *Action research as a living practice* (pp. 265–280). New York: Peter Lang.

Smith, D. G. (1999). Brighter than a thousand suns: Facing pedagogy in the nuclear shadow. In D. G. Smith (Ed.), *Pedagon: Interdisciplinary essays in the human sciences, pedagogy, and culture* (pp. 127–141). New York: Peter Lang.

Smith, D. G. (1999). *Pedagon: Interdisciplinary essays in the human sciences, pedagogy, and culture*. New York: Peter Lang.

Smith, D. G. (2006). *Trying to teach in a season of great untruth: Globalization, empire and the crises of pedagogy*. Rotterdam/Taipei: Sense Publishers.

Taylor, C. (1991). *The malaise of modernity*. Concord, ON: Anansi.

Varner Gunn, J. (1982). *Autobiography: Toward a poetics of experience*. Philadelphia: University of Pennsylvania Press.

Wang, H. (2004). *The call from he stranger on a journey home: Curriculum in a third space*. NewYork: Peter Lang Publishing.

KAREN MEYER AND CARL LEGGO

IMAGINING OTHERWISE

Tantalizing Tales from the Centre

To endure is to live with promise, with possibilities. It is to believe, with the weed, in the value of living in a crack in the cement. It is to blossom where no blossoms were expected. It is to say that the world might be made habitable. But such faith often is not enough. Perseverance requires the creative. It calls for improvisational acts in a concrete world. (Pelias, 2004, p. 77)

To administer is to minister, to serve. (Huebner, 1999, p. 385)

Dwayne Huebner (1999) refers to imagination as "the storehouse of human possibility–ethical, intellectual, political" (p. 436). In this sense, imagination is the capacity to bring forth new realities, assuring renewal and at least the possibility of what Hannah Arendt (1977) called "setting right" of the world (p. 189). As educators, we begin by asking: What kinds of responsibilities are demanded of us when imagination takes on a significant role in education? In this chapter we take up this question by exploring narratives of "imagining otherwise"—a backward glance at the accomplishments and struggles of an active 'counter-community' located in our Faculty of Education at the University of British Columbia. Huebner invites narrating personal journeys "to help us think about the others with whom we work", and asks, "can we look at students as we look at ourselves: on a journey, responding to that which calls them into the world" (p. 382)? Our narratives, as the former Director and Graduate Advisor of the Centre for the Study of Curriculum and Instruction, are recounted alongside reflections inspired by Huebner's further claim that "imagination is the manifestation of human freedom" (p. 436).

LIVING IMAGINATION AT THE CENTRE

In *The Prophetic Imagination* Walter Brueggemann (2001) claims that imagination is a "legitimate way of knowing" (p. x). It manifests within insight beyond the ordinary, the expected, and the knowledge structures of what the world is. Following a prophetic tradition that advocates what could be different, prophetic imagination offers possible realities counter to the dominant reality that Brueggemann argues "enjoys institutional, hegemonic authority but is characteristically uncritical of itself" (p. xi). Such alternative realities often become realized in counter-communities whereby members share a willingness to be critical of the dominant reality, as the

P. Lewis and J. Tupper (eds.), *Challenges Bequeathed: Taking up the Challenges of Dwayne Huebner*, 39–50.
© 2009 sense publishers. All rights reserved.

way things are, and engage alternative practices of what could be different. In this case, a community knows and experiences itself to be in a position of tension with the dominant community, which responds to counter-communities "at best as an inconvenience, at worst as an unbearable interruption" (p. xvi). In any best or worst case scenario, the tension is felt most markedly at the border between the counter and dominant communities. The inside and outside of each is clear. The ethos of each can be poles apart.

Karen: Unbearable Interruption. I came on board July 1, Canada Day. The hiring process had been a political whirlwind. Someone was needed to fill the position of Director for the Centre. It had to be someone 'from within' the Faculty because hiring a new person wasn't financially possible. There had been two interim directors in the past two years keeping the Centre community of graduate students viable. Since the Centre's conception it had been surrounded by controversy concerning the need for its existence. It was unusual compared to bordering departments and centres in the university. Usually centres are research units rather than program units. The Centre had a large graduate program similar to a department, but no faculty positions. While still following the rules of program requirements— what it takes for students to be admitted, graduated, etc.—the Centre's 25 year-old structure was intended particularly to promote interdisciplinarity. In that way, advisors and instructors would come to the program from across other departments. A good idea, but in reality it was tough for faculty members to cross their own departmental borders for many reasons. Those who did teach courses and supervise students in the Centre, jumped across borders from time to time.

Over the years, this arrangement created and sustained a strong student commitment because full and part time students, rather than faculty, constituted the heart and soul of the community. Students weren't positioned at the bottom rung of the hierarchical ladder like in most departments. The Centre attracted students whose research was interdisciplinary, 'outside the box' of traditional scholarship, and creatively expressed. Some students had transferred to the Centre from other departments. The evolution of such a community in a student-centred structure enabled and fostered a robust student voice concerning the never-ending politics surrounding the Centre, as well as active participation in their own learning. As one might expect, the community frequently collided directly with dominant positions of institutional authority, particularly in the form of knowledge expertise—who has it and who does not. This is where that story began....

Charges Laid

when I walked into my office for the first time
I didn't feel like I knew how to be in charge
of anything
though I'm a teacher and parent
–both 'in charge' callings–
they feel part of my nature
not this

I was given the charge to create something
out of a ship that was about to sink
not by design
but by reconfiguration and political charges
all I could imagine to do
was to re imagine

Carl: Bearing Witness. Even in the beginning, when I first joined UBC in 1990, I was a staunch supporter of the Centre for the Study of Curriculum and Instruction. I recognized that the Centre was a location for creative and innovative research, a location where graduate scholars with diverse backgrounds and interests gathered. Eventually, I served on the faculty committee that recommended to the Dean that Karen become the next Director. When Karen presented her vision for the Centre, she spoke about the metaphor of a café, evoking the hope for a space where scholars could linger together and learn together. I was immediately entranced, ready to order an espresso with all the intense bursting of flavor that Karen's vision promised.

I subsequently served on the advisory committee for the Centre. Around this time, I had just returned to campus from my first sabbatical leave, and I had decided that I would focus more of my energy on creative writing, especially poetry. During the sabbatical year, I grew convinced that I didn't want to be caught up in the politics of the academy and I certainly didn't want to be involved in administration. Instead I wanted to continue to grow as a writer, and to pursue writing without the kind of nagging encumbrances that I was sure characterized administrative positions. Then, Karen called a meeting of the advisory committee, and indicated that she needed a Graduate Advisor for the Centre. She also informed us that she was not having much success finding a colleague to fill the role. Following the meeting, I carefully considered Karen's request, and sent an e-mail indicating that I was willing to become the Graduate Advisor. Even at the time, and certainly often since then, I have been impressed by how little I actually wanted the position. I received a two-course buyout from teaching in order to serve as Graduate Advisor, but since I love teaching, I did not see any actual advantage in surrendering teaching in order to write memos and go to meetings and diplomatically manoeuvre the often complex and tangled stories that graduate students sometimes find themselves in. I offered to become the Graduate Advisor because I admired Karen and because I was enthused with her vision for the Centre. Karen wanted to nurture a community of scholars who were creative, courageous, and collaborative. So, for the next several years I stood beside Karen as she devoted herself to fostering a vision that would define the Centre even while knowing the Centre would never be at the centre of the academy.

Carl: Acknowledging Mystery and Profundity. Wendell Berry (2001) claims, "we are involved ... in a profound failure of imagination" (p. 40). The Centre was all about imagination, all about dreaming possibilities. Some colleagues probably thought Karen and I were naïve, romantic dreamers who used words like celebration and wonder too much. But, we were compelled by a profound sense of education as transformative. Like Berry (2001) we understand that "education is not properly an industry, and its proper use is not to serve industries, either by job-training or by industry-subsidized research. Its proper use is to enable citizens to live lives that are economically, politically, socially, and culturally responsible" (p. 9). Karen and I are about the same age. We grew up in different countries on different coasts of North America, but, in adolescence and young adulthood, our daily and living rhythms were steeped in the energies of the revolutionary 70s. And we have never lost our optimism that change is possible. Under Karen's leadership, the Centre was devoted to promoting practices and policies of pedagogy as transformative, integral, holistic, ecological, spiritual, radical, and critical.

Karen: Hybrid-Hybird. Canadian Thanksgiving is around mid October, a good time for a Monday holiday and dinner at White Spot if you're so inclined. Traditionally it's a day to feast together in various communities, especially families. I wonder if full-blown turkey dinners are waning some these days. My first attempt at turkey away from home meant numerous phone calls to Mom. She would be on the other end of the line describing to me how a thoroughly cooked turkey easily pulls apart. That button thing, that was supposed to pop out when the turkey was done, never really worked.

The Centre was a community brimming with diversity. Many of its members came from different countries to study along side Canadian students, leaving behind families and traditions for several years. So, the sharing of each other's celebrations mattered. In our community that meant food, music, dance and a seminar room transformed into a café with the help of special fabrics and objects from all over the world. In education contexts, these kinds of events are often criticized as being superficial and stereotyping to cultures. There is a critical point to that claim, and when the charge came to our attention, the community took it seriously. We formed a study group called "de-colonizing conversations" intending to learn more about the severe impact of colonialism (now called globalization) on cultures and people. Some members of the group spoke first hand about their homeland. During the first gatherings, we took up issues of racism, particularly related to the recent history of residential schools forcibly imposed upon First Nations communities in Canada. This study group lasted the entire year, and we got through some tough and important conversations. We concluded, however, that sharing celebration was appropriate and vital to our community.

Consequently, early in October we decided to have a potluck for Canadian Thanksgiving. Our colleague from Nigeria asked if she could cook the turkey. It was a big job to volunteer for indeed. The budget could afford a small bird, but we bought a large one because our potlucks and cafés usually gathered over 30 people. It was T-day. As I headed to the potluck, I saw a familiar group sprinting along side a moving cart—with a large towel-covered mass on top—down the hallway to the seminar room where people had begun to gather. The group looked like an emergency room crew in a hospital corridor. An interesting aroma followed behind them and filled my imagination; it wasn't exactly reminiscent of sage. It occurred to me this was a Canadian free-range turkey with special Nigerian spices—a hybrid-hybird.

As the group rushed the turkey in, they met with applause. However, just when the crew decided it was time to ceremoniously carve the bird, they discovered that nobody had brought a ceremonial knife. The 1970s electric one I inherited from my mom was left on a shelf at home. All we had were 'safe' plastic cutlery, thankfully with serrated edges. So the turkey was ceremoniously carved with a white plastic knife, and with the help of a few bare hands, it pulled apart easily. The seminar room was decorated in café style with all the round tables we could find in the building. At one table, all five people came from different continents. I was thankful to learn more about hybridity and ways to respectfully celebrate its inherent/inherited integrity.

HEART AND MIND CONVERSATIONS

The Centre was a location for heart. In *Becoming Human,* Jean Vanier (1998) observes "we have disregarded the heart, seeing it only as a symbol of weakness, the centre of sentimentality and emotion, instead of as a powerhouse of love that can reorient us from our self-centredness, revealing to us and to others the basic beauty of humanity, empowering us to grow" (p. 78). When we were students in school, we often spoke about "learning by heart." We spent most of our time committing definitions, dates, facts, and formulae to heart, storing them in memory like a squirrel stores nuts for the long winter. What would research be like if we acknowledged the heart as "a powerhouse of love" that enthused and energized all our searching and becoming? According to William Sloane Coffin (2004), "the longest, most arduous trip in the world is often the journey from the head to the heart. Until that round trip is completed, we remain at war with ourselves" (p. 126). The Centre was a location for exploring the intricacies of the heart. Above all, it was a place where we told one another stories. Berry (1990) observes that,

> most of us no longer talk with each other, much less tell each other stories. We tell our stories now mostly to doctors or lawyers or psychiatrists or insurance adjusters or the police, not to our neighbors for their (and our) entertainment. The stories that now entertain us are made up for us in New York or Los Angeles or other centers of such commerce. (p. 159)

In the Centre, we told stories about Newfoundland, California, Pakistan, Malawi, Cameroon, India, Japan, and we learned from one another.

Carl: Learning to Live Well Together. One late afternoon I attended a presentation by a scholar of Islam who had been born in Palestine and grew up with a commitment to Christianity. He spoke during Ramadan. After a long and tiresome day, I arrived at the Centre a little late for the presentation as everybody else was just turning their attention to an introduction of the speaker. I hadn't eaten since early morning, and it was now about 4:30 or 5 o'clock. I saw food laid out—a bright-coloured feast. As I raced to an empty seat tucked in a far corner, I grabbed a cherry tomato and popped it in my mouth. When I sat down, eagerly looking forward to biting the tomato, I noticed that nobody was eating. Finally, I realized that the Ramadan fast would continue till sundown, some time after the invited speaker's presentation. Once more I learned that I seldom get it right! But I also knew my Muslim and non-Muslim colleagues would all hold me generously and generatively in that space where we were all learning to live well together, a space that celebrated the capaciousness of the heart.

Karen: The Whole Is Greater than the List. The round table in my office gathered stories, news, questions, attempts at answers, advice, laughter, tears, complaints, more attempts at answers, and lots of brainstorming about research. It was a plain issue, wood-grain veneer and chrome, four-foot table. It sat near the white board that never completely erases, and large windows facing North with mountains in the distance; the closer in view held large maple trees. I witnessed the cycle of red leaves to bare branches to spring buds to pristine chartreuse leaves five times. In those years, I spent at least half my time around the round table deep in conversations, leaving piles of unattended administration on my desk. [Most of the other half went to faculty meetings in various dull fluorescent-lit rooms around the building.] While the rest of my office was cluttered, the table sat tidy with a Pakistani cloth and a Japanese ikebana flower arrangement on top, both gifts from students.

This table was one familiar place where I came to know individuals within the Centre community, and where the community came to know me. I was a member and advocate for this community. My administrative skills—I use the word loosely, took a backseat to time spent in the community. Some colleagues outside the community were annoyed that I didn't return email or a phone call in two minutes. It was my practice never to answer the phone when my table had a visitor. I recall some long afternoon conversations there that lasted until we noticed dusk had settled in the naturally lit room. It was a privilege for me to learn about so many different disciplines, research preoccupations, homelands, family contexts, cultures, backgrounds, orientations, beliefs, and spiritualities.

Once during a formal review of another department, the review committee, who were deans and administrators from other universities, asked me to speak about the Centre. We sat at a long rectangular table in a room with no windows. The committee was curious about the Centre's connection to the department under review. We both had curriculum in our titles. Students interviewed from that department spoke about the Centre's vibrant community. One of the deans asked me what was the secret to my community; he'd like to 'bottle it up' and take it home to his faculty. I thought it was a curious question and comment. Should I provide a list? All I could think of to say was that I took the time to know each person in the community from over 20 different countries (Canada, Cameroon, Kenya, Malawi, Nigeria, Pakistan, India, Viet Nam, Japan, Maldives...) and uncountable disciplines (dance, creative writing, technology, drama, literature, counseling, music...). I wasn't about to say that I spent most of my time deep in conversation at a little round table near large windows to the outside and beside a white board that never fully erases. I must have given an unprofessional shrug before I abruptly heard, "Thank you very much, we have what we need."

WHO RATHER THAN WHAT

Arendt (1958) reminds us that "the moment we say who somebody is, our very vocabulary leads us astray into saying what he is; we get entangled in a description of qualities he necessarily shares with others like him; we begin to describe a type or 'character' in the old meaning of the word, with the result that his specific uniqueness escapes us" (p. 181). When we name ourselves or when we are named by others, we are created (constructed or re-inscribed) with identities, and these identities are multiple because we always occupy many subject positions— educator, poet, drummer, scholar, mother, father, daughter, son, wife, husband.... We have written ourselves and been written in multiple identities. Sometimes these identities are conflictual, possibly even contradictory, constantly in a process of change, malleable and tentative. When we consider that everyone we meet is like us, constituted in the play of language, always writing and being written in changing configurations, we see the shadow of chaos fill the blue sky, and we almost despair that notions of community are romantic dreams with no substance. How can a person who walks daily in plural stories ever hope to find places for meeting other people who walk in their plural stories? We then turn to Coffin (2004) who observes wisely that, "diversity may be both the hardest thing to live with and the most dangerous thing to be without" (p. 34).

The Centre was a location for humanity. Brueggemann (2001) notes that, "where passion disappears there will not be any serious humanizing energy" (p. 32). The Centre was a place of humanizing passion because it fostered "a story-based culture", acknowledging how "story is essential to human survival" (Baldwin, 2005, p. 19). We came together in the Centre from around the world, from diverse locations of identity, including race, ethnicity, language, sexual orientation, spirituality, and class. We learned to attend to one another as *who,* to hear one another's stories. We learned like Christina Baldwin (2005) that "breaking silence changes the world" (p. 87).

Carl: Remembering. Is there a paucity of leadership because nobody knows how to relate? Are leaders failing to lead well because nobody knows how to respond to one another? The Centre was enthused by Ted Aoki. Countless times, Ted invited Karen and me to his favorite sushi restaurant where we discussed the challenges of innovation in the academy. Ted had once been the director of the Centre, and he had been an administrator at the University of Alberta for many years before his retirement. Now in his late seventies, he continued to teach and to mentor graduate students. Above all, he was delightfully devoted to supporting younger scholars.

Vowels
(for Ted Aoki)

with Ted I walk in the moment,
a tangled line of metonymic moments,
making the momentous story
where moments are still and eternal

always in motion, he lingers long
in locations where he stands steady,
sturdy, in the dizzy, always
shape-shifting landscape of holes
like a floating archipelago, best
navigated by memory, and faith
in the mysteries of the alphabet

in his words I am rendered
pneumatic, with feet dangling
in both the earth and the heart's
imagining of poetic possibilities,
still waiting for names

he holds the vowels that breathe
life in our consonants, constantly
ready to know the I in our writing,
the metonymic wildness of I

he knows the messy texture
of lived experiences, and follows
the line of discipline to know
the oblique, porous, capacious
line that is no line

Ted lives in language, and
language lives in Ted,
drawing us to see what we
overlook, focuses attention
on tension, both tending
and attending, throwing out
lines, here and there, enamored
with the fecundity of conjunctions

reminds us that grammar, the letter,
the law are chimerical, even comical,
like an alchemist of gramarye,

transforms stone and water
into pigments for re-presenting
the world in words, always
both familiar and unfamiliar,
a seer who teaches us to see

with Ted I walk in the moment,
a tangled line of metonymic moments,
making the momentous story
where moments are still and eternal

Where There Is Hope. Walter Brueggemann (2001) writes,

> it is only a poem, and we might say rightly that singing a song does not change reality. However, we must not say that with too much conviction. The evocation of an alternative reality consists at least in part in the battle for language and the legitimization of a new rhetoric. The language of the empire is surely the language of managed reality, of production and schedule and market. But that language will never permit or cause freedom because there is no newness in it. (p. 18)

Neither is there hope. The language of hope has to express immediacy. It is promise rather than critique, explanation, or even strategy. Hope is the spirited and faithful tug that arouses us to refuse an unacceptable reality by way of imagining otherwise. Hope doesn't survive in consuming apathy or cheerful optimism, but lives within inspired disobedience that embodies power to dismantle what is fraudulent, and within courage that re-imagines 'what if'. Thus the deep potential of hope is in the now—expressed in language, visualized in imagination and enacted in ways we participate in the world.

The Centre was a location for hope born out of the evocation of alternative realities where we embraced a lot of words that begin with H, words that are too seldom heard in the academy, such as: heart, humanity, happiness, humour, humility, hospitality, honour, health, history, home, hearing, and holism.

Carl: Refusing to Forget. Ken Schram was a medical doctor, psychiatrist, and homeopath. In his seventies he was pursuing a PhD in the Centre. Then on a late September day, he died, suddenly, too soon.

Psyllium
(for Ken)

Ken shared books, show and tell.
He always carried a big bag of books,
more books than I will ever read:
poetry, philosophy, history, theology, literature.

Ken wore his intellect like a rumpled coat.

We sat outside Benny's and ate gelato,
sat in silence, savouring the gelato,
the pleasure of being together.

He loved me with heart-breaking constancy.

He laughed with joyful abandon.

He told me he had Henry Wadsworth Longfellow's nose,
acknowledged his genealogical connections to the poet
who had to be both embraced and challenged.

In autumn air I said good-bye,
as if good-bye is ever possible,
connected to Ken like rhizomes
    without end.

And in autumn air
  through winter air
    into spring air
I walked the dike along the Fraser
    remembering Ken.

The best gift an older man
can offer a younger man
is the same gift a younger man
can offer an older man:
love, bountiful love.

Ken was a poet who saw
connections everywhere
so all our relations rendered stories
in a continuous present
that breathed always.

Ken knew the healing in roots.
He healed me many times.
I'm still taking the psyllium he recommended.
And every morning when I drink a glass
of pineapple juice with psyllium
I remember Ken, hear his light.

                MINDFUL OF THE GAP

In *Eyes of the University* Jacques Derrida (2004) asks, "Who are we in the university where apparently we are [if indeed we are 'we'; if indeed we know our position]? What do we represent? Whom do we represent? Are we responsible? For what and to whom" (p. 83)? He further claims that if there is a university responsibility, it begins when there is a need to hear these questions as a call to responsibility whether or not a response is forthcoming. What matters is that this call comes from within the institution, which will question itself. In our academic experience, however, these are not questions we often hear in faculty gatherings. Nor are these questions a *curriculum vitae* concerning individual achievement addresses, or questions that precede dissemination of disciplinary knowledge. Nonetheless, we are the participants who play a key role in institutional authority and consciousness. We do teach about social justice, but without living it institutionally (within policy making, administrative language, and the politics of teacher/student relationships). It would appear we are in the business of reproducing ourselves rather than asking how we might re-imagine ourselves.

Building upon Arendt's essay, "The Crisis of Education", Natasha Levinson (2001) proposes that "introducing newcomers into a weary world while preserving the possibility that students might undertake something new in relation to this world requires that teachers meet students in the gap between past and future" (p. 30). Meeting students in the gap means introducing them critically to the world 'as it is' while preserving their capacity as newcomers to imagine and create otherwise. Here in the gap between the past and the future lies the significance of imagination as proposed by Huebner (1999): "The imagination makes connections between present and future, present and past, and future and past" (p. 436). He argues that imagination shapes possibilities from which we perceive, know and act; and that "by encouraging the imagination, freedom is affirmed". In hearing Derrida's questions and the following words of Arendt (1977), we are reminded that our primary responsibility as educators lies in nurturing human freedom:

> Education is the point at which we decide whether we love the world enough to assume responsibility for it and by the same token save it from the ruin, which, except for renewal, except for the coming of the new and young, would be inevitable. (p. 193)

Karen: The Worth of Community. It took me all day and all night to pack up my office. I couldn't imagine this place empty. Living here had been about living outside the box. Filling the empty boxes with things I brought with me five years ago wasn't hard. But packing away what I had collected was, especially the gifts. Most came from places in the world I've never been. From time to time, people in our community traveled home during a break and returned with cultural gifts like fabric, jewelry, and souvenirs. I tried one last time to erase the whiteboard, but faded graffiti still bled through. I remembered thinking about having all four walls as solid whiteboards. I was crazy with ideas back then. I looked around a long last time. In my head I heard the scores of conversations that took place around my round table. That's where learning happened.

Imagining Still. In those five years ten babies were born. A wedding assembled our blessings. Some of us separated from family and home to be here. One of us left and couldn't return. There was illness and wellness, retreat and celebration, questions and answers and more questions. We came together around a common intention—nothing more significant than reminding the world of our preoccupations about what matters. We gathered our presence, our potential, our language. We were a community. We remember that much.

And in the midst of our remembering, we are especially glad and grateful that the creative scholarship of the Centre continues to unfold with imagination and hope. The graduate scholars who were a part of the community of the Centre when we were the Director and Graduate Advisor now occupy positions of education, scholarship, and leadership throughout the world. More students have joined, and continue to join the Centre, always in a process of transformation, with a new name (Centre for Cross-Faculty Inquiry), new directors, new visions, and new hopes. May the Centre continue to thrive as a location for scholarship that, in the spirit of Dwayne Huebner, imagines otherwise.

REFERENCES

Arendt, H. (1977). *Between past and future*. New York: Penguin Books.
Arendt, H. (1958). *The human condition*. Chicago: Chicago University Press.
Baldwin, C. (2005). *Storycatcher: Making sense of our lives through the power and practice of story*. Novato: New World Library.
Berry, W. (2001). *In the presence of fear: Three essays for a changed world*. Great Barrington: The Orion Society.
Berry, W. (1990). *What are people for? Essays*. New York: North Point Press.
Brueggemann, W. (2001). *The prophetic imagination* (2nd ed.). Minneapolis, MN: Fortress Press.
Coffin, W. S. (2004). *Credo*. Louisville, KY: Westminster John Knox Press.
Derrida, J. (2004). *Eyes of the university*. Stanford, CA: Stanford University Press.
Huebner, D. (1999). Challenges bequeathed (1996). In V. Hillis (Ed.), *The lure of the transcendent, collected essays by Dwayne E. Huebner* (pp. 432–445). Mahwah, NJ: Lawrence Erlbaum Associates.
Huebner, D. (1999). Teaching as a vocation (1987). In V. Hillis (Ed.), *The lure of the transcendent, collected essays by Dwayne E. Huebner* (pp. 379–387). Mahwah, NJ: Lawrence Erlbaum Associates.
Levinson, N. (2001). The paradox of natality: Teaching in the midst of belatedness. In M. Gordon (Ed.), *Hannah Arendt and education* (pp. 11–36). Boulder, CO: Westview Press.
Pelias, R. J. (2004). *A methodology of the heart: Evoking academic & daily life*. Walnut Creek, CA: AltaMira Press.
Vanier, J. (1998). *Becoming human*. Toronto, ON: House of Anansi Press.

LEAH FOWLER

IMAGINATION AND INNER LITERACIES OF A TEACHING CONSCIOUSNESS

Imagination is the storehouse of human possibility – ethical, intellectual, political (Huebner, 1999, p. 436).

Shaping educational processes around the known diminishes the need for the imagination, for then the future is no longer a field of imagined possibilities (Huebner, 1999, p. 436).

The role of the imagination is not to resolve, not to point the way, not to improve. It is to awaken, to disclose the ordinarily unseen, unheard, and unexpected (Maxine Greene as cited in Pinar, 2004, p. 190).

BEYOND 'EIKASIA' IN CURRICULUM CONSCIOUSNESS

Imagine Dwayne Huebner at an intimate dinner-party with William Pinar, Jan Zwicky, Madeleine Grumet, John Kabat-Zinn, Maxine Greene, Jane Hirshfield, John Ralston Saul, John D. Caputo, Kieran Egan, Fraser Mustard, Cynthia Chambers, Wislawa Szymborska, Northrop Frye, Gregory Cajete, Mary Warnock, Mikhail Bakhtin, Samuel Taylor Coleridge, William Blake, John Dewey, Jeddu Krishnamurti, Rumi, and Plato. Others were invited, but unable to attend because they had previous commitments.

Huebner is the host, with his work of "the lure of the transcendent": entirely appropriate for this company of minds, themselves out of the imagination of God or "The Imaginative Source", however you take the beginning of All This to be. Appetizers involve introductions, discussions about who should sit next to whom. 'Tell me a little about yourself' they speak to those on their left and right as they unfold their napkins and clasp the bases of their wine glasses (one or two of the older ones getting a professional development update on stemware). Before they commence, Huebner says grace.

Well before the entrée they are, of course, talking about imagination and education in their contemporary, current re/publics. There is linguistic talk of definition, etymology, semantics, and pragmatics: is it power to create in one's mind? Is it "the capacity to consider sensible objects without actually perceiving them or supposing that they really exist? There is playful talk: One mentions while

P. Lewis and J. Tupper (eds.), Challenges Bequeathed: Taking up the Challenges of Dwayne Huebner, 51–65.
© 2009 sense publishers. All rights reserved.

choosing the sheep or goat's cheese: "According to Aristotle, 'the soul never thinks without a mental image [*phantasma*]'" (De Anima, 431a 15-20). Laughter ensues and double entendres are shared about the dark nights of the soul and what pictures over all time persist in that abyss.

There is teacher talk: One of the more pedantic souls among the dinner guests tries to teach others with an impromptu lecture about stages of imagination and understanding given in Plato's *Republic*, (vi. 509-11), conceived and written of course immediately before the famous myth of the cave. Remember: "At the bottom is the world of images, known only by 'eikasia', a term used by Plato to refer to a human method of handling appearances. Objects of sense are known by 'pistis' or opinion; mathematical, scientific objects by 'dianoia' or reasoning; and at the summit the forms are known by 'noesis'." (answers.com, 2008). Imagination surely must include all of these layers of images in a teaching consciousness.

"Very fancy", opines another, admiring the double-smoked maple-basted lox. "More, I think, "it is the ability to perceive, whether a perception is an image or something else. It therefore allows us to perceive that a dream or memory or a reflection in a mirror is not reality as such."

"Too much cheap Wikipedia-ing," declares a more serious philosopher among them, munching on tender fresh mint and basil leaves in the balsamic dressing. "Go to my website <philosophy of mind> and you will see that 'traditionally, [imagination] is the mental capacity for experiencing, constructing, or manipulating mental imagery. Come, come, poets, will you not agree?" Rumi breaks into laughter here and Northrop Frye is secretly annoyed that literature is not mentioned, and wonders why they haven't read his *Educated Imagination*.

"I am so sorry I have missed the 21st Century," Coleridge muses through half-shut eyes, smoke from a dubious tobacco enwreathed about his head. "As I maintained earlier, 'the imagination I consider either as primary, or secondary. The primary imagination I hold to be the living Power and prime Agent of all human Perception.... The secondary, I consider as an echo of the former, co-existing with the conscious will... It dissolves, diffuses, dissipates... yet still at all events it struggles to idealize and to unify.'" [Yo, Dude, Wiki Coleridge]

The waiter clears the salad cutlery and whispers to Fraser Mustard, "I looked imagination up in the dictionary. My grade one teacher taught me that. It said '1. Conception; image in the mind; idea. ☐2. Contrivance; scheme formed in the mind; device.' Most of the people I work for taught me the second definition. Ya gotta watch out for these clever people."

Blake is troubled as usual with his visions unbidden, even in this good company of strangers commenting on the ginger carrot soup with organic yogurt swirled on the surface, and begins quoting scripture: "'Thou hast seen all their vengeance, and all their imaginations against me'", although in Genesis 6 we hear of imagination as the very first motion or purpose of mind. All the guests wonder about imagination as the first motion or purpose of mind with their own work.

All could agree, while cleansing their palates with grapefruit and ice wine sorbet, with the idea often mentioned in most dictionaries that the space of imagination, in itself, is actually boundless. It involves original and insightful thought and a wider range of mental activities including the non-actual, such as supposing, pretending, "seeing as", thinking of possibilities, and even being mistaken.

The curriculum scholars among them, sipping the dregs of the first course Pinot Noir, love this kind of complicated conversation. They laud the perennial ability to visualize, be resourceful, creatively act, or use a particular part of mind...especially on the right side of the head if you believe in the bicameral mind. Jaynes, absent, could not say more about that.

Szymborska offers Hirshfield advice as they discuss a concentration of mind around how difficult it would be to write a poem about imagination – say a haiku or blessing –with words like intelligence, awareness, wittiness, insight, mental agility, visualization, fancy, or dramatization.

Three or four of the teachers watching the kitchen entrance, recall and share classroom exercises attempting to define and teach something about imagination. They recall notes they put on the board – slate, black, green, white, or SMART® – for students to copy in their notes from the Oxford English Dictionary. One of the pedagogues runs to the laptop in the corner of the dining room and reads aloud to the others as they accept their plates of quail, tofu, chicken, salmon, and venison as ordered and engage in this etymological debate about Greek and Latin roots. They wonder aloud to each other about new meanings of imagination.

The writers and poets sigh again and remember why they struggled in school: too much talk and note-taking while they looked out the window and imagined all the pain, possibility, and desire in life which seemed so far from the classrooms in which they found (or lost) themselves. Several of them at the table want to scream: "Log off the World Wide Web now: we are having dinner together. Blackberry and cell phones off please. There needs to be a curriculum of manners or there will be need for social and relational triage soon."

Every one present well knows the dark side of the imagination, especially on the Net, and the attendant dangers of dysfunction and abusive fantasy. More than one of these diners has spent time considering the construction of a new personal avatar for the current gaming engagement with on-line "Second Life". True the benefit for some with disabilities, is that imaginatively they can simulate and almost experience a normal life of dancing, hiking, working at an active job, or being more involved at social functions in this imaginary on-line hobby. But misuse of imaginative literacies is thieving lived and real time away from productive human work, authentic research, and imaginative being. The draw of becoming our dreamed personas is powerful but the question is: how do we develop and use these imaginative literacies in (educational) life?

Talk trickles off and they speculate absent-mindedly about possible synonyms for imagination: conception, idea, conceit, fancy, device, origination, invention, scheme, design, purpose, contrivance, and antonyms: being, entity, existence, material, reality, substance, truth!!

A professor from a small university in Western Canada asks if they might agree that there needs to be a strategic affirming of the imagination as their host suggested, to develop literacy of imagination for teachers now, to enhance their own boundaries of consciousness through several modes. While the main dinner is enjoyed, she invites others to tell of their adventures in imagination in teaching.

Imagination, a vital part of Wachtel's (2007) "hum inside the head" (p. 15), has saved my life. I have been one of the lucky ones. As a child, woman, partner, friend, Canadian, teacher, education professor, citizen, and human being born in the middle of the 20th Century, survival and 'thrival' has been possible because of imagination: mine and Others. Dream, thought, fantasy: these are the modes of releasing the imagination, of legendary Maxine Greene's (1995) depiction of the educational process. "Releasing the imagination means moving into the future, at least as the contents of dream, thought, and fantasy are split-off fragments of self" (Pinar, 2004, p. 128).

We do need to release and educate the imagination: Now is the time in this difficult world to re-affirm, integrate, and employ the imagination in ways that Dwayne Huebner invited. We all might agree the world is in serious trouble as a whole organism. Its survival and those of its inhabitants depends on imaginative and restorative thought, theory, education, practice, and work. Three quarters of the world's people go to bed hungry, unsafe, and inadequately housed every day. This is NOT a CLICHÉ or METAPHOR: This is an urgent plea for the human collective imagination to get to work on these problems now. Let's find out now what each of us need to learn and teach to work well on needs of safety, poverty, health, and peaceful community everywhere. This is at the heart of every lived curriculum in the world.

All our distinguished guests nod in agreement. Krisnamurti leans forward with his large kind eyes and interjects at this sober place in conversation: "When there is that intelligence born of compassion and love, then all these problems with be solved simply, quietly." I want to believe him.

Canadian writer Timothy Findley (1990) moves us beyond 'eikasia' with attention on only the appearance of (temporal) things (so characteristic of current vernacular of politics) and inspires us toward a more meaningful dwelling that can be applied to more restorative kind of curriculum:

> I know that human imagination can save us: save the human race and save all the rest of what is alive and save this place—the earth—that is itself alive. Imagination is our greatest gift…if you can imagine harmony, you can achieve it. Harmony, after all, can be well defined as an absence of cruelty. If I am a hiding place for monsters—and I am—then I can also be a hiding place for harmony. At least, I can imagine such a thing. (p. 300)

For my part, I imagine and invite thinking about several imaginative teaching literacies that can contribute to a restorative and mindful education.

AFFIRM IMAGINATION WITH AN AWARENESS LITERACY

> It's hot in the imagination today,
> Partly cloudy in the memory,
> Humidity rising

In tomorrow's teaching selves.
The barometric pressure
Saturates the consciousness:
Re/markable.

If a class of my own.
If a Principal; superintendent; head trustee;
If on the Board. Well, someone with clout
If a new library.
If laptops for every child,
If music, art, theatre programs,
If counsellors.

If I, if we, if we all…

If money were no object.

If I were King, Queen, Dalai, Yahweh,
Buddha, Mohammad, God, Imaginative Source?

If a peaceful world, healthy
If a literacy of sustainable plenitude –
Then what could a currency of imagination provide—
The transcendent lure?

Wherever illiteracy is a problem, it's as fundamental a problem as getting enough to eat or a place to sleep.

Northrop Frye, *http://www.frye.ca/english/northrop-frye/frye-quotes.html*

I began naively teaching the way many do, illiterate in the ways of imaginative and empathic teaching. I started for the children, I thought, to save them, teach them, grow them. Not being able to change the world, I wanted to believe that my teaching work matters and makes a difference to This One Particular Starfish from the wrecked beach that I can return to the living waters. Everything from loaning students my pen to write, to the think-pair share and jigsaw classroom strategies, to using film as adjunct to text, I thought of myself as an imaginative teacher. When they got stuck and asked for guidelines and suggestions for doing their work, I would cheerfully say, "Use your imagination". I passed the buck. I asked them to do what I could not imagine myself, or do in the time I gave them to do it. They were game, resilient, and resourceful so we all passed from each year. But I needed to build an awareness literacy I did not have. And because I imagined that I, and teaching could be better, I went back to school as a teacher.

All teaching begins in imagination. As Huebner (1999) reminds us, "[Imagination] is central to all aspects of human life and is at the core of educational phenomena. It is not an add-on to the educational project. It undergirds everything an educator thinks and does" (p. 436).

Like Maxine Greene, in her life and imaginative work, countering indifference with current curriculum by arguing for the essential and increased role of the arts in education, I am curious how we could learn more about the essential and increased role of the imagination in a teaching consciousness, whether in pre-service teacher education or with experienced educators. Space should be structured in curricula to explore new literacies of the imagination of a teaching consciousness into practices of learning and being.

In the practice of teaching, especially with new teachers, the entire project of educational design, plan, development, implementation, and evaluation of meaningful, engaging learning opportunities presses our imaginative capacity to the educational wall of possibility not-yet-lived. The momentum of a teacher's imagination can open or close the educational turn. With a restorative education of imaginative literacy in our new and experienced teachers, we can re-imagine schooling, learning, and integrated balanced dwelling in our beleaguered planet with innovative curricula of self, Other, and the world. All this begins with imaginative awareness.

My early imaginings of teaching began inside me as I learned to plan lessons, units, year-long plans. Naïve-I could see myself at the front of the room, standing with the loving teacher-gaze. I wanted them to love me, and I wanted to love them as their "in loco parentis" professional. I wanted to be a significant bearer of meaning to their lives. Although I did not choose teaching as my first career, I am determined to be inventive and resourceful about engaging my students in a relevant curriculum, instructing and exchanging with them skills, knowledge, and attributes.

But I noticed my verbs of teaching around "I want" and "I'll give", and how it was about me, so I imagine deeper into my conscious thought and emotion about teaching and seek to educate deeply my imagination – a literate and mindful human consciousness, attuned to disappearing self within the community of learners and all inner work so needing to be done. A literacy of awareness is just the beginning.

AFFIRM IMAGINATION WITH A PSYCHOLOGICAL LITERACY

Imagination is a manifestation of human freedom – a cultural birthright.
(Huebner, 1999, p. 436)

The fundamental job of the imagination in ordinary life, then, is to produce, out of the society we have to live in, a vision of the society we want to live in.

Northrop Frye, http://www.frye.ca/english/northrop-frye/frye-quotes.html

"Ninety per cent of what happens to us occurs inside our heads" reflected the late and much-loved Canadian literary icon Carol Shields (as cited in Wachtel, 2007, p. 15). Inside our skulls resides the real possibility of being and freedom, and for an educator, so ensconced in institutional life with multiple stakeholders demanding so much, imagination is crucial in restorative and explorative teaching.

Literacy and imagination are double strands of the helix of human consciousness. We need to ring the alarum about the need to include and affirm imagination as an essential literacy for teachers in the field now. A literate imagination is crucial to good teacher education, healthy curriculum thinking, and authentic professional development as part of a collective effort and will to heal the earth and its populations. Imagination as Huebner conceived and wrote about can provide foundations for better human lives and communities. Let us explore why and how we might represent the imagination in the educational enterprise. Can we re-imagine education, teaching, and learning with the embodied, ethical, intellectual, and political work which that would require? Yes. YES. We must.

I often joke with colleagues and friends that "I have a rich inner life", and I do. That powerful life of the mind began and developed in experiences with literature and in school. Spending my formative years in a small prairie town as I did would have caused me to perish without those books and classrooms. It is where I explored the emotional and cognitive realms of people all over the world. I went to the Kroeller-Mueller museum in Holland to see van Gogh's paintings because of a book. I went to Stonehenge for physical angles of light; Canterbury to see the union of stone and ecclesiastical space; Ypres to Braille my fingers over the names of the son-soldiers on the memorial wall; and Weimar to see where Goethe's young Werther pined for his love. So much action in my life arises from the imaginative life that comes of deep learning. Without the imaginative work of writers and map-makers, perhaps I would not have left my own home town. That would have resulted in a lost life.

All the disciplines we study, learn and write about are in existence because of highly refined imaginations writing, reading, speaking, listening, viewing, and representing what we know. All the work of deconstruction and reconstruction of inner knowledge takes place with the imagination as we neurologically travel in our brains (capable of such plasticity and growth).

Imaginative cognition is required in teaching, just as in literature, art, music, science at the edge of the known world. In teaching and learning there is a mapping of the new frontiers of thought, questions explored together about what else could be known, and done, and why? What is it that we cannot imagine because we have not thought about it yet? Imagination enables us to cultivate patience and hope about finding solutions to the enduring questions. Philosopher Jan Zwicky (2003) explores that imaginative phenomenon "'seeing-as' because it encapsulates the mystery of meaning" (p. Left 1), and "All genuine understanding is a form of seeing-as: it is fundamentally spatial in organization" (p. Left 3).

The inner understanding of a teacher involved in thinking about (imagining, envisaging, projecting forward in time) curriculum, for example, runs on the motor/field/energy of imagination. The very quality and effectiveness of teaching depends upon the imaginative literacy of the mind of the educator. How we model, guide, develop, play, extend, and elaborate literacies of the imagination is the central work of faculties of education all over the world. With the exception of practicum placements for student teachers, preparation of teachers all happens in the mind.

Our lives, our communities, our world depend upon the kind of imagination that Dwayne Huebner writes about in his call to affirm the significance of the imagination in education curriculum theory and studies. The education of such a teaching imagination begins in inner space, like artists, musicians, and scientists at the edge of discovery, with a willful pre-conceptual leap between hope and knowing.

In the inner literacies of the teaching consciousness, imagination forms the hub of that interior wheel of educational thinking. When awakened gently and thoughtfully, our imagination is available always for invention, repair, invitation, problem solving, healing, understanding, empathy, inspiration, and hopeful being. Part of teacher education must provide opportunities to develop a literate imagination to explore, study, model, guide, independently play and work with creative extensions.

Many may argue that if imagination only happens in the mind, then it is not real, and that literal experience is required. Time in schools does clearly teach apprenticing educators, but time in the imaginative mind is the deep preparation that provides knowledge, skills, and attributes to serve the learning young and their communities.

Imaginative affect is also needed in the teaching consciousness of an ethical educator. As Parker Palmer (2007) writes in *The Courage to Teach*:

> As good teachers weave the fabric that joins them with students and subjects, the heart is the loom on which the threads are tied, the tension is held, the shuttle flies, and the fabric is stretched tight. Small wonder, then, that teaching tugs at the heart, opens the heart, even breaks the heart — and the more one loves teaching, the more heartbreaking it can be. The courage to teach is the courage to keep one's heart open in those very moments when the heart is asked to hold more than it is able so that teacher and students and subject can be woven into the fabric of community that learning, and living, require (p. 11).

There are qualities of the heartmind needed: from empathy, kindness, compassion, and tenderness, to wide open-eyed awareness about desire for power or control or will to damage from anger which is nearly always born from fear and grief.

AFFIRM IMAGINATION WITH PSYCHOTHERAPEUTIC LITERACY

Everything changes, everything is connected; pay attention.

Hirshfield, (2005)

A professor recently visiting as an oral examiner to one of my students had returned from Liberia. She told the story of a library there, started from the remnants of two rooms in a building that had been shot up and riddled with bullets, then cleaned up and made into the library. The military soldiers of the government could go there to get their soccer scores so it became a protected zone, and continues to grow slowly. They imagined that a library could be the re-beginning of an education, of peace, safety, and sustainable life; not a pub, not a clinic, not, an internet café, not a store... a library. After living through many layers of hell there, imagining and creating a library has given many a safe house – literally and mentally, where freedom to be is made possible.

And I remembered Pablo Neruda who imagined heaven to be a kind of library.

I imagine now, as I write and you read this, those Liberian children in Monrovia, slipping quickly and quietly in and out of a bullet riddled two-room library, choosing one of four books to huddle and read right there. I imagine refugee camps in Afghanistan; I imagine all the desolate places near my home. Imagine less harm.

Imagine if it could be otherwise.

Some books have had to go into hiding. I do not mean the ones officially censored by the limited minds of bored boarder guards or frightened people who have put themselves in charge of "protecting the public from offensive corruptions by the printed word"-protecting them from imagination. In many countries books have lost their citizenship and remain couched in the back of closets, under floor-boards or holes in the walls where they hopefully will not fall into the wrong hands.

The educational space within a classroom, school, university can be a problematic household, a problematic country: one of my deep challenges as both a privileged and a marginalized member of those learning institutions is to get in touch with my own inner fascist. The hardest lessons I encounter inside its walls are those around imagining and understanding issues of my own inner government. Given that I do not have the right as a conscious feminist educator to colonize my students or colleagues by curriculum or position, a central part of my reflective and imaginative teaching practice is to study my own inner legislative, executive, and judicial branches of self–government within my teaching consciousness. I need to attend to how I live and become literate with that imagination that governs my teaching from planning to evaluation, from curriculum to community, from self to Other to the world and back.

I, like bell hooks (1997), want an engaged pedagogy, where education is a libratory practice that teaches us to transgress the status quo that is always limited, usually silencing, and often destructive to people's lives. As a personal, academic, and public being who dwells amid others here on the planet, I want to hear and tell both autobiographical and theoretical discourse, to hear and tell both the Grand Narratives and the petit récits. I want to engage memory, perception, and imagination so that the everyday world as problematic is opened, questioned, and re-understood – to enlarge both the boundaries of discourses, and the meaning and quality of our lives.

Like Maxine Greene (2008, homepage), I want a

vision …[that] is to generate inquiry, imagination, and the creation of art works by diverse people. It has to do so with a sense of the deficiencies in our world and a desire to repair, wherever possible. Justice, equality, freedom– these are as important to us as the arts, and we believe they can infuse each other, perhaps making some difference at a troubled time.

Teaching has changed in this post-modern, multi-vocal, self-interested, cyber-bound, grasping society, I think it is necessary for imaginative educators to develop an extraordinary set of literacies in order to navigate the complex matrix of the classroom, the institution, and the surrounding cultural community. To do that I sempiternally hold two questions as a focus in my work in the field of education, where we have honed matronizing to a fine and terrible art: What psychotherapeutic literacies do I need to continually develop? And, how shall I govern myself in my own discipline and teaching practices?

What cognitive and affective literacies might we need, to attend to the dissonances of being? I think of several: relational, ethical, environmental, metaphoric, narrative, economic, theoretical, and, of course, political. The reason for developing these literacies in ourselves, and perhaps by living example in our students, is to avoid re-inscribing traditional, patriarchal, hegemonic, colonizing practices so that all people, (especially marginalized people), are brought into the social conversation and community with a full right to be and to participate equitably. I do think a good inclusive classroom can be one of the remaining bastions of participatory democracy, which takes into account the difficulty of power and evaluation, but insists on the larger conversations of greater good.

Which brings me to my second question: that of self- government and self-education, with a belief/hope that others will learn to govern and educate themselves as well. In that enterprise, imagination is central to the direction, scope, and content of that intellectual and character work.

As a professor I do have power: expert, evaluative, titular, contractual, and relational. What shall I do with it? How shall I act with ethical responsibility when I am teaching students, graduate or undergraduate? As instructor of a class, how do I explicitly and implicitly hold the dialectics of care and resistance, empathy and challenge, guided practice and growth toward independence, tender invitation and rigorous, voiced debate?

Perhaps the strongest of power literacies is relational, which I can share with my students deliberately, visibly, educatively. The roots of relationships again are held by imagination in the capacity for empathy, compassion, and attunement with others. If I run into trouble, as I certainly will if I am any good at provoking assumptions and creating cognitive and affective dissonance, then I also must have ready to hand, some methods of reading my students and myself as essential texts of any course I teach.

How? One way is to get in touch with my inner fascist. I use my imagination for a moment to consider how I may cause harm to others in the course of my educational work. I use my imagination to call into question my own relations of power and the ways in which I invoke that power. I must imagine: Who is the self that teaches? I have neither the right nor the interest to co-opt other people's personal power, so what does it mean now to teach at all? I cannot and will not get daddy or big brother or principal or Dean in to help me sort things out if I struggle with issues of power and control that interfere with the goal of passionate studying and inspired learning. So how do I go on authentically as a feminist and as a knower, researcher, and teacher? Imagination is the cognitive field of energy where

I learn to stay with difficulty and work it out with the other mortals I encounter in Pinar's *complicated conversations* of learning and teaching.

With a student who troubles our classroom, what shall be my approach? Of course I can say, as Shakespeare may have: "There's the door; there's the way: get thee hence." And what would that response teach? Marginalization? Anathema to feminist theory, I think.

To a misogynist male student, I may be tempted to say, "Yes, dear, I see you have a penis, but you have already used up your share of oxygen, so we need to hear from someone else now" but what would that response teach? That patronizing and misogeny have been replaced by matronizing and *pisogeny*? Worst kind of pedagogy of the oppressed. To a pre-conscious female student who insists she does not need feminist theory and analysis because she has a really nice boyfriend who lets her drive his truck, we may want to roll our eyes and snort in exasperation. And what would that response teach?: that her voice does not matter? Not helpful in moving anyone up the evolutionary beach of consciousness. Affirming the imagination to engage in more humane and skilful ways would move the educational project much further in evolving, beyond anger, resentment, fear, sarcasm, censure, toward shared enterprises, belonging, and worth.

Of course, I am less comfortable saying: "Yes Leah, I see you have a Ph. D. and you have also taken up your share of the oxygen in this classroom, and now it is time for someone else to speak. What might that response teach? But perhaps visibly and self-consciously I need my imagination to govern myself to do just that…in order that others may do the same. I think we need to use our relational power in the classroom as (feminist, imaginative, liberal) scholars: I want to work hard to invite ALL the narratives and personal experience, mine and the students, in relation to the topics at hand. We share the work of thought and writing and discussion. Collectively we try to open classroom and community difficulty to the whole class and labour together as mortal citizens amid that lived curriculum.

In the interests of psychotherapeutic literacy we might explore a feminist hermeneutics that continually asks, what is really going on here? Whose interests are actually being served and why? What other interpretations might be made about this? How can we reduce harm and suffering? How shall we live generatively amid difficulty? How can imagination in the teaching consciousness give us a space to call necessary things into question? Let's talk, read, write, listen, view, represent together about that in our classrooms.

AFFIRMING IMAGINATION WITH NARRATIVE LITERACY

(There are two halves to literary experience)…imagination gives us both a better and a worse world than the one we usually live with, and demands that we keep looking steadily at them both.

Northrop Frye (1963)

A literate imagination comes into fruition most in narratives. Story, thought-progeny of memory and imagination, constitutes the content of all the disciplines.

Sciences, social sciences, and the arts begin and continue in imagination that arises from the stories of the people and research and writing and conference events in these subjects. What we notice is what constitutes the narrative; literal detail of the actual is not required, but the specificity of storied detail does give our accounts the density of the real. The narrative line of each human being needs an aural and loving home, where every story there matters. The narrative line of each discipline is an invitation to the young to participate in the great chain of being, to find a generative place for contributing to the actual and possible world.

AFFIRM IMAGINATION WITH HERMENEUTIC LITERACY

Different Pedagogy in a Difficult World

In a literate and exemplary teaching consciousness, a hermeneutic imagination is essential. John Caputo (1987, 2006) asks us, in *Radical Hermeneutics* and *The Weakness of God*, for example, to face up to the profoundly difficult and complex mortal situations in which we find ourselves. He urges responsibility together with imagination and intelligent, playful interpretations that look directly at what is actually before us. A hermeneutic imagination notices what is being missed, not said and yet necessary, notices the cracks and fault lines in deep structure of thought, being, and text that may reveal what has been concealed. The openings from hermeneutic imagination no doubt trouble us but there is vividness in that Foucaldian *parrhesiast* enterprise of uncovering original difficulty in speech, belief and justice, and making visible what is true. The most needed sites show themselves and guide human work. This is a courageous enterprise in keeping with Rumi's advice "Don't turn your head, keep looking at the bandaged place, that is where the light enters you." We must learn to interpret curriculum with imaginative, pedagogic, and transformative literacies.

AFFIRM IMAGINATION WITH A DIFFERENT CURRICULUM LITERACY

> "You know, it is quite interesting, to sit together for an hour and talk over our problems without any pretence, without any hypocrisy, and without assuming some ridiculous facade. To have a whole hour together is really extraordinary, because so rarely do we sit and discuss serious matters with anybody for a whole hour. You may go to work for a whole day, but it has far greater meaning to spend sixty minutes or more together in order to investigate, to seriously examine our human problems hesitantly, tentatively and with great affection, without trying to impose one opinion upon another." Krishnamurti, 1981, p. 279

Imagine a room in the world where all the curriculum scholars could sit for an hour and talk over the need for imagination in the curriculum, not unlike the imaginary dinner table in this chapter. Again from the 12th Century Persian poet Rumi, we are reminded of the need to affirm the imagination, which he speaks of as a second kind of intelligence:

> A spring overflowing its springbox. A freshness
> in the center of the chest. This other intelligence
> does not turn yellow or stagnate. It's fluid,
> and it does not move from the outside to inside
> through the conduits of plumbing-learning.
> This second knowing is a fountainhead from within you, moving out.

It is a time for *Coming to our Senses* (Kabat-Zinn, 2006) in the educational projects of learning institutions all over the world. That requires using our imagination to engage in a different pedagogy than before. We must consider the qualities required for approaching curriculum so desperately needed: beauty of existence without intentional harm, restorative health and education, truths about politics, history, and ecology, and socio-economic justice.

My University's Board of Governors, to which I belong, has been going through the process of developing a strategic plan for the university's future: it has been very instructional imagining and thinking about the vision and mission and mandate of a university. We are in a small city in the very south end of the province of Alberta, with half our student teaching placements in rural schools and half in small towns and cities. So that location contextualizes what we have as organizational, teaching, research, and community service goals. I was impressed with the good will at work while imagining what those communities and our students need to learn and do in the future, as 'they become what they are not yet' Our university's vision and core value is "to build a better society". At the root of that desire for post-secondary education, that better world, is imagination.

There is much within such strategic plans of most universities and schools (again the future tense always implies acts of imagination to propel our being and doing into the realm that is not-yet-become) that requires an active, developed, and literate imagination. There is plenty of room for the imagination in all those statements, which guide curriculum, pedagogy, and research.

Back to our imagined ideal curriculum dinner party: Toward the end of the evening Huebner suggests that the company of diners retires to the library where they form a talking circle while they take their cultural beverages. They go around the circle and ask for one word or phrase from each of these heart-ful thinkers to suggest a connection between imagination and what qualities of the teacher with a newer, more generative pedagogy might be like: illuminative, lively, responsible, collegial, egalitarian, authentic, sentient, hermeneutic, poly-cultural, feminist, inclusive, restorative, reconstructive, meta-reflective, communicative, empathic, insightful, provocative, care-full, multi-modal, ethical.

Not one of those lovely dining scholars is or was unaware or uncommitted to the good of the world...they have all worked together in their lives and texts, shirtsleeves rolled up, with an imagination about the good ahead, the better world possible.

Insight, imagination, and mindfulness can make it possible to see accurately and deeply what is going on, listen with attunement, notice compassionately the struggles and happiness, desires and griefs, tears and laughter, heavy demands and Herculean social work and participate generatively without being taken too much from ourselves. We need not be exhausted by continually being too little for too much. We are as we are in any moment, doing the best we can. Perhaps in the stillness of mindful insight, we can 'save' our own being in its best form by paying attention simply to what is, without having to rescue or fix it or take it over. We then can look and find our place and work that could be of most use.

We commit to being alert, attuned, and aware to all that transpires in our daily lives. That can be more possible if we travel lightly in our daily journeys. Insight and mindfulness are ways of being present and living our lives to the fullest. Teachers especially require this I think because we study so many disciplines, have such keen interest ourselves in the entire world, and could have had so many other lives and choices. Teaching allows us to live all the possibilities in a strange and beautiful way. May we develop those literacies of awareness, cognition, ethics, narration, relationship, and hermeneutics in a new consciousness of teaching.

May we dwell imaginatively together in learning.

REFERENCES

Answers.com (2008). Retrieved July 1, 2008, from http://www.answers.com/topic/forms-1
Barks, C. (2006). *A year with Rumi*. New York: Harper Collins.
Calvino, I. (1988, 1995). *Six memos for the next millennium*. Toronto, ON: Vintage.
Caputo, J. D. (1987). *Radical hermeneutics: Repetition, deconstruction, and the hermeneutic project*. Bloomington, IN: Indiana University Press.
Caputo, J. D. (2006). *The weakness of God: A theology of the event*. Bloomington, IN: Indiana University Press.
Findlay, T. (1990). *Inside memory: Pages from a writer's notebook*. Toronto, ON: ECW Press.
Fowler, L. (2006). *A curriculum of difficulty: Narrative research and the practice of teaching*. New York: Peter Lang.
Frye, N. Retrieved from http://www.frye.ca/english/northrop-frye/frye-quotes.html
Gallas, K. (2003). *Imagination and literacy: A teacher's search for the heart of learning*. New York: Teachers College Press.
Greene, M. Retrieved from http://www.maxinegreene.org/
Hasebe-Ludt, E., & Hurren, W. (Eds.). (2005). *Curriculum intertext: Place/language/pedagogy*. New York: Peter Lang.
Hirshfield, J. Retrieved from http://blogs.csmonitor.com/the_poetic_life/2005/05/
hooks, b. (1994). *Teaching to transgress*. New York: Rutledge.
Huebner, D. (1999). Challenges bequeathed (1996). In V. Hillis (Ed.), *The lure of the transcendent: Collected essays by Dwayne E. Huebner* (pp. 432–445). Mahwah, NJ: Lawrence Erlbaum Associates.
Krishnamurti, J. Retrieved from http://www.kfa.org/
Palmer, P. (2007). *The courage to teach: Exploring the inner landscape of teacher's life*. San Francisco: John Wiley & Sons, Inc.
Pinar, W. (2004). *What is curriculum theory?* Mahwah, NJ: Lawrence Erlbaum.
Plato. Retrieved from http://www.philosophypages.com/ph/plat.htm

Richardson, L. (1977). *Fields of play: Constructing an academic life.* New Brunswick, NJ: Rutgers University Press. (See Writing Matters, p. 86)

Rumi. Retrieved from http://oldpoetry.com/opoem/38198-Mewlana-Jalaluddin-Rumi-Two-Kinds-of-Intelligence-wbr-

Scott, D. (2008). *Critical essays on major curriculum theorists.* London: Routledge.

Wachtel, E. (2007). *Random illuminations: Conversations with Carol shields.* Frederickton, NB: Goose Lane.

Zwicky, J. (2003). *Wisdom and metaphor.* Kentville, NS: Gaspereau Press.

JAMES MCNINCH

SCHOOLING MEMORIES: SURPASSING THE TECHNICAL WITH EDUCATIONAL LARGESSE

Memory: And in one of these houses- I can't remember whose- a magic doorstop, a big mother-of-pearl seashell that I recognized as a messenger from near and far, because I could hold it to my ear – when nobody was there to stop me – and discover the tremendous pounding of my own blood, and of the sea. (Alice Munro, 2005, The View from Castle Rock, p. 349)

INTRODUCTION

It might seem odd that Huebner's call to temper the technical and rational in education has prompted me to an auto-ethnographic response, but such navel-gazing may be just the antidote for the empirical maladies affecting our schools. Huebner's comment that technical and positivistic modes of reflection "do not depict the complexity, or even begin to approach the mystery of the human condition" (Huebner, 1996, p. 432) struck a deep chord with me, an educator with more than 35 years experience as a school and university teacher and administrator. Is it simply the process of aging that makes long term memory seem more vivid as short term memory grows more vague, or is this the brain's way of helping us sort through what is really important about having and living a life and making sense of ourselves and others? If the educational process is a critical aspect of that mystery, as Huebner contends, what are some non-technical and non-rational ways we might explore this mystery?

At this stage of my life and career I am convinced more than ever that it is through story and metaphor that we begin to understand significance. As Lewis (2007) has noted, "creative symbiosis between story and human life, that living together, is always present, alive, always at work (p. 2). O'Reilly-Scanlon (2002), inspired by Haug (1987), suggests "as Self is socially constructed through reflection: one of the major goals of memory work is to uncover the ways in which individuals build their own identities" (p. 75). So, I have a few stories about school to share that have meaning not just for my own construction of self, but for the larger issues that shape education. These fragments are out of context because they

P. Lewis and J. Tupper (eds.), Challenges Bequeathed: Taking up the Challenges of Dwayne Huebner, 66–81.
© 2009 sense publishers. All rights reserved.

are not continuous and they do not integrate with my out of school memories. They are not complete or completely coherent, but they do signify.

These episodes tell me that the content of schooling, broadly understood as constituting curriculum and instruction, is much less significant than we educators would like to think. This is despite our knowledge of cognitive and learning theories that have informed and "improved the sequencing of educational materials and led to the construction of diagnostic instruments" and our power to "fabricate [rich] educational environments has increased many fold in the past fifty years. This is a wonderful and significant achievement." (Huebner, 1999, p. 434). My contention, based on my own memory work, is that it is the social and emotional elements of schooling that are affectively fundamental, and it is how we feel, how we learn to feel, and what we do with those feelings where schooling has the most impact. The "real", the most impressive, stories are found not in curriculum documents or instructional strategies or in the results of achievement scores and mental testing. Rather it is the complex relations among students and between students and teachers that should most concern us. The affective domain is embedded dialectically in the official and unofficial discourses of schooling and stimulates identity in the educational context. LeCourt (2004) discussing Foucault and Deleuze in her analysis of student writings adds, "knowledge is produced through power relationships, and power is actualized through knowledge" (p. 56).

This chapter illustrates these contentions by starting with six vignettes from my memories of elementary schooling. Goodson (2006) argues that if life stories are contextualized within social space and historical time this can "heal the rupture between the individual life narrative and the collective and historical experience" (p. 9). I would add that any stories I re-create here might serve to resonate with others who will bring their own point of view to my constructions of the past and my musings upon them. "[A]s readers...we bring yet another point of view to a story thereby creating a reciprocity of viewpoints" (Lewis, 2007, p. 36). In auto-ethnography there is also reciprocity between object and subject, between observer and observed, since they are one and the same person where this separation is mediated by retrospection (Goldie, 2008). It is this reciprocity which illustrates the relational and affective dimensions of education that serve to counter-balance the technical and the rational Huebner worried about. Relational constructs and identities compel us to de-centre the rational and empirical to celebrate the imaginative and emotional. "It is from our relationships within interpretive communities that our constructions of the world derive" (Gergen and Gergen, 2003, p. 597). Schools are just such interpretive communities and our experiences in them need to be understood from multiple perspectives because it is the quality of our relations with others and how we treat one another and how others treat us and how we approach teaching all of this, explicitly and implicitly, consciously and unconsciously, in our schools that matters most.

SCHOOLING MEMORIES

Kindergarten in Winnipeg, 1952-53

With hindsight, the impact of kindergarten on my formation now seems profound if only because I have so few pre-kindergarten memories. It is as if a light-bulb suddenly was turned on in my life and a great narrative began: I was going to school! Schooling had a kind of legitimacy and importance that other experiences did not. Is this testimony to the power of schooling to shape, mould, create an identity and a personality? Why, for example, can I vividly remember "playing" with the large wooden boot ("There was an old woman who lived in a shoe"), carefully undoing the laces, un-cris-crossing them to get at the many children inside and then having to carefully lace up the boot again when it was time to "stop playing" (and learning how, in a pre-Velcro age, to tie my own shoe laces)? I have a much more visceral memory of doing this (perhaps because of the repetition of it over many days) than that day in the summer before kindergarten when my friend, Linda Lindsay, and I hand in hand crossed a busy street against a red light and sent a car careening into the front of a dry-cleaning store to avoid hitting us.

The making of my first Mother's Day card now seems fraught with significance. A crepe paper carnation was glued on the front. I remember mine wasn't as tight as it should have been, but we got to spray some Midnight in Paris (or at least something from a blue bottle) onto the flower to give it a "real" scent. And inside to print VERY carefully and formally "To Mother Love Jimmy". Two years later I argued with the teacher who printed MOM on the board. I insisted it should be MUM, unaware of the Canadian dilemma poised then between American and British English and assuming that phonics ruled: we say mUm (rhymes with bum) not mOm (rhymes with bomb). It is not the kindergarten teacher that I remember, nor the other children. No, it is me, my relationship with myself, negotiating myself through a rich and complicated space and unrolling a mat to lie on, listening to songs being played on the radio and often falling asleep.

At the hands of this faceless teacher I also experienced my first vivid memory of public humiliation, although I realize now that no one probably noticed or cared about my shame. Was it part of the health curriculum to form a circle and show our hands – first palms up and then palms down – in an inspection for cleanliness? It seems to me a hand puppet was involved in this surveillance. My fingernails, a mess because I gnawed on them to the quick, were always raw and sore looking. In addition, we were supposed to produce a clean handkerchief from our pockets and I never had one, not even a paper tissue.

Grade one in Arrowood Alberta, 1953-54

Learning to read, I met Dick and Jane and Sally and Spot and Puff in grade one and was aware that their world, like that inhabited by the Bobbsey Twins, was an artifice, but I did relate to Dick because he was the eldest kid in the family and like me assumed a kind of superiority that came with being the eldest and a boy. Here was my formal introduction to phonics and sounding out the letters of the alphabet in large and small case carefully printed across the (real slate I now realize) blackboard on permanent lines. Above the board were letters on cardboard with images to recognize: A is for Apple, B is for Bee, and so on. For some reason the letter "n" was made to look like a Singer sewing machine but without any reference to an initial "n" sound. I remember the teacher being unable to provide me with an explanation of this.

Grade 3 in Devon Alberta, 1955

This teacher would draw a large clock on the black board and we learned our times-tables by rote, with the multiplier number in the middle and the teacher pointing with a stick at the numbers around the clock. "Five times one is five. Five times two is ten. Five times three is fifteen" we would recite in unison. There was some excitement to this drill. She would point at the numbers randomly to test our memory and change the multiplier to review previous sets. Then she would tell us all to stand by the sides of our desks and then select one student at a time for a solo performance. When you made a mistake or hesitated too long you had to sit down. The last person standing was the "winner". This drill was followed by practice in workbooks. I never was the last person standing because the seven and nine times tables were a mystery so I never discovered if there was a prize for not making any mistakes.

Grade 3 in Burnaby BC, 1956

We moved to British Columbia near the end of the school year and I remember feeling vaguely alien. A substitute teacher, an older man in a dark suit (the principal?), distributed paper and poster paints which I had never worked with before and told us to paint "a picture from our imagination". My father had started a job as a navigator flying on overseas routes to Hong Kong and Australia. I painted a grey plane over a wash of blue and tried to distinguish the ocean with whitecaps and the sky with cumulous clouds. I was frustrated by my ineptitude with the medium and kept hiding my efforts from the teacher as he walked up and down the aisles between the rows of desks inspecting student work. He said something to me that made my ears burn red but I can't recall what he said. I remember my desk was covered in paint and the piece of paper thick with attempts to re-do my efforts until it had become a sodden mess. My anger at myself and my irritation at the teacher who couldn't seem to help threw me into such a black mood that I crumpled the paper and marched to the front of the class and threw it in the wastepaper basket and took some satisfaction that the man in the dark suit wasn't the "real" teacher.

Grade 4 at Second Street School, Burnaby BC

We learned to write cursively using nib pens dipped in ink wells recessed into a hole on the top right hand side of the desk. I was left handed. I learned quickly to crook my wrist up and over so that I didn't smudge the page with my hand and arm and still maintain the compulsory right angle required of the "MacLean Method" of hand-writing we were practicing in little half note-books ruled with solid and perforated lines to guide the formation of upper and lower case letters. My grade 4 teacher was a young woman named Miss Robinson. She had wavy hair and glasses and noted on several report cards that "Jimmy talks too much in class". The girl who sat in front of me was named Linda Wheeler and she had buck teeth and a pony tail. I enjoyed pulling on her pony tail to get her attention and whisper in her ear. I sat at the back of row one nearest the windows. I realize now that Miss Robinson seated students by their academic achievement. The kids on the far side of the room were poorly dressed and didn't answer teacher's questions. We were also divided for reading into three groups: the Bunnies, the Beavers, and the Blue-Jays. I remember making comments to Linda about other students in the class.

This was the year a boy in my class from row five whose name I didn't even know jumped on me after school and pinned me down on the cement and wouldn't let me up and I wasn't strong enough to get him off me. He didn't do anything and eventually just let me go. Another day, Miss Robinson sent me to the cloakroom at the back of the class because I was again "talking too much". My sense of injustice soon had me choking back tears. I looked at the double rows of coats on their hooks and decided if I was banished I would simply leave and grabbed my jacket. By the time I got home there had been a phone call to my mother who was expecting me. I was relieved and surprised that she didn't scold me. All she said was, "Miss Robinson was worried about you". Although, thankfully, Miss Robinson didn't speak of the incident the next day, there was a rift between us that lasted the rest of the school year. It should be noted, however, that I did stop "talking too much in class". I was such a needy arm-waver and finger-snapper vying for attention and wished I could sit at the front near teacher's desk. In June, we were given a note from the PTA to take home asking us to contribute $2.00 for a gift (a dinner service set) for Miss Robinson who would be retiring from teaching to be married that summer. My mother's only comment was $2.00 was excessive and people should only be asked to give what they could; I was given one dollar to take to school. There was a presentation of the gift in class, mothers were invited, and there was punch and dainties. I was glad my mother did not attend.

Grade 5 at Armstrong School, Burnaby BC, 1957-58

A new school and a new beginning in September with Mr. Crawford. My first male teacher. My first crush on a teacher. Mr. Crawford in the class picture is not as handsome as I remember him. But he liked teaching art and arranged for us one fine day in June to go to Stanley Park to paint the huge bowed cedar known as Lumberman's Arch. I loved that. I loved a lot about Mr. Crawford. One lunch-time a friend and I went to the staff parking lot behind the school to look at Mr. Crawford's car. It was a 57 Ford Thunderbird convertible with a continental kit. The ultimate. I tried a door and it wasn't locked. Inside, we sat on leather seats – a first for me – and pushed the buttons on the "automatic" radio. I pulled open the ashtray and discovered cigarette butts with red lipstick on the brown filters: proof that Mr. Crawford had a GIRLFRIEND! It is hard to explain the impact this new knowledge had on me. For the first time a teacher was connected to the social world outside the school. He was a real person, not just a young teacher in a tweed sports jacket. I felt giddy with this new knowledge of a teacher's private life, and now understand why the party and gift for Miss. Robinson's impending wedding did not have the same impact: hers was a public social event, this was the surfacing of a secret – one of life's apparently important mysteries. My memories of Mr. Crawford are tied to another vivid image of my three friends, Glen, Gordon, and John. We were the four most popular boys in class according to the number of Valentine's Day cards we each received. (I had the third most). We were jumping up and down using the beds in my bedroom as trampolines and listening to the first 45 rpm record I had bought: the Everly Brothers' *Wake Up Little Suzie* and *Bye Bye Love*. John, a head taller than the rest of us (and by the card count the most popular boy in the class), showed us that he had hair growing around his penis. Mr. Crawford, his car, and his girl-friend who smoked and wore lipstick are embedded in these same pre-pubescent stirrings.

Grade 6 at Grauer School, Richmond BC, 1958-59

I moved schools again – to suburban Richmond, after the term had started late in Fall. My teacher was "old", that is she had grey hair, but had a kindly demeanour if that means anything anymore. She wore white blouses and dark skirts and was pencil thin. I had decided that instead of Jimmy, I should be called Scott, a name I thought quite dashing. So I introduced myself to the teacher as Scott, but of course the principal had told her my name and she asked me if I wanted to be called Jim or Jimmy. I didn't dare say "actually, I would prefer Scott" and sunk into my seat. For some reason I assumed she was not married, even though we called her "Mrs.", and I also believed she had suffered some personal tragedy (such as the loss of a child in its infancy?). I remember nothing about instruction except for Health which focused completely on the Red Cross. We did first aid, pretending to have broken limbs and severe bleeding, and other students splinted our legs and applied tourniquets to our arms. We also learned about international initiatives and organized penny drives and bake sales for worthy causes. I remember seeing Lotta Hitschmanova speaking on (black and white) TV for the Unitarian Service Committee and its 56 Sparks Street Ottawa address and thinking our Red Cross work must be part of this effort.

What I more vividly remember was that all the grade sixes were involved with square-dancing. It had to be more than just a phys ed class because there were outfits and everything, and I had somehow missed out and resented it. Was there no partner for me? Was it an extra-curricular club? I remember standing outside the gymnasium door and looking in at the boys with white shirts and string ties and the girls with bouffant crinolined skirts do-se-doe-ing and a la main left and right to the calls of an ancient man in a cowboy hat above the amplified music from a record player. I ached to be part of all the glamour of this group, but never even imagined how I might do so, because I had not been invited in, and it never occurred to me to ask a teacher about this.

I could go on, into the morass of junior high and the pretence of high-school or I could retrace my steps and provide more details from the elementary years, but I hope you get the picture of elementary memories: a fundamental shaping of my being through schooling. This is the "real" content of curriculum. Identity emerges from the discourses one is caught in. It is obvious that grades four and five mark a significant growth of my sense of the social, a connectedness to others, including teachers with "real" names, and "real" lives. It is in and through these memories of identity formation that I "know" who I think I am. Code calls such sites "epistemically responsible knowing centres" (as cited in Goldie, 2008, p. 231). As I have been writing this chapter I have prompted friends and relatives to share a memory of schooling with me. I am distressed that their immediate memories are often very negative and sometimes involve abusive students and abusive teachers. I am also surprised that while I "loved" school, because at least academically I thrived there, many of my peers "hated" it. This "hatred" is a legacy of the modernist era in North American education that has emphasized the empirical and technical to the detriment of the affective.

STOP RUNNING AND START GARDENING

....It's/easy to see how/the act of expression/grows/from an awkward/stutter-/ step, the point where/chaos becomes/chance, becomes/order, becomes/time. (Mooney, 2008).

I read about a young Newfoundland poet, Jacob Mooney, extolling the virtue of "infinitely exhilarating pluralism" at the launch of his latest book of poetry, and that afternoon I see a young university student in a hijaab and below her burka the brightest of red high-top runners with Velcro straps. My mother would mutter "incongruous" (under her breath) to describe "such a get-up". But appreciating that the discourses of life and schooling are "incongruous", complicated, often contradictory (and sometimes humorous) is consistent with Doll's call (1993) for the new 4 Rs in curriculum: richness, relations, reflection, and rigor. These 4 R's, it seems to me, may be useful criteria by which to assess and evaluate the complexity of engagement in schooling. The stories I have shared are intended to illuminate in a small way the complexity of that engagement. In a recent brain-storming activity at a provincial meeting on assessment and evaluation we were asked to quickly jot down an "outcome" we would hope to be the result of a student's engagement in schooling. I wrote without hesitation, "the ability to love and be loved". The truth, as Huebner understood it, is the really important things in life are the most difficult to teach, but if we ignore these "mysteries" we fail the students who are entrusted to us. Rhetoric about academic leadership and success contributes to the diminishment of the incongruous, the magical, the mysterious.

The post modern paradigm considers human endeavours to be connected with the natural world rather than separate from Nature. Ecological metaphors for human activities have replaced the machine. Yet so much of schooling and ideas about curriculum and instruction are still framed and constrained by modernity. Betts (1992) used the phrase "paradigm paralysis" to describe our dependence on thinking that is based only on what has gone before. Lewis (2004) contrasts some of the differences between the modern and the post-modern in education and the tension inherent in working in an environment shaped by both. The standard style in educational publishing, for example, is APA which assumes from scientific modernism that what has been written most recently must be the most germane, and eschews first names of authors based on the modernist notion that names and sex are irrelevant to higher values like neutrality and validity. A post-modern view counters that knowledge of the person who writes is critical to understanding. APA is silent of course on how to cite poetry. Another example of this tension is found in the discussion of boys and schooling. Modernism asserts that boys (or actually only certain boys, but surely the majority) will excel the more structured and competitive school environments are and quantitative research can be used to prove this. In this construct, queer students become the exception that proves the rule. In contrast, post-modernism posits teaching and learning as playful and relational. The study of boys should involve qualitative research using induction to move from the particular to the general and illustrate the diversity of boys' experiences through case studies and narrative life stories. Gay-Straight Alliances in high schools celebrate students' rights to be different and unique in a way that the debating society or the football team do not. Schools reflect modern/post-modern tensions roiling in the culture at large. "Success" of "leaders" is still seen as an individual accomplishment. So-called reality TV and game shows and singing competitions produce winners and losers that we vote for as modern democrats, and yet we network post-modernly, like ants in cyberspace on Face Book and in chat-rooms connecting to tribes of people "like us" or anonymously bully them with text messages to put them down so we might be "up". If life is simply a contest or game show (and the person with the most toys "wins", as the bumper stickers say) then schooling that emphasizes group work, sharing, and co-operation must be the theatre of the absurd.

In our post-modern world, as Goodson (2006) has noted, grand or meta-narratives no longer ring true even though they still seem to maintain the status of truth in curriculum. Because "isms" from across the spectrum have been interrogated and found lacking, we revert to the individual. Modernist notions of educational leadership in a post-structural environment have similarly been queered. One construct –there are those who are born or destined to lead – continues to exist in cultures that are based on inheritance and title and wealth and lineage, including European cultures, and permeates educational discourse, albeit sotto voce. It used to be assumed, for example, that men inherited this right, and therefore female pre-service elementary school teachers had no need for courses in educational administration. In the modernist age, the "natural" leader was replaced by another grand narrative of "the self-made" man, who pulled himself up by his bootstraps, as my Irish Protestant relatives were fond of saying, and who rose above "their station" with purse-lipped determination, hard work, (and hard drinking). In the 21st century both these models of leadership are hollow and yet both are imbedded in the ways in which we organize and manage our schools and the intended learning. Today, bourgeois parents and their children inherit a sense of entitlement to success and leadership and "prove" this entitlement through achievement in schools. In light of this we are compelled by Huebner's challenge to understand how each of our own life narratives are the product of a multiplicity of complex factors, including the critical experiences of twelve years of formal schooling, where "inherited privilege" and "sheer determination" do not explain the roots of concepts like success or happiness and our development as human beings.

If we understand that positions of leadership in schools are always ambiguous, always provisional, and always dependent not on grand narratives like the Hero in History but on private people agreeing to do public work along side others, we might better understand the tensions between the personal and the public implicit in the act of teaching. Much of the rhetoric of educational leadership derives from the world of business, which is still driven by modernist notions. An advertisement in the *Globe and Mail* for an investment company nails this modern macho ethos:

> If you want to stay in [the] business [of education], you had better plan to stay sharp; lose focus and you're done. Especially if you're out in front where there's no one to show you the way, and there's always someone coming up fast. (Business Section, March 29, 2008, p. 3)

The visual image accompanying the text is of a male jogger re-tying his shoe and looking back, not as a member of a team, but as a solo runner ready to go the distance and beat all comers. Such an aggressive discourse turns schooling and education and training into key elements of such things as Canada's competitiveness in a global environment. It is this discourse, which in turn animates the emphasis on standardized testing and other technical benchmarks by which we compare ourselves to others.

In contrast, for those who believe like Huebner that we must move beyond the technical, I wish to offer another image, grounded or rooted (sorry) in my own love of gardening. To me, and many others, the image of the gardener is more apt a metaphor for an educator than the distance-runner. Competing to "win" reduces life to a race that is all about the finish line as if it is the outcome not the process that is important. Gardening is in microcosm and macrocosm all about process, about rhythms, cycles of rebirth, growth, death and renewal, of each part of Nature intimately part of an inter-locking and interdependent system of great complexity and yet stunning simplicity. Much has been written about self-reflection and awareness of pedagogy through finding metaphors for our teaching and as much again has been written about the metaphor of the teacher as gardener. (Cf. Holge-Hazelton & Krojer, 2008; Vernon, 2007; Song and Taylor, 2005; Lewis, 2004; May, 2003; Agger, 2002; Baptist, 2002, Gayle, n.d.). A gardener cannot control, but she can nurture and encourage; a gardener tends, attends, and tenders within natural and aesthetic parameters. But while the garden is a seductive metaphor for education, it may also be dangerous if, in its allure, it masks other realities. Easy images are comfortable and need to be interrogated.

More than 30 years ago in Pinar's (1975) edited collection, Curriculum Theorizing: The Reconceptualists, Herbert Kliebard described three clusters of metaphors related to curriculum theory: production, travel, and growth. The modern or mechanical metaphor is the one of production – the student is transformed from raw material to finished product by the experience of schooling, most aggressively prodded and made on a production line, or more passively or benignly sculpted like driftwood by the incessant waves of the sea. In the metaphor of travel, education is seen as a journey of discovery where Baptist (2002) notes "both the nature of the road and the nature of the learner are considered in determining the course of the experience" (p. 20). The teacher is more like a Sherpa guide in the Himalayas, someone who has gone before and knows what to expect. Here it is the journey not the destination that defines the experience of being a learner however sage the guide.[i] In the metaphor of the garden, students are regarded as seeds and then plants with potential and promise that can be nurtured in a specific context. The most generous and eco-friendly view of teachers as gardeners is that they encourage each plant to learn to survive, even to thrive in the environment they find themselves in, and are then able to adapt to even more exotic or alien locations.

I have often observed that schools are like hot-houses, artificial sites of heat and humidity and light where some students, the most social, flourish and thrive and others, the least social, wilt and wither in such intensity (McNinch, 2004). Pre-service teachers have a hard time, for example, realizing that they are very much exceptions: they flourished in the hot-house environment of schooling while many of their peers did not; they felt a sense of their own agency while many of their peers felt "done to" and put upon. The garden is a mediation imposed on Nature; it is by definition, like teaching, an intervention. A garden is not passive: like school a garden is replete with decisions made by "others". Rousseau-ian ideas about what might be construed as "natural", if only children were left to their own devices, have permeated the thinking of educators like Mead and Dewey and Montessori. If we need to remind ourselves of the romanticism of these ideals, we need not necessarily disparage them. Like schools, there are many different kinds of gardens. Private gardens are just that – a reflection of individuals connecting in different ways and for different reasons with Nature. Public gardens are about community and definitions of who we choose to be collectively. In each garden there is a promise of an aesthetic experience, some connection to artistry as envisioned by Greene (1995) and Eisner (1991). Gardens, like schools and curriculum, reveal an infinite variety, ranging from the most pristine to the highly planned and controlled to the completely neglected and overgrown. Weeds, by definition, in this context are simply plants not wanted in a particular setting. We must interrogate our schools' penchant for weeding out the undesirable.

But the garden is not "natural"; by definition it involves human intervention and reflects culturally and historically embedded discourses about style and meaning, in the way that schools do. Like schools, gardens reflect the intention of the architects and designers whether it be Louis XIV at Versailles, or the nouveau riche who envisioned a designed but "natural" New York landscape known as Central Park, or the Wascana Park authority in my own city of Regina, Saskatchewan that has made an integrated connection between the city and the surrounding landscape of sloughs, fields, marshes, and creeks. The same is true of every experiment in education, whether it be un-graded classes or schools without walls or the (re-)segregation of boys and girls. Planning is based on values embedded in concepts of leadership and definitions of success.

So as landscape architects (the educational planners and administrators) or as gardeners (the classroom teachers), when we think of all that has gone wrong in schools and indeed how little the experience of schooling has affectively changed for students in the past fifty years, we must ask ourselves in what ways we are part of the problems inherent in schooling, even as we flatter ourselves that we are part of the solutions. All is not well in the garden. Literacy rates and high school completion rates, directly related to poverty and social inequities throughout the world, are no where near where they could or should be. There is much work to be done at both the macro (design) and micro (tending) level. That work for all of us starts by paying attention to the needs of each seed or plant, each one unique, each vulnerable to larger forces – the winds of whim and change – of so many things beyond their control (parents, technology, the economy, to name just a few). We must remember that all the seedlings respond to some special attention, some pinching off, some propping up, some cutting back, some encouragement, some enrichment, some connection, some love. Gergen and Gergen (2003) put it this way: "Individual selves are not prior to, or constitutive of relationships, but rather a process of relatedness precedes the conception of individual minds" (p. 599).

THE ACCIDENTAL GARDENER

"they nourished seeds to flower for a while in me" (O'Siadhail, 1999).

I wish to extend this teaching as gardening metaphor to its most important point. As gardeners, as educators, we are often completely unaware of the impact of our actions and we need to heed the incidental and the accidental. Recently at my university, a grounds crew inadvertently sprayed trees and surrounding grass with a liquid laced with Roundup™ with devastating results. Overt and conscious decisions about curriculum decisions, planning for instruction and assessment, and the intended outcomes of these actions are nothing in comparison to the daily impact we make accidentally in the lives of students for both good and for ill. Unlike music, sports, or other media stars' influences on the young, teachers are largely unheralded and often ignored. Not only does our work go largely unnoticed and unrecognized, we are often simply unaware of the difference we make in the lives of young people. We live in double jeopardy: planning for the intended and living with the consequences of the unintended.

Out of the blue last year I was contacted (thanks to the internet) by Kelly Damphousse, a student I had taught in my first years of teaching in the late nineteen-seventies in Lac La Biche, a town in north-eastern Alberta. This student is now an Associate Dean of Sociology at the University of Oklahoma. He had been nominated for an excellence in teaching award at his University and was asked about influences on his life and he remembered me, his grade 9 and 10 English teacher. As he remembers, it goes like this:

> *It was the first day of 10th grade and I was acting the goof in English Lit. I had skipped kindergarten (because I could already read), so I was always the youngest in my class. Being the chubbiest kid didn't help things and I learned that "smart was not in" and not much was expected of kids in Lac La Biche. I discovered that being drunk and being a goof was the best coping skill for me. Not much of a future for a 15 year old.*

> *Mr. McNinch, who I remember as having hair to his shoulders and granny glasses, like John Lennon, after asking me a question I couldn't answer said, "What happened to you over the summer, Mr. Damphousse, that turned your brain to mush?" Even though I was a bit embarrassed by his comment ('how did he know about bush parties and sex and booze and drugs over the summer?'), I was shocked* **since it was the first time that anyone had suggested that I had more to offer than what I was giving**. *His comment also suggested that some time during my 9th grade, I had shown some good – at least to him.* **That Mr. McNinch would think me at least a little worthy meant more than I could express.**

> *For some reason, that comment stuck with me and has encouraged me over the years Every time I was tempted to do the bare minimum to get by, his comment came back to me. It was as if he was saying, "I know you can do better than that".*

> *Your words, so innocently spoken, have continued to inspire me for thirty years. When people ask me about my favorite teacher, your name is the first to my lips. Whenever I think about blowing off some student who has failed to live up to my expectations, I think of you. Whenever some one asks (as someone did this past week) who inspired me to do well, I mention you.*

It is these "accidental" moments repeated every day in every classroom that define the educational experience, as much as any technical attention to lesson planning or evaluation rubrics. As the director of a Teaching Development Centre I hosted annual "Inspiring Teaching Awards" banquets. University students were asked to choose both a K-12 and university teacher that had made an impact on them. Although many students had difficulty selecting a university teacher, all of them were able to quickly identify at least one school teacher who had had a profound affect on them. We have no idea of the impact we make on our students. This is both a burdensome responsibility and a wonderful opportunity. I know that for every student like Kelly Damphousse that I may have inspired, I have also "injured" just as many with my penchant for irony and sarcasm. My own memories of schooling that I have shared and Kelly's story confirm the significance of minor incidents that create not just memories but lasting impressions that help to shape who we are. This is not about a "hidden curriculum", but it is about the very human, relational affective nature of teaching that has been over-shadowed and often silenced by technical concerns for finding the right program or strategy for students in order to "produce results" and prove our "accountability".

I am drawn, once again, to van Manen's (1991) articulation of "pedagogical tact and thoughtfulness" (p. 8) that is less about instructional techniques and more about "a personal appropriation of a moral intuition" (p. 9); I am reminded of Palmer's (1998) view of identity and integrity: "subtle dimensions of the complex, demanding, and lifelong process of self-discovery" (p. 13). Palmer praises teachers' ability to connect: "they are able to weave a complex web of connections among themselves, their subjects, and their students so that students can learn to weave a world for themselves" (p. 11). Palmer describes identity and integrity as "that familiar strangeness we take with us to the grave, elusive realities that can be caught only occasionally out of the corner of the eye" (p. 14). This resonates with Huebner's (1999) concern for understanding schooling as "the beauty and tragedy of the new human being's journey with others" (p. 432). As educators, our search for insights is crucial for building effective relationships with students. In turn this search depends on an intentional grasping for integrity so that purposeful, as well as the accidental and the incidental, connections we have with students will serve them well. "Pedagogy is a self-reflective activity that always must be willing to question critically what it does and what it stands for" (van Manen, 1991, p. 10). It is this critical stance and the stories we tell ourselves, and others that will help us surpass the technical foundations of education. I have written previously (McNinch, 2007) about eros as the passionate desire animating teaching and about maintaining my integrity and identity as a queer teacher. I do so "in continuing to be charmed, intrigued, captivated, enchanted, in short – seduced – by youth in all their brave, frustrating, naïve, sweet ignorance... [and] to accord to them, and celebrate with them, the majesty they desire" (p. 212).

CONCLUSION

"The generous are still a glow within" (O'Siadhail, 1999).

Life stories (including their stance or view as well as their discourse) cannot be understood if they are de-contextualized. The critical pedagogy based on identity and integrity that van Manen and Parker speak to needs to be seen through multiple periods of time: the large chunks we construct, like the Modern and Post-modern Eras and our appreciation of how difficult it is to understand the historical period we live in. There is also generational or cohort time: the Cold War fifties and turbulent sixties that helped shape the boomer generation I belong to, for example. Just as crucial for education, there is cyclical time, the stages of life from birth and youth to adulthood and work, and perhaps children, through to the death of our own parents, and retirement and eventually our own death. This intensely private and yet universal and public cycle is the garden we occupy and it is the relationships we cultivate with others there that create meaning. This kind of garden, this kind of schooling, needs constant tending.

My own integrity and identity demand that I come to terms, for example, with why I hated my dyslexic attention-deficit brother's athletic ability and why he hated me for being a "brain" and why we remain estranged to this day. And then there is my sister's struggle with alcohol, stemming in part, from a deep sense of her own mediocrity that her experience in school reinforced. As I write this, my partner's gay nephew, who came out in high school to much trauma, has just spent a night in jail and is now charged with assault following a back-alley fight with his friend. My brother dropping out of school and my sister's low self-esteem, and the nephew's rages are not just signs of failure on the part of an individual or a family. They also represent and reflect the failures these individuals experienced in schools, including the lack of any "real" or authentic relationship with a teacher.

Such failure is an indictment of the teaching profession as a whole and must serve as an incentive to those who know, like Huebner, why we must surpass the technical foundations of education. Teacher education programs must help pre-service teachers to be prepared to make every school day as rich and exciting for students as the anticipation of the very first day of school. Huebner implores us to go beyond the rational. Where does that lead? "I suspect into ever greater levels of suspicion of the protocols of intellectual discourse, and into exploration of the limits of the genre of 'academic knowledge'" (Frow as cited in Gergen and Gergen, 2003, p. 583). The pendulum swinging in education, from its current position as a (social) science back now towards a position animated by the humanities and social justice, is part of the modern/post-modern tension. We must acknowledge that learning and schooling are both "real" and "constructed" because they are situated in specific contexts. By definition that context is political in the sense that it concerns issues of power, leadership, decision-making, choices, and values, belief systems, and ideologies. As educators, we must be vigilant to ensure that our educational systems are not self-serving to those of us who construct and then inhabit them. We must ensure that educational bureaucracies created by educational leaders are not barriers to children's engagement in learning and their ability to make real and sustained connections with other students and teachers. In the personal and the public realm, largesse will help us temper the technical and aspire to Doll's (1993) rubric of richness, relations, reflection, and rigor. Above all we must instil in and bequeath to others the generosity, the "largesse" as O'Siadhail (1992) calls it, which has been extended to us by others over the years, including, if we were lucky, some tender teacher-gardeners.

Largesse

The generous sink into traces they leave in us
In tiers of personality, gestures, words we use,

Flashback to small confirmations, that hand lain
On a shoulder. The generous are still a glow within.

Confident, they knew nothing diminished their glory,
As they nourished seeds to flower for a while in me.

The jealous I begin to forget, frightened spirits
Nipping the bud of younger and younger threats.

The turning-point and I face both ways like Janus
Recall how terribly you needed praise. Then choose.

-Micheal O'Siadhail (1999)

NOTES

[1] "In Sherpa country every track is marked with cairns and prayer flags, reminding you that Man's real home is not a house, but the Road, and that life itself is a journey to be walked on foot." Bruce Chatwin, (1989, p. 273) *What am I doing here?* London: Picador.

REFERENCES

Agger, B. (2002). Sociological writing in the wake of postmodernism. *Cultural Studies ™Critical Methodologies*, 2(4), 427–459.
Baptist, K. W. (2002). The garden as metaphor for curriculum. *Teacher Education Quarterly*. Retrieved March 26, 2008, from http://findarticles.com/p/articles/mi_qa3960/ is_200210/ai_n9121971
Betts, F. (1992). How systems thinking applies to education. *Educational Leadership*, 50(3), 38–41.
Code, L. (1988). Experience, knowledge and responsibility. In M. Griffiths & M. Whitford (Eds.), *Feminist perspectives in philosophy* (pp. 187–204). Bloomington, IN: Indiana University Press.
Doll, W. E. (1993). *A post-modern perspective on curriculum*. New York: Teachers' College Press.
Eisner, E. W. (1991). *The enlightened eye: Qualitative inquiry and the enhancement of educational practice*. New York: MacMillan.

Gayle, V. (n.d.). Teaching teachers in a learning garden: Two metaphors. *The EcoJustice Review*. Retrieved July 15, 2008, from http://www.ecojusticeeducation.org/index.php?option=com_content&task=view&id=55&Itemid=46

Gergen, M. M., & Gergen, K. J. (2003). Qualitative inquiry: Tensions and transformations. In Y. S. Lincoln & N. Denzin (Eds.), *The landscape of qualitative research* (pp. 575–610). London: Sage.

Goldie, T. (2008). *Queersexlife: Autobiographical notes on sexuality, gender, and identity*. Vancouver, BC: Arsenal Pulp Press.

Goodson, I. (2006). The rise of the life narrative. *Teacher Education Quarterly*. Retrieved March 26, 2008, from http://findarticles.com/p/articles/mi_qa3960/is_200610/ai_n17197621?tag=content;col1

Greene, M. (1995). *Releasing the imagination: Essays on education, the arts, and social change*. San Francisco: Jossey-Bass.

Haug, F., et al. (1987). *Female sexualisation: A collective work of memory* (E. Carter, Trans.). London: Verso.

Holge-Hazelton, B., & Krojer, J. (2008). (Re)construction strategies: A methodological experiment on representation. *International Journal of Qualitative Studies in Education*, *21*(1), 19–25.

Huebner, D. (1999). Challenges bequeathed (1996). In V. Hillis (Ed.), *The lure of the transcendent, collected essays by Dwayne Huebner* (pp. 432–445). Mahwah, NJ: Lawrence Erlbaum Associates.

Kliebard, H. M. (1975). Metaphorical roots of curriculum design. In W. Pinar (Ed.), *Curriculum theorizing: The reconceptualists* (pp. 84–85). Berkeley, CA: McCutchan.

LeCourt, D. (2004). *Identity matters: Schooling the student body in academic discourse*. New York: State University of New York Press.

Lewis, N. (2004, Summer). The intersection of post-modernity and classroom practice. *Teacher Education Quarterly*, 119–134.

Lewis, P. (2007). *How we think, but not in school: A storied approach to teaching*. Rotterdam, NL: Sense Publishers.

May, G. (2003). Gardening in cyberspace: A metaphor to enhance online teaching and learning. *Journal of Management Education*, *27*(6), 673–693.

McNinch, J. (2007). Queering seduction: Eros and the erotic in the construction of gay teacher identity. *The Journal of Men's Studies*, *15*(2), 197–215.

McNinch, J., & Cronin, M. (Eds.). (2004). *I could not speak my heart: Education and social justice for gay and lesbian youth*. Regina, SK: Canadian Plains Research Center.

Mooney, J. M. (2008). *The new layman's almanac*. Toronto, ON: McClelland and Stewart.

Munro, A. (2005). *The view from castle rock*. Toronto, ON: Penguin.

O'Reilly-Scanlon, K. (2002). Muted echoes and lavender shadows: Memory work and self-study. In *The fourth international conference on self-study of teacher education practices* (Vol. 2, pp. 74–78). Herstmonceux, East Sussex, England. Retrieved July 12, 2006, from http://educ.queensu.ca/~russellt/sstep4/Volume2.pdf

O'Siadhail, M. (1999). *Poems 1975–1995*. Highgreen, England: Bloodaxe Books.

Palmer, P. (1998). *The courage to teach*. San Francisco: Jossey-Bass.

Smith, D., Shortt, J., & Cooling, T. (2000). Metaphor, scripture and education. *Journal of Christian Education*, *43*(1), 22–28.

Song, J., & Taylor, P. (2005). Pure blue sky: A soulful autoethnography of chemistry teaching in China. *Reflective Practice*, *6*(1), 141–163.

van Manen, M. (1991). *The tact of teaching: The meaning of pedagogical thoughtfulness*. London: Althouse Press.

Vernon, T. (2007). Beyond bricolage. In P. C. Taylor & J. Wallace (Eds.), *Contemporary qualitative research: Exemplars for science and mathematics educators* (pp. 205–216). New York: Springer Press.

Weber, S., & Mitchell, C. (1996). Drawing ourselves into teaching: Studying the images that shape and distort teacher education. *Teaching and Teacher Education*, *12*(3), 303–313.

BARBARA MCNEIL

GIVING VOICE TO THE VOICELESS: ADVOCACY FOR TRANSIENT CHILDREN AND YOUTH

INTRODUCTION

More than two decades ago, noted curriculum scholar Dwayne Huebner (1999) posed an irresistible ethical and moral challenge by boldly asking: "Who in this culture speaks for children and youth?" (p. 443). Huebner's challenge was at once a necessary reprimand, a challenge, a reminder, and task that reveals the contradictions of the troubling situation of living in a part of the world—in a wealthy country such as Canada that constantly proclaims its love for and caring commitment to children and yet allows 16.5 per cent of them to live in poverty (Campaign 2000). Huebner himself often spoke on behalf of children and youth. As a social reconstructionist, Huebner "places human problems at the centre of his concern" for children and youth and is a Christian crusader of the highest order. In the field of education, he is a staunch advocate for learners and the amelioration of their possibilities through education as a form of individual and joint social action. Huebner believes that "[e]ducation is the lure of the transcendent—that [that] which we see is not what we are for we could always be other" (p. 360). I take this to mean, that education, if prudently guided and used, has the potentiality to make us better, to make us more than we are at present. I share Huebner's conviction and like him, I believe that "education is the protest against present forms that they may be reformed and transformed" (p. 360)—especially for the well being of children and youth—the collective potential of people everywhere.

Consequently, I step away from the shadows of silence with an energized and urgent voice, in order to speak on behalf of a particular oppressed group—transient children and youth. In order to bring attention to the situation of transient learners, I draw and build on a qualitative research study that I conducted with elementary school teachers (Pre-K-Grade 8) in a mid-sized city in western Canada (McNeil, 2006). The research focused on teachers' perspectives on transience and literacy and grew out of a desire to gain insight from their lived experiences in "community schools" which principally served low-income, racial, cultural, and linguistic minority students who were often transient. According to the teachers in the study, they taught many students who were highly transient and they believed

P. Lewis and J. Tupper (eds.), Challenges Bequeathed: Taking up the Challenges of Dwayne Huebner, 82–98.
© 2009 sense publishers. All rights reserved.

that the students were caught in an atypical pattern of schooling that had a deleterious impact on their literacy development.

I begin my exposition of this atypical world of schooling by briefly examining the materiality of student transience. To do so I look at some of the social and political superstructures that give rise to and maintain systems of domination in which some students are winners and others, such as those who are transient, are losers in the sweepstakes of schools (McLaren, 1989).

Using my lens as a literacy educator, I draw upon Huebner's (1999) "Language and teaching: Reflections on teaching in the light of Heidegger's writings about language" to name and reveal the implications of transience for the development of literacy amongst these students. I argue that access to school literacy, or the lack of it, is inextricably linked to the "political economy of curriculum and human development" (Huebner, 1999, p. 285). It is paramount to understand the current political economy of curriculum and of child development in contemporary schools. These "will not tell us how to educate young people but how the current structures of production and consumption intrude upon the social relations among people, young and old, near and far, rich and poor, black and white" (p. 297).

In Huebner's writings, education and curriculum are broadly construed; they are rich and expansive. Because Huebner's work is informed by a diversity of traditions, philosophies, and disciplines (e.g., Marxism from political science and sociology), it provides a powerful vehicle for capturing and expressing the complexity of factors that create the phenomenon of student transience.

THE POLITICAL ECONOMY OF STUDENT TRANSIENCE

Transient students are those who, because of punishing poverty and other hardships, including racism, experience the socio-educational disadvantage of making multiple, non-promotional, non-routine, and usually unplanned changes in the school year (Bruno & Isken, 1996; McNeil, 2006). Transient students in particular are "alienated in and from the institution" of school—a socio-political institution "constructed with children and youth in mind" (Huebner, 1999, p. 407). Student transience is an educational atrocity that is seldom talked about. The plight of legions of poor, cultural, linguistic and racial minority children and youth often goes unnoticed and unacknowledged. Their plight cries out for, and deserves critical attention and advocacy. Advocacy is needed because the marginalization of transient children and youth is not only due to their non-adult, hence, non-power broker status, but is undeniably linked to their alienation, isolation, and exclusion from elementary and secondary schools that are products of capitalism (Freire, 1970; Apple, 2004; McLaren, 2003).

McLaren (2003) suggests that under the influence of global capitalism "'free market revolution, driven by continuous capitalist accumulation of a winner-take-all variety, has left the social infrastructure of the United States in tatters (not to mention other parts of the globe (e.g., Canada)" (p. 154). He explains that "business has been given a green light to restructure schooling for its own purposes" and now "the image of *homo economicus* drives educational policy and practice, [and] corporations and transnational business conglomerates and their political bedfellows become leading rationalizing forces of educational reform" (2003, p. 157).

Huebner (1999) recognized that Marxist class analysis of macro economics and its "historical, dialectical, and material content" were essential to understanding the political economy of schools and curriculum under capitalism, which in the words of Freire (1998), is "responsible for the aberration of misery in the midst of plenty" (pp. 94–95). For Huebner and for Freire, "schools and other structures of education reproduce the labor force and class distinctions within the capitalist economy and the political and social institutions which accompany it" (Huebner, 1999, p. 286).

Ensnared at the macro level by the vicissitudes of avaricious capitalism, transient children and youth are among the most wretched of the school world. They are voiceless and often invisible; they are students whose contact with schools, the institutions built specially to socialize and educate the young in our society, is fragile and fleeting. Their material reality is rarely remarked by the telling systems of schools (newsletters, websites, or public announcements by school boards). The socio-educational disadvantage of transient students is also not remarked by the capitalist, consumerist media to which the children and youth are hooked into and hooked on and thus is not reflected back to them for critical scrutiny, neither in nor out of schools.

The political economy of school is such that it impinges on the child at the macro (political and economic) as well as at the micro level (interpersonal or intersubjective). At the macro level of analyses for example, transient students, are caught up in a political and socio-economic system that demands critique and social transformation. Within this general Huebnerian framework, Marxists and Marxist-influenced individuals and groups are tasked with developing class consciousness and the political organization of the working class to fulfill its mission of class struggle in order to disrupt and transform an unjust social order in the interest of transient and other oppressed human beings.

The mobilization of large segments of people for political action to end socio-political domination is "important" and is not the sole purview of Marxist educators alone. Instead, it is the responsibility of all those who are in the world with and alongside children and youth because to care for them is to work praxically (Freire, 1970) toward transforming the abject existential, material conditions of the lives of transient and other disadvantaged children and youth. However, Marxian tools are necessary for understanding the totality of the schooling experience. For example, the elementary teachers I interviewed about transience and literacy did not have, but would have benefited from, Marxist influenced analyses to develop an awareness of the asymmetries, power, and privilege differentials between their social class and that of their students. Such analyses would allow the teachers to take political, economic, and social action for educational transformation.

In addition to the importance of Marxian analyses for understanding the political economy of schools, Huebner makes it clear that the relationship between teachers and students is the centerpiece of schooling (1999, p. 295) yet this is what is decentred and disabled by student transience. For many teachers, it is a substantial deviation from the traditional paradigm of schooling and it is here that it is most destructive. As one teacher expressed it:

> Because you're working with the child and he's come a long way ... In a little while he trusts you.... You begin to get to know him because he is there every day and you know, he wants to go to school ... So, you sort of give them that structure I think that they don't have at home, a routine. And so it's sort of sad at times when they say, 'teacher I have to go, I'm moving'... (McNeil 2006, p. 12).

The teacher describes the establishment of social relations, between adult and child, the building and development of care and trust, the importance of school to the child, the difficult life of the learner, and the rupturing of that relationship when the student conveys that he must leave. These written words do not capture the sadness in the teacher's cadence, the eyes made bright with tears, and the deep sigh of frustration and pain when she described the child. Furthermore, the teacher and I both knew that what she said did not, could not come close to revealing the hurt and anguish of the child as he realized that he had to change schools and home yet again.

The multiple school changes experienced by transient students disrupt the possibilities for creating meaningful, positive social relationships with teachers and peers, unnecessarily and painfully separating them from the social and cultural spaces of schools. Consequently, as teachers "our fundamental concern is and must be the quality of that social life" (Huebner, 1999, p. 297). The distortion of transient students' social relations with teachers and peers severely limits their social collaboration, social activity and productivity. Thus, from the standpoint of Huebner's genetic Marxism, transience limits:

> the developing power of the person for self and social production, the evolving social relations of the person, the relationship of self activity to social activity, the evolving functions of language as manifestations of social relations and consciousness, including class consciousness, the functions of production and ownership, and use-value of the materials of production for children, relationships of these materials to the schemata of assimilation and accommodation of the child, and the relationship of these materials to the productive forces within society (1999, p. 297).

Schools work well for most members of the dominant sociocultural group. But how can schools work for transient youth if they do not have time to develop intersubjectivity? Teachers and students need to have time to develop intersubjectivity—consciousness of each other and each other's intentions in order for schools to work more successfully. Huebner tells us that consciousness, in what ever form it takes, is a social product—it emerges from relationships developed as a result of social interactions in social contexts. In situations of student transience, students do not tend to have time to fully develop consciousness of themselves as learners, the particularity of their relationship with their schools and classroom worlds, and to recognize those with whom they are in relation with critical clarity; rather, school mobility typically results in distorting the few relationships that they might manage to develop (Huebner, 1999, p. 295).

TRANSIENCE AND [DIS]ORIENTATION

Huebner (1999) reminds us that "[a] person is not an isolated individual, but can exist only in relation with others" (p. 293). Student transience keeps learners "isolated" from, and out of relations with teachers and peers, partners needed for the development of intersubjectivity at schools. Student transience can be complicating and corrosive on the developing consciousness of learners. As children mature, they need to move "outward into diverse realms of experience in [their] search for meaning" (Greene, 2004, p. 138). In their search for meaning in school contexts, transient children, like many others encounter pre-set, pre-established curricula. In this search for meaning, children, and in particular the transient child, experience strong feelings of "separateness, of strangeness when [he] is confronted with the articulated curriculum intended to counteract meaninglessness" (Greene, p. 140). This is a "strangeness" that is exacerbated for transient children because:

> Learning to read has to be a continuous process and they're [the students] jumping from here to there. That's how their learning is…they might be in a classroom where they're doing one, then they're in another classroom where they're doing something else, and some kids might not be able to make the connections. They are disconnected (McNeil, 2006, p. 92).

The above statement paints a picture of children who frequently journey into unfamiliar terrain, and who are often estranged from the pre-set curricula of schools. And to paraphrase Shutz (2004), the transient child is like a stranger to his or her new classroom.

> When a stranger comes to the town, he has to learn to orientate in it and to know it. [Few things are] self explanatory for him and he has to ask an expert…to learn how to get from one point to another (as cited in Greene p. 140).

For children and youth the situation of the stranger is even more intense because of their limited frame of reference in the world. When a newcomer first arrives at a new location, "his peculiar plight ought not to be overlooked" and neither should his 'background awareness' of "being alive in an unstable world…" (Greene, 2004, p. 140). Yet the newcomer brings consciousness of his "primordial' world, and in the case of transient students, that which they can remember of other school sites they have experienced, and marshals these (consciously and unconsciously) to "bring into visibility" that which he seeks, needs, and is necessary to find meaning in his new world (p. 140).

Theorizing on "curriculum and consciousness" opens up pathways for us to see that on the "micro-level", when a transient child enters a new school site "his focal concern is with ordering the materials of his own-life world when dislocations occur, when what was once familiar [is changed and] abruptly appears strange" (Greene, 2004, p. 140). The narratives from the teachers interviewed in my research suggest that the "impermanence", the transience that highly mobile students experience with school, ineluctably "penetrates and tinctures [their] consciousness[es]", thereby "radically affecting" the way they "relate to other people, to things" and possibly, "the entire universe" of school (p. 141). It may be fair to say, that it is "far more likely" for transient children, than those who engage with schools in more conventional ways, to routinely "experience moments of strangeness, moments when the recipes they have inherited for the solution of typical problems no longer seem to work" (p. 141). Furthermore, for the newcomer in situations of transience, "[d]isorder . . . is continually breaking in; meaninglessness is recurrently overcoming landscapes which once were demarcated, meaningful" (p. 141).

The circumstance of the transient learner as newcomer is rendered even more intensely poignant and encrusted by meaninglessness because he is not the abstract, or generic child that typifies curricular documents; he is raced, classed, gendered, and cultured. The history of colonialism and its multiple forms of oppressions in western Canada, means that the strangeness of the transient child as a raced, classed, and cultured being is deepened when he encounters the hegemonic, generally monocultural, and monolingual sites of mainstream schools.

In moments of disorientation and strangeness that not only arises from differences in schools, classrooms, teachers, and peers, but also in culture, language, race, gender and social class, transient children are likely to reach "out to reconstitute meaning, to close gaps, to make sense once again" (Greene, 2004, p. 141). Greene (2004) argues that at such times individuals,

> will be moved to…disclose or generate structures of knowledge which may provide unifying perspectives and thus enable [them] to restore order once again. [Here] learning [is a kind of] orientation—or reorientation in a place suddenly become unfamiliar. [A] place is a metaphor, in this context, for a domain of consciousness, intending, forever thrusting outward, 'open to the world' (p. 141).

This means that it is up to the teachers to lead the students to lend the curriculum their lives (Greene, 2005, p. 141). Since the disclosure and development of the students' consciousnesses are indisputably linked to their willing engagement and their willing participation in "generating the structures" of knowledge, it is imperative that they are presented with learning situations that incorporate "the background of [their] original perceptions, with a clear sense of being present to [themselves]." Huebner (1999) makes a similar argument, when he points out that "[t]hrough listening and speaking, the teacher helps the student see the present as a moment of vision, a moment when the past and the future come together to disclose the present as possibility" (p. 155).

If the past and the future of transient students are to "come together to disclose the present as possibility" then, they cannot be constructed or engaged as generic learners. As a way of making the personal (e.g., identity, culture, and language), and political realities of transient students apparent and integral to what transpires in classrooms, teachers and the instructional systems they represent need to acknowledge in caring, conscious, and critical ways, the "existential predicament and primordial consciousness" (background and experiences) of the students (Greene, 2005, p. 145). This means that the teachers need to adopt approaches to curriculum that will consider and respond to the totality of the students as persons experiencing systemic hardships that arise from the social and political context of their schooling. Such approaches address the fundamental interdependence of transient students and their teachers and the need for the teachers to root their work in an ethic of love that marries caring with justice and equity—orientations that are at times complementary and conflicting but must nonetheless be present at all times (Noddings, 1999).

In this regard, Huebner (1999) reminds educators of our moral calling and responsibility and stolidly stipulates that we need "consciousness of our own complicity in the forces of domination, and a critical methodology which will inform and be informed by our practice as educators. That critical methodology, and practice, is social, dialectical, and materialistic" (p. 296). Additionally, he explains that "by social [he] mean[s] that individuality is only possible because we are, have been, and will be in relation with others; and that our fundamental concern is and must be the quality of that social life" (p. 296). To show the mutuality and interdependent nature of the adult/teacher and child framework, Huebner adds that

> [o]ur activity and that of the young is part of the continuing transformation of energy and material for the sake of collective life. To have that activity turned into alienated activity, for someone else rather than for the person and the collective which he/she chooses, is the beginning of distortion of the social relations, of domination, and of language which no longer expresses truth and possibility (p. 296).

In the above, Huebner beckons educators to strive for the development of consciousness with the students in their classes, to act with the consciousness of teachers as part of a collective committed to moral vision for the transformation of "energy and material for the sake of the collective." With such a vantage point, educators are encouraged to substitute their traditional solidarity with their social class, in favor of a teaching one that is oriented toward the children and youth in their classes. The development of traditional class-consciousness and its movement toward solidarity with those with whom teachers live and work in classrooms (children and youth) can help teachers and students unleash the hopeful and socially just possibilities of schools and classrooms for transient students and others.

LANGUAGE AND LITERACY

Huebner's conceptualization of language exhibits richness and complexity. He proposes that the "foundation of language is discourse or talk" suggesting that "language is not simply a tool, not simply discourse, it is a gift to man that 'has the task of making manifest in its work the existent, and of preserving it as such'" (p. 146). Here, we see evidence of Huebner's philosophical and ontological viewpoints on language, which together rejects any solely technical-rationalist understanding of language.

The casting of language as "gift" is important and can be interpreted as part of the larger architecture of Huebner's work. Language, a uniquely human entity has the power to create and preserve. Huebner exudes reverence (but not worship) for language; it is seen as a gift of creation, a purposeful, ethereal offering, necessary for the fullest and moral articulation of human experience. This view of language is carefully and compellingly nuanced and is authored by one who embraces and humbles himself to the divine and the spiritual that is part and product of creation.

> Language is not simply an entity within the world. It is grounded in a basic characteristic of man, his capacity for speech or discourse. In discourse man discloses his being there in a given situation; through his mood, his state of mind, man discloses his throwness into a world. It makes manifest 'how one is, and how one is faring.' Through his understanding he projects his own potentiality for being, the possibilities which are his. Through discourse man articulates his being-in-the-world as thrown and as possibility. Discourse puts into words the totality of significations, the related instruments and entities which man can use for his own sake. In all talk, man [sic] talks about something. At the same time, his being is expressed and "explicitly shared" with others (Huebner, 1999, p. 147).

Huebner's (1999) ethical, moral, and philosophical view of language is apparent in his assertion that language is more than a tool, it is "a way of being with students" (p.146). It is in language that the "teacher lives with students." Hence for Huebner, language as divine gift, is maker, broker of the interaction, the relationship that exists between students and teachers. "But language is not only a relationship among people; it is also a relationship between the person and his world" (p. 145). The Huebnerian view of language has fullness and rigor and I present it here to illustrate why student transience, one of the grotesque manifestations of poverty, is perceived to have such an insidious and deleterious impact on the school literacy development of transient students. As a result of transience, many children and youth do not get to access and acquire the "gift" of school language—one that is needed for the fullest participation with the majority located in and outside of school.

Huebner states that "[l]anguage provides procedures, customs and/or rules for the structuring of interactions among people throughout a period of time (p. 145)." The sociocultural context of language learning for transient students is rendered unstable, irregular, and chaotic by the frequent changes in school and stifled school language development. Confirmation of this viewpoint can be seen in the following remark, from my research, by a Grade Two teacher in speaking about the oral language of a transient student,

> The children who stay here have the routine. They have sort of a safe house and security. So they have that, they pick up so much more...many more words. They can just learn lots when they're safe and secure and they have a good self-concept and they're not going anywhere. They know their daily patterns, every day is going to be this way it's good...and they feel really good about themselves and their homes. But the student that does not live that way...doesn't care [and] doesn't see the point....

As the excerpt suggests, transient children and youth, by virtue of numerous school changes, rarely get to adequately learn socio-literacy (Gee, 1996), the routines, procedures, customs, and or rules of school sites—all of which are learned through oral and/or written language. In addition, they are further thwarted because one of the reasons they are in school is to learn words to help them negotiate the interpersonal, physical, and the textual worlds of those sites and they lose out; doubly penalized since they do not get to "pick up" the words, the ways of thinking, and acting that they need for socio-linguistic, and socio-cultural participation in mainstream schools.

It is important for transient children and youth to have sustained contact with, and to be embedded in the language communities of mainstream schools. Gee (1996) points out that in "socially situated language use one must simultaneously say the 'right' thing, do the 'right' thing, and in the saying and doing express the 'right' beliefs, values, and attitudes" (p. 124). Vulnerable children such as those who are transient are not from the dominant classes and groups (Kerbow, 1996; McNeil, 2006) whose social capital and practices are paraded as neutral and natural (Delpit, 1995, McLaren, 1989) in public schools. Transient students do not always say and do the right thing in the socially situated language situations of schools. Although transient students bring their own social capital—their rich sociocultural resources to classroom spaces (flexibility, good listening skills, cultural knowledge, understandings about language variety, drawing, facility in reading their world etc.)—this capital is generally undervalued in schools. Because they are frequently on the move, these students do not always learn the socially accepted codes and linguistic practices expected of them or the power that accrues from such knowledge. It is in this way that transience helps to maintain the privilege of those who acquire the "right" kind of social capital by virtue of the strength of their contact with schools.

This abominable state of affairs finds confirmation in comments from a research participant who, in describing the oral school language of transient children said, "I think it would be safe to say that their vocabulary is not, as I said, not as developed. They do not know many words, you know, not so many words." This teacher (and many others with whom I spoke) indicated that she was "frustrated" by the constant intrusion of transience in classroom lives because it continuously undercut attempts to scaffold the literacy learning of the students. The teachers' instruction did not stick. In addition, it seemed to me that the teachers were "frustrated." Because child poverty is neglected by the society the teachers are part of, they found themselves thrust into a teaching paradigm that deviated from the myths they held about 'doing' school (that most children come in September and stay put in the same class and same school until the end of June). The teachers were not prepared for how transient students were forced to "do" school and could not bring themselves to adjust to it.

Student transience was in sharp relief to the teachers' view of schooling. It led them to bemoan their situation, to have some empathy with their students but continually frame these transient children and youth within the now, all too familiar paradigmatic scripts of cultural and linguistic deficits rather than seeing them as victims of an economic system that advantages the teachers' social class.

Emerging from the teachers' comments about oral language, is indication of an unacceptable situation. Transient children and youth, unlike many of their peers do not get to learn the words, the talk, the tools to build on the rich sociocultural resources (knowledge of stories, prayers, icons, proverbs, expressions, songs, ways of being, and doing etc.) they bring to school in order to contribute to the learning community, to construct meaning with others, and to name and understand the world in order to change it (Freire, 1970).

Transient children miss out on what Huebner describes as the "talk in teaching" that allows teachers and students to actualize "being-with-others in communication" (p. 147). I believe this to be of enormous consequence to transient students. The "talk in teaching" to which Huebner refers is not only concerned with the "passing along of common language" though this, of course, is of importance; it is also concerned with the search for meaning, the development of consciousness, and the ability for material transformation. Language/Discourse is an instrument of personal, social, and political power and since there is general belief that it is fair and just to have this power distributed equitably, it behooves schools and teachers to do all they can to teach students about the workings of language, how it relates to power, and how that power, as "capital" can be used to up-end the current system to create a more socially just world. This means, teaching about language as an entity that is "present-at-hand as something in the world" and is to be conceptually and theoretically differentiated from language that is "ready-to-hand" (Huebner, 1999, p. 147).

> It is as present-at-hand that language is the content of teaching. In books and in the speech of the teacher language shows itself as something. It is not hidden or absorbed in its use, but is visible as an entity. One of the tasks of the teacher is to make the present-at-hand usable for the student; to help him absorb it within the totality of instruments for his use—to turn the present-at-hand into the ready-to-hand. It must become an instrument to be used by the student in his dealings with the world" (Huebner, 1999, p. 147).

LITERACY INSTRUCTION FOR TRANSIENT STUDENTS

There is an emphatic value in using language, but also of studying, analyzing, and unpacking it explicitly so as to make it "visible" as an entity for learners. The goal of unpacking, and deconstructing language is to demystify it, to render it more pliable and useable, to "turn the present at hand into the ready-to-hand" thus enabling and empowering students in their "dealings with the world." All children and youth benefit when language is taught explicitly; when the rules and codes of school language are not taken for granted by those already privileged by school language. Analysis of data that I obtained from teachers about student transience revealed that as members of the in-group of school language, teachers did not teach it with the visibility and the explicitness needed by transient students. Thus, their literacy instruction fell short of what is required for the scholastic success of transient children. Conversations with the teachers clearly revealed that it was not their intention to teach in ways that were not particularly productive for transient students; nonetheless, that was the result. All children need to be in classrooms where

> [l]anguage as present-at-hand can be articulated as an instrument, as a happening of truth (a work of art) or as the thought of thinkers. By stepping out of the language within which he teaches to look at and talk about it as an instrument, as a happening of truth, or as the thought of thinkers, the teacher can project more clearly the language situation within which he teaches (Huebner, 1999, p. 151).

The explicitness in teaching of school language and its genres (poetry, prose, narrative, factual, fictional etc.) are particularly necessary for those learners whose primary Discourse differs from the one used in schools and who, in addition, are pushed to the outer limits of school engagement because of transience. At the risk of sounding too prescriptive, this type of practice would involve teaching students about language registers—the social aspect of literacy—socio-literacy to better support transient children and youth in their valiant efforts to be functionally and critically literate.

Literacy cannot be critical without reflection on language that is "present-at-hand. And, given the connection between language and social and political power, there can be no question that knowledge and use of "language-at-hand", that is to say, making language the object of study, is critical to unfolding the potentialities of all children and youth. When students do not receive the full instructional program of the school for literacy learning, they seldom become proficient knowers and users of school language. They do not benefit from the empowerment that language bestows. Without such knowledge, transient children and youth are less able to fully name their world in the language of and in relation to those who have power and are responsible for their suffering. Without the social and political power that can emanate from knowledge of the language of the powerful social and political groups in mainstream society, it is difficult to see how transient students and their families can help enact the deep structural changes needed to transform our unjust social order. And it is only the transformation of the current economic, social, and political order in favour of those currently oppressed that we can eliminate school and residential transience and the misery they impose on transient students and their families. Therefore, knowledge of and fluency in school language is very important for transient students. Huebner (1999) points out "language as already in the world wherein one finds himself is part of the totality of instruments available for use" (p. 146). He adds that in the teaching situation, language that is "ready-to-hand" is language that is "accessible, serviceable, and reliable." Therefore, for language to be "ready-to-hand, the student must be as at ease with the language as with a hammer when driving nails, or a typewriter when writing a letter." From a review of the literature on student transience/mobility (Alexander, Entwisle & Dauber, 1996; Besnon, Haycraft, Teyaert, & Weigle, 1979, 1981; Bruno & Isken, 1996; Hefner, 1994; Kerbow, 1996; Liecty, 1996; Ream, 2001) and my own study (McNeil, 2006) it appears that school language cannot be considered to be "ready-to-hand" for the majority of transient children and youth because it is not accessible or serviceable.

The reasons for its inaccessibility are these: transience severely restricts access to the site where school language is learned and developed; by keeping learners on the move and out of schools between moves, transience impedes the progress of language learning by interfering with the extended periods of practice and immersion that students need in order to flourish linguistically, and because the majority of their teachers are monolingual, they sometimes struggle with scaffolding the students' language(s) with school language. Without the sensitive, caring, and strategic scaffolding of home language(s) or primary Discourse(s) of transient children and youth with the secondary Discourses of schools, linguistic attainment is constrained. This is especially the case in contexts where embedment in classrooms is denied to the students. In each of these instances of accessibility, language does not empower transient children and youth, it "overpowers" them and is neither accessible nor serviceable.

In addition, teachers are failing "to serve language" (though not necessarily consciously so). A teacher

> serves language by welcoming the origins and the beginnings disclosed by language in the speech of students. Serving language by bringing the past and the future into the present, he serves the student by leaping ahead of him in solicitude that the student might live authentically in language. (Huebner, 1999, p. 150)

Such conceptualizations of language are powerful and have relevance for transient students and their teachers since some teachers are less than welcoming of the home languages of students when they differ from the language of school. The point underscored here is that language hegemony pervades schools and that there is not enough space created to welcome "the origins and beginnings disclosed by language in the speech of students" (Huebner, 1999, p. 150). Although schools serve students who bring a variety of languages and literacies to classrooms, many schools remain traditional and obstinate in clinging to monolingualism instead of actively engaging with multilingualism and multiliteracies.

Another teacher in my study referred to the language of transient students as the "language of poverty." The teachers' description of the students' language reveals an instance when she was not "with students in language", not "alongside them" but standing apart from them (Huebner, 1999, p. 149). This kind of positioning on the part of the teacher is ethically undesirable when what is needed is "ethical valuing."

> Ethical valuing demands that the human situation existing between student and teacher must be uppermost, and that content must be seen as an arena of human confrontation. This human situation must be picked away at until the layers of the known are peeled back and the unknown in all of its mystery and awe strikes the educator in the face and heart, and he is left with the brute fact that he is but a man trying to influence another man...Awareness of the power to influence may lead to hubris, the demonic state of false pride in the educator's own omnipotence, or the humbling recognition that with the power to influence comes the life-giving possibility of being influenced. The humble acceptance of his power to influence and to be influenced makes possible his freedom to promise and forgive and his willingness to do so. An act of education is an act of influence: one man trying to influence another man. Educational activity is ethical when the educator recognizes that he participates in his human situation of mutual influence, and when he accepts his ability to promise and forgive (Huebner, 1999, pp. 111–112).

LANGUAGE AND POWER

Through willingness to accept their power and their responsibility to levy linguistic influence (not judgment) with care and respect for the cultural identities of transient students, teachers can engage in "ethical valuing." Examination of the transcripts of some of the teachers in my research leads me to suggest that the students' languages (the varieties of the English language they spoke), were unwelcomed, treated with disdain, and were perceived as something that needed to be rooted out. Without the use of, and access to the language they bring to school, how can transient students communicate and participate in classroom discourse? The teachers I interviewed said that the majority of their students did not. The result was that the classroom site was one of monologue rather than dialogue; it was rarely a linguistically democratic space (Darder, 2001; Delpit, 1995; Freire, 1998; McLaren, 1989). Consequently, transient children and youth experienced further institutional alienation that was thickly layered on top of the frequent ruptures they already endured in schools.

Within such a narrow and autocratic structure, transient learners struggle to "bring the past and the future into the present" and would be well served if their teachers would leap ahead of them "in solicitude so the student(s) might live [more] authentically in language"(Huebner, 1999, p. 150). For transient learners this would mean the encouragement and freedom to use their primary Discourses/home languages while receiving caring support to bridge it with school languages, and to be able to learn the latter through uninterrupted, prolonged contact with schools. Educators need to heed Huebner's gentle wisdom to "gingerly" serve language, but to remember that language is evolutionary and changing. Teachers are also reminded that

> [a] teachers' concern for the institutions and traditions within which he lives is not made manifest by guarding the language as if it were a museum piece, beyond the touch and the use of the student. His concern is a temporal concern, a concern for the evolution and development of those traditions and institutions, for their history and their destiny. His concern is with the future as well as the past" (Huebner, 1999, pp. 149–150).

By respectfully weaving together students' linguistic past, which is a very special part of their present and their future, with school language as a language of the future that is to be extended and developed, teachers help to make language accessible as well as serviceable to transient students—two important aspects of "language that is 'ready-to-hand.'" The careful grafting of school language on the language that students bring to schools grants them access to, and use of two languages. Knowledge of two or more discourses empowers students and allows them to project their "possibility into the opening" that schools can create for equitable social change (Huebner, 1999, p. 151).

As a way of closing my foray into Huebner's "language as ready-to-hand, I draw attention to "reliability", its third characteristic. Huebner (1999) states that, "serviceability is of no consequence unless language as ready-to-hand is also reliable." Language that is reliable "helps the student adhere to the world opened to him" and provide hand-holds for the student to grasp his world and project his own possibilities for being in the world" (p. 153). Captured here is the exquisite recognition that language is fluid, ever changing, and ever growing and that teachers need to work alongside students to ensure that their linguistic saws are kept sharpened. "By failing to keep his language instruments sharp and precise, the student loses his 'grip' on the world and is no longer where the action is. Understandably then, reliability is a relative quality; as new instruments are produced, old ones lose their purchase" (p. 153).

Although school is not the only site for keeping linguistic instruments sharp, it is a significant one. My conversations with teachers of transient students revealed that with regard to mainstream developments in young people's literature that swept North America for instance, the students, though very interested, did not have the linguistic knowledge needed to talk about social capital engendering events in popular culture such as J.K. Rowling's (1999, 2000, 2001, 2003, 2005, 2007) series about "Harry Potter the boy who lived," and Daniel Handler's (1999, 2000, 2001, 2002, 2003, 2004, 2005, 2006) "A series of unfortunate events" as well as some of the academic language that is associated with Information Communication Technologies (ICTs). Of equal or greater importance, is the reality that transient students do not get sufficient opportunities to practice showing what they know about social capital producing language related to fishing, camping, hiking, community gardening, hip-hop, rap, comics, video games, sports, bicycles, cars, hunting, skateboarding, knowledge of what is happening in their communities, and much more. And as long as student transience of the kind described in this paper exists, transient students will continue to need teachers who recognize "that the child and teacher share the same human condition." The child and the teacher are

> explorers, constantly striving to order their feelings and sensations; that they encounter others through speech and conversation; and that they must assume responsibility for building a world in which each may realize his potential. This means, above all, that in the classroom children need the freedom, within limits imposed by the teaching situation, to converse and to discover, and to own the instruments of power created and conserved by others (Huebner, 1999, p. 46).

Transient students need to "own the power" of language that is "created and conserved by others." Transience, as I have argued throughout this chapter denies children and youth access to "language experiences, [those which] are [the] most significant experiences of the school day" (Huebner, 1999, p. 46). Huebner makes the case that although 'the basic language patterns are formed in the home...the school program should be designed to extend the language competence of the child and to bring to his awareness the power and beauty of language." Undeniably, the "significance of language...extends beyond the skills of reading, writing, speaking, and listening" that is generally stressed in schools. Huebner cuts to the heart of the matter and explains the power and possibilities of language when he states that:

> Language is an intimate link between the various forms of knowing, and the child's thinking, perceiving, and feeling. Not only do children have the potential to use language skillfully in reading, writing, speaking, and listening; they can also become aware of the increased power and freedom to act in the world so created, controlled, and enjoyed. With increased awareness, power, and language, children can become more sensitive to the development of knowledge and the channeling of imagination. Children can recognize that language is indeed 'a pathway to the realization of ourselves' (Huebner, 1999, p. 47).

CONCLUDING REMARKS

I have used the insights of philosopher, educator, and curriculum scholar Dwayne Huebner to respond to one of the five challenges he issued: to speak out on behalf of children and youth. I did so by focusing on those who are transient—those caught in the cycle of frequently changing schools. Huebner's ideas provided a congruous means for excavating the context and complexity of language/literacy learning for these students. On my journey toward the end of this chapter, I telescoped on the constructed nature of student transience and the havoc that it wreaks on the learning and developing of school literacy practices for transient students. As I approach the conclusion of the chapter, I dedicate time to look at one of Huebner's most profound messages about language in teaching contexts. He implores us to see that language is a "way of being with students." Huebner states that

> [i]n speaking, the teacher is being-in-the-world with others; he is there among and with others as only man can be—in language. Language is the medium within which he lives, grows, and projects his possibilities for being. Language is his culture, as agar medium is the culture of microorganisms. Language sustains man, opens up possibilities for being-in-the world, comforts him, preserves truth, and provides the platform to jump momentarily beyond himself. Language also hides man from his world and from himself. As it opens possibilities it covers others. The veil torn from some aspects of the world conceals others (p. 145).

To summit Huebner's flag of meditation, the tablet on which he inscribes the importance, instrumentality, serviceability, life sustaining/engendering, transcendent quality of language, I point to his perspicacious belief that "[i]t is in language, 'the most dangerous of possessions' that the teacher lives with students" (p. 144). For children and youth, transient and non-transient alike, it is critical that we heed Huebner's call for understanding and responding to the significance of language in our lives (as a medium for life, as culture, as opener of possibilities).

It is important for teachers (and others with power) to heed Huebner's (1999) view to be "alongside" children and youth in language because as relational human beings, children and youth require the best of us, but even more so when daily life includes incessant marginalization, disadvantage, and oppression. There are indeed many ways of being with people in the world, however, teachers have a special responsibility since for "the most part, when we teach we are in the world with others by way of language"—it is crucial to teaching" (p. 144). As a way of being in the world with students, our ethical vocation as human beings, as teachers, is to look after, care for children, to the extent that they feel they are cared for (Noddings, 2005), to use dialogic means (Freire, 1970) to solicit their understandings, and respond to them "concernfully" (Huebner, 1999). By virtue of their age, size (in many case), status as subservient to parental and/or state authority/ies, socio-economic, socio-emotional dependence, and general absence of power in society, children are vulnerable and require a plethora of support in order to fully underwrite and propel their processes of being and becoming, more fully human (Freire, 1970), more transcendent human beings. One strategic way of supporting transient children and youth is to become tireless advocates on their behalf, to give full voice to the voiceless by speaking out, up, for, and alongside them as long as oppression and injustice exists. It is by doing so that we (citizens and educators) can ethically and responsibly respond to the challenge bequeathed by Huebner. We must collectively speak up and ask for social justice on behalf of transient and other marginalized students because failure to do so results in "the closing of the asking mouth and the shutting of the wondering eye [which can] lead eventually to the hardening of the responsible heart" (Huebner, 1999, p.12). We must never let that happen.

REFERENCE

Alexander, K., Entwisle, D., & Dauber, S. (1996). Children in motion: School transfers and elementary school performance. *The Journal of Educational Research, 90,* 3–12.

Benson, G. P., Haycraft, J. L., Steyaert, J. P., & Weigel, D. J. (1979). Mobility in sixth graders as related to achievement, adjustment, and socioeconomic status. *Psychology in the Schools, 16,* 444–447.

Benson, G., & Weigel, D. (1980–1981). Ninth grade adjustment and achievement as related to mobility. *Education Research Quarterly, 4,* 15–19.

Bruno, J. E., & Isken, J. A. (1996). Inter and intraschool site student transiency: Practical and theoretical implications for instructional continuity at inner city schools. *Journal of Research and Development in Education, 29,* 239–255.

Campaign2000.ca. (n.d.). *2007 Report card on child and family poverty in Canada: It takes a nation to raise a generation.* Retrieved from http://www.campaign2000.ca/rc/rc07/2007_C2000_NationalReportCard.pdf

Darder, A. (2001). *Reinventing Paulo Freire: A pedagogy of love.* Cambridge, MA: Westview Press.

Freire, P. (1970). *Pedagogy of the oppressed.* New York: Seabury.

Freire, P. (1993). *Pedagogy of the city.* New York: Continuum.

Freire, P. (1998). *Teachers as cultural workers: Letters to those who dare to teach.* Boulder, CO: Westview.

Gee, J. P. (1996). *Social linguistics and literacies: Ideology in discourses* (2nd ed.). London: Taylor & Francis.

Gee, J. P. (1996). *Social linguistics and literacies: Ideology in discourses* (2nd ed.). New York: RoutledgeFalmer.

Greene, M. (2004). Curriculum and consciousness. In D. J. Flinders & S. J. Thornton (Eds.), *The curriculum studies reader* (pp. 134–147). New York: RoutledgeFalmer.

Hefner, M. (1994). What is the effect of the rate of transfer on the academic achievement of fourth grade students? (*ERIC Document Reproduction Service.* No. ED364866).

Huebner, D. (1999). Language and teaching: Reflections on teaching in the light of Heidegger's writings about language (1969). In V. Hillis (Ed.), *The lure of the transcendent: Collected essays by Dwayne E. Huebner* (pp. 143–158). Mahwah, NJ: Lawrence Erlbaum Associates.

Huebner, D. (1999). Toward a political economy of curriculum and human development (1977). In V. Hillis (Ed.), *The lure of the transcendent: Collected essays by Dwayne E. Huebner* (pp. 285–298). Mahwah, NJ: Lawrence Erlbaum Associates.

Huebner, D. (1999). Challenges bequeathed (1996). In V. Hillis (Ed.), *The lure of the transcendent, collected essays by Dwayne E. Huebner* (pp. 432–445). Mahwah, NJ: Lawrence Erlbaum Associates.

Huebner, D. (1999). Curricular language and classroom meaning (1966). In V. Hillis (Ed.), *The lure of the transcendent, collected essays by Dwayne E. Huebner* (pp. 101–117). Mahwah, NJ: Lawrence Erlbaum Associates.

Huebner, D. (1999). Education and spirituality (1993). In V. Hillis (Ed.), *The lure of the transcendent, collected essays by Dwayne E. Huebner* (pp. 401–416). Mahwah, NJ: Lawrence Erlbaum Associates.

Huebner, D. (1999). Knowledge and the curriculum (1962). In V. Hillis (Ed.), *The lure of the transcendent, collected essays by Dwayne E. Huebner* (pp. 44–65). Mahwah, NJ: Lawrence Erlbaum Associates.

Huebner, D. (1999). Knowledge: An instrument of man (1962). In V. Hillis (Ed.), *The lure of the transcendent, collected essays by Dwayne E. Huebner* (pp. 36–43). Mahwah, NJ: Lawrence Erlbaum Associates.
Huebner, D. (1999). Religious metaphors in the language of education (1985). In V. Hillis (Ed.), *The lure of the transcendent, collected essays by Dwayne E. Huebner* (pp. 36–43). Mahwah, NJ: Lawrence Erlbaum Associates.
Huebner, D. (1999). Spirituality and knowing (1985). In V. Hillis (Ed.), *The lure of the transcendent, collected essays by Dwayne E. Huebner* (pp. 340–352). Mahwah, NJ: Lawrence Erlbaum Associates.
Huebner, D. (1999). Teaching as a vocation (1987). In V. Hillis (Ed.), *The lure of the transcendent, collected essays by Dwayne E. Huebner* (pp. 379–387). Mahwah, NJ: Lawrence Erlbaum Associates.
Kerbow, D. (1992). *School mobility, neighborhood poverty and student academic growth: The case of math achievement in Chicago public schools.* Paper presented at the annual meeting of the American Educational Research Association, San Francisco, CA.
Kerbow, D. (1996a). *Patterns of urban student mobility and local school reform: A technical report.* Chicago: The Center for Research on the Education of Students Placed at Risk.
Kerbow, D. (1996b). *Pervasive student mobility: A moving target for school improvement.* Chicago: Chicago Panel on School Research.
Kincheloe, J., & McLaren, P. (2000). Rethinking critical theory and qualitative research. In N. K. Denzin & Y. S. Lincoln (Eds.), *Handbook of qualitative research* (2nd ed., pp. 279–313). Thousand Oaks, CA: Sage Publications.
Liechty, S. J. (1994). The effects of mobility on fourth grade students' achievement, attendance, and behavior (Doctoral dissertation, Drake University, 1994). *Dissertation Abstracts International, 56,* 10.
Luke, A. (1998). Getting over method: Literacy teaching as work in "new times". *Language Arts, 75,* 305–313.
McLaren, P. (1989). *Life in schools: An introduction to critical pedagogy in the foundations of education.* New York: Longman.
McNeil, B. (2006). *Teachers' perspectives on transience and literacy.* Unpublished doctoral thesis, University of Regina, Regina, SK, Canada.
Rowling, J. K. (1999). *Harry Potter and the chamber of secrets.* London: Bloomsbury.
Rowling, J. K. (2000). *Harry Potter and the prisoner of Azkaban.* Vancouver: Raincoast Books.
Rowling, J. K. (2000). *Harry Potter and the goblet of fire.* London: Bloomsbury.
Rowling, J. K. (2001). *Harry Potter and the sorcerer's stone.* New York: Scholastic.
Rowling, J. K. (2003). *Harry Potter and the order of the phoenix.* London: Bloomsbury.
Rowling, J. K. (2005). *Harry Potter and the half blood prince.* London: Bloomsbury.
Rowling, J. K. (2007). *Harry Potter and the deathly hallows.* London: Bloomsbury.
Schutz. (1967). Problem of rationality in the social world. In Natanson, (Ed,), *Collected papers II* (pp. 66). The Hague: Martinus Nijhoff.
Snicket, L. (1999). *The bad beginning.* New York: HarperCollins Publishers.
Snicket, L. (1999). *The reptile room.* New York: HarperCollins Publishers.
Snicket, L. (2000). *The austere academy.* New York: HarperCollins Publishers.
Snicket, L. (2000). *The miserable mill.* New York: HarperCollins Publishers.
Snicket, L. (2001). *The ersatz elevator.* New York: HarperCollins Publishers.
Snicket, L. (2001). *The hostile hospital.* New York: HarperCollins Publishers.
Snicket, L. (2001). *The vile village.* New York: HarperCollins Publishers.
Snicket, L. (2001). *The wide window.* New York: HarperCollins Publishers.
Snicket, L. (2002). *The carnivorous carnival.* New York: HarperCollins Publishers.
Snicket, L. (2003). *The slippery slope.* New York: HarperCollins Publishers.
Snicket, L. (2004). *The grim grotto.* New York: HarperCollins Publishers.
Snicket, L. (2005). *The penultimate peril.* New York: HarperCollins Publishers.
Snicket, L. (2006). *The end.* New York: HarperCollins Publishers.

VALERIE MULHOLLAND

AND CARRY ON AS THOUGH NOTHING HAPPENED

INTRODUCTION

In response to Dwayne Huebner's fourth challenge to "engage in public discourse in education" (1999, p. 432) I look at art in common spaces in schools and the broader landscape as texts, as public expressions of a curriculum that privileges some and disadvantages many others. In the province of Saskatchewan, where I live and work, public discourse about education is suffused with the "settler-invader mythology of the barren land" (Wetherell & Potter, 1992) and the "fantasy of originality and origination" (Bhabha, 1994) which allows colonizers to believe they were first to live on a land and first to build a civilization. In addition to postcolonial theory, I use Madeleine Grumet's definition of curriculum as "the collective story we tell our children about our past, our present and our future" (In Graham, 1991, p. 120), a definition that provides a generous space to do as Huebner calls university educators to do: "to participate in the larger discourse about education" (1999, p. 441). The story of the past that children are told in Saskatchewan, in schools and in public discourse, is pre-dominantly from a white, male Euro-American perspective. Colonization is an on-going process, reified by institutions of power, and I argue, told as a national story that is inscribed and continually re-inscribed on the landscape.

Two quotes from Huebner's essay "Challenges Bequeathed" (1996) are used as titles for the major sections of the essay. In the first section, *Other Discourse Systems, Not Part of the University*, I show some of the ways that the story of the past told in school and Saskatchewan society more broadly is colonial, a story of invasion that continues to be reproduced in the provincial language arts curriculum. In the second section, *Education Happens*, expressions of history inscribed on the landscape are discussed, to confront the contemporary ramifications of discourses that marginalize First Nations people as well as recent non-European immigrants to the province. A sample of photographs of public art is included to illustrate ways the white-settler version of history permeates not only curriculum but also common public spaces where citizens teach, learn and live.

OTHER DISCOURSE SYSTEMS, NOT PART OF THE UNIVERSITY

My work as a teacher-educator includes observing pre-service teachers during their internships at a variety of rural and urban schools. In those minutes between my official contact with the office, a metonymous term for school authority held by the principal, and the beginning of my observations, I have time to study the common public spaces of the school, to see what is and is not there. In Canada, most schools display portraits of power, such as Queen Elizabeth II or her representative, the Governor-General, the Prime Minister or the Pope near the entrance to the main office. Occasionally, a version of the medicine wheel claims pride of place. Most schools also have showcases with trophies, plaques and photographs to acknowledge distinguished students, past and present, and to represent collective stories of achievement that honour individuals, the school and the greater community. Some schools have collections of art by local artists as well as talented student artists, and often these grace the public spaces of school, too, signifying an additional story of influence and authority. At the very least, what is designated as art or worthy of public display may be seen as an expression of what is valued and by extension, of who is valued in particular school communities. To some extent, these artifacts are expressions of power. They provide a visual cue to the discourse systems that are at work in the school.

Figure 1. The iconic figure of a lone white-settler, with grain elevators in the distance and sunflowers in the foreground; a curious mixture of myth and kitsch

Recently, on a visit to an urban high school in Regina, I was struck by a wall-size mural depicting a lone pioneer man breaking the soil with a horse drawn plough in an impossibly green field, flanked by a startlingly abundant crop of sunflowers (see Figure 1). I had visited the school many times before, but my immersion in postcolonial reading at the time, caused me to refocus the image, to subject it to closer scrutiny. The familiarity of its subject was simultaneously comforting and disturbing. I was conscious of having seen many similar historical representations in the foyers and halls of schools and public buildings in Saskatchewan, but I was seeing the image with new eyes. As a descendent of white-settlers, I am accustomed to seeing my family's history glorified in formal and informal ways. On this particular occasion, I saw a remnant of my history and a symbol of oppression that was misleading in its simplicity.

In general, the human figures featured in these ubiquitous depictions of Saskatchewan history are male, usually white, and engaged with a limited variety of occupations, such as agriculture (breaking the land, harvesting), surveying (a man pointing into the distance, at vast empty spaces) or some other process associated with hewing wood and drawing water (mining, lumber). In other words, the work the men are doing evoke an historic period when the most robust era of European settlement occurred in Saskatchewan, roughly between 1880 and 1930. Women are noticeable for their absence. When First Nations people are represented in these artistic representations, they are most often male, usually passively observing or welcoming European settlers (meeting with a military officer, signing a treaty). Daniel Francis (1992) writes extensively about the creation of these phenomena in *The imaginary Indian: The image of the Indian in Canadian culture*. Much of what he says is relevant to this paper, but I interrogate the images of white-settlers and their implication in dominant discourses. Homi K. Bhabha (1994) asserts: "An important feature of colonial discourse is its dependence on the concept of 'fixity' in the ideological construction of otherness" (p. 94). It reflects an imagined past, not the lived present. In Saskatchewan, a number of communities have commissioned murals with historic subjects to decorate the sides of buildings in dying downtowns, in an effort to attract tourism dollars, but also, I think, to glorify a time gone by.

In the history of Western art, murals have a distinguished past; traditionally, their subjects were mythological, religious or historical topics or events. The scope of the subject was matched by the size of the work; which is to say, the more important the subject, the larger the art form. Murals, and publicly funded sculpture, are used to tell *the* officially sanctioned story. When I visit schools, I make it a practice to pay attention to how the buildings are decorated, to what official story is told through the choices of art hanging on the walls or displayed in glass enclosed display cabinets. Such things inscribe what is valued and recognized as achievement, and whose names appear on the plaques represent systems of power and privilege. Recently, I have noticed the occasional portrait of Michaëlle Jean, Governor General of Canada, Haitian-born and brilliant, appearing in schools, which I interpret as an expression of change in the social order in Canada. However, the official story of white-settler history and of white-settler dominance more broadly, remains largely in tact amid the trophies, the highlights from student art shows, including the labored muddy-glazed pottery, and the murals painted by students.

The image of the lone pioneer man behind the plow lingered in my mind's eye until the class I had come to observe began. I sat poised, ready to record my version of the unfolding events. Instruction of the grade twelve class began with the students receiving the results of their Chaucer quiz from the previous week. The teacher had since moved on to a novel study of *Catcher in the Rye*. How the two texts were linked remains a mystery to me. Within minutes, the intern managed to engage the students in a spirited discussion of innocence and disillusionment, as these concepts related to Holden Caulfield. "When we start *Hamlet*," the intern said, "many of these universal themes will emerge again. You'll see the connections." According to the course syllabus, the major texts of the World Literature course included Chaucer, Shakespeare, English poetry and Salinger's coming-of-age novel *Catcher in the Rye*, organized thematically as prescribed by the provincial language arts curriculum. Overall, it was a highly restricted sample of the literature offered by the world. Given the literature curriculum of the class, the mural adjacent to the Principal's office was oddly coherent. Almost exclusively English, with a dollop of American literary culture, the course content was canonical: historical, male, white. Just like the pioneer man in the mural.

At other schools, urban and rural, I have observed many similar murals featuring white-settlers arriving in Saskatchewan by covered wagon, presumably at the turn of the 20th century. Covered wagons were a significant part of the settler-invasion of the American prairie west, but not of Saskatchewan. The majority of 19th- and 20th- century white-settlers arrived in Saskatchewan by train. In the 18th century, some Métis ventured into what was then officially the North West Territories from Manitoba by Red River cart. In the 1930s, my grandfather showed my father the ruts made by those carts on the prairie, and when I was a little girl in the 1960s, my father showed them to me. The North West Mounted Police arrived by horseback dressed in striking, but given the climate, unsuitable red serge. The early European fur traders of the 17th and 18th centuries traveled the waterways of the North West by canoe, accompanied by guides from various First Nations. Covered wagons appeared in Saskatchewan mainly on television. Nevertheless, they are iconic images from the colonial past, just as the presence of British and American literature in English language arts curricula are a vestige of colonization.

Implemented in 1999, the current high school English language arts curriculum in Saskatchewan includes themes such as "Frontiers and Homelands" and "Marginal Voices" as required topics of study. Within the latter category are the sub-themes "Aboriginal Voices" and "Multicultural Voices" for which there are teacher guide questions to support the teaching of these voices. For example, "What Aboriginal or Indigenous voices are making their way into mainstream literature?" And "How is the multicultural nature of Canada captured by her authors?" (Saskatchewan Learning, 1999, pp. 317–318). Two debatable assumptions inform these statements. The first, that First Nations writers are regularly read and recognized as art in contemporary Saskatchewan classrooms. The second, that Canada is benignly multicultural, a descriptive, but contentious term. In a province like Saskatchewan there are many homogenous communities populated almost entirely by white-settlers. When I visit classrooms, I am as likely to observe units on Native Mythology or a novel study of *Obasan* as I am to see an integrated multicultural program of study that does not render non-white-settler literature exotic or other. As a little girl growing up in Saskatchewan I read a series of Copp-Clark readers with remarkably similar topics; in grade six I studied literary selections from the anthology *All Sails Set*, which offered the sub-themes entitled "Pioneer Days" and "The Sun Never Sets." From the table of contents, I see that my teacher's efforts to be multicultural were restricted to Rudyard Kipling's "How the Rhinoceros got his Skin." And we are likely to agree that Kipling is famous for his glorification of the British Empire. In the fifty years that have passed since the Copp-Clark Canadian Reading Development series was published and since the revised 1999 program of language arts study was implemented in Saskatchewan, it is reasonable to argue that the sensibilities governing literature instruction have changed little in the intervening years.

In Saskatchewan, Canadian literature was not a required course for graduation from high school until the curriculum reform of 1999. Until then, two credit courses in English at the grade-twelve level were required. The first was a British literature survey course that typically included Beowulf, Chaucer, Shakespeare, the Romantic poets and a Victorian novel. The second course combined American and Canadian literature with the aim of introducing students to modern literature and six modes of writing. Gauri Viswanathan (1989) in *Masks of Conquest: Literary Study and British Rule in India* traces the history of English as a course of study designed to educate a class of Indian bureaucrats, well versed in the language and culture of the Empire, which was adopted throughout the British colonies the world over, "enabling the humanistic ideals of enlightenment to coexist with and indeed even support education for social and political control" (p. 3). Viswanathan defines curriculum as a discourse that distributes and validates cultural knowledge. The teaching of English in public schools in Canada has been used for similar purposes, to dominate a variety of groups of marginalized people, as each new wave of immigrants invaded the great Dominion of Canada. Proponents of colonial education saw the study of English literature as "an instrument for ensuring industriousness, efficiency, trustworthiness, and compliance in native subjects" (Viswanathan, 1989, p. 72). In John Willinsky's (1998) *Learning to Divide the World: Education at the Empire's End,* colonial education is described as a "mission." Inspired by Macaulay's proclamation that "a single shelf of a good European library was worth the whole of native literature in India and Arabia" (as cited in Willinksy, 1998, p. 97), the study of literature in colonial Canada's free and compulsory education system was intended to ensure that the values and culture of the Mother Land were preserved.

Initially, colonial education was committed to "providing native populations with the full scope of an English education" (Willinsky, 1998, p. 102). English functioned as part of the colonial identity kit, a method of "suppressing Indigenous populations and steeling colonial servicemen against the temptations of a 'native' culture" (Murray, 1995, pp. 5–6). The Canadian government, aided and abetted by Catholic and Protestant churches, created and operated a system of residential schools, the most obvious and egregious example of colonial education (Dieter, 1999; Monture-Angus, 1999).

Prior to the western treaties, the official Canadian policy was to protect, civilize, and assimilate the Indian. The Gradual Civilization Act, passed in 1857, called for the eventual assimilation of Indians into Canadian society. It was later consolidated with other acts dealing with Indians and Indian lands into the Indian Act, 1876. This Act was actually in force before the treaties in the west were signed, but it was never mentioned to the Indians during treaty negotiations. The Indians were led to believe they could continue their traditional way of life, and that the provisions made by treaty would merely add to what they already had (Dieter, 1999, p. 14).

The suppression of First Nations people was necessary for white-settlers to invade and occupy land inhabited by others. It was necessary to see the land as empty and undeveloped and the people living there as uncivilized and rapidly disappearing. Edward Said's (1993) *Culture and Imperialism* explains the connection between the study of literature and the creation of history that I have described through an analysis of colonial systems of education:

The settler makes history and is conscious of making it. And because he constantly refers to the history of his mother country, he clearly indicates that he himself is the extension of that mother country. Thus the history which he writes is not the history of the country which he plunders but the history of his own nation in regard to all that she skins off, all that she violates and starves (Fanon as cited in Said, 1993, p. 270).

Julia Emberley (2007) writes: "Colonial cultures do not, then, have a history of their own but remain like the category of 'primitive art' in a separate space in the museum, a prehistoric and yet timeless symbol of European history" (p. 26). The story Saskatchewan children are told about the past, the present and the future is limited by a version of colonization that is "fixed," characterized by a reluctance to name the gaps and absences in the official story of colonization, populated by stereotypes of lone pioneer men, passive First Nations people and the narrative arc of progress. Bhabha's (1994) definition of stereotypes and their purposes is useful in this context:

The stereotype is not a simplification because it is a false representation of a given reality. It is a simplification because it is an arrested, fixated form of representation that, in denying the play of difference (which the negation through the Other permits), constitutes a problem for the representation of the subject in significations of psychic and social relations (p. 107).

The images I discuss in this essay are implicated in the creation of white-settler identity. They are part of a curriculum of amnesia.

If we can accept that images are a basic unit of meaning, the imagery of public art may be read as an indicator of the ideology at work in schools and in the communities in which schools are situated. The school mural of the lone pioneer at work behind the plow clearly has an historical subject since in contemporary Saskatchewan, farming is done with massive, industrial-scale equipment and mythic because men working alone did not accomplish the settlement of the prairie west. Agriculture has always been a collective enterprise, which in the course of human history relied largely on the labour of women in the planting, gathering, harvesting and preserving of food. Similarly, the fur trade in Canada relied on the expertise of First Nations women, whose knowledge and labour were fundamental to the survival of traders and of the trade alliances established between First Nations and Europeans at the time of contact (Van Kirk, 1980). Furthermore, sunflowers are not a common commercial crop in this part of North America. An artist has no special responsibility to be more factually accurate than does a writer of fiction; both pursuits result in social constructions. I am contesting the effects of realist representations of the past that are used to reify a particular version of our collective story. Bhabha writes that:

> Such art does not merely recall the past as social cause or aesthetic precedent; it renews the past, refiguring it as a contingent 'in-between' space, that innovates and interrupts the performance of the present. The 'past-present' becomes part of the necessity, not the nostalgia, of living (Bhabha, 1994, p. 10).

The pioneer narrative is not limited to the literature students study or the art that decorates schools. It is one of the fictions of a dominant version of the imaginary Saskatchewan that privileges white-settler history. However naïve the technique or perspective of the individual artists, the rhetorical effect and discursive implications of the works are not neutral. These works of art contribute to the on-going processes of colonization.

EDUCATION HAPPENS

Huebner's statement "Education 'happens' to everyone through informal and formal activity" (1999, p. 441) is taken as a title for this section to identify ways the discursive production of white-settler identity and history shape not only schools, but also the landscape of Saskatchewan. I use the term landscape both figuratively and literally. The imagination as landscape is invaded not only by curriculum, as defined in this essay, but by immersion in a landscape filled with museums, historical markers and folk art that are very literal representations of a white-settler history and identity.

The most pervasive historical narrative in Saskatchewan is of the pioneer past. As with all synonyms, there is an imperfect relationship of meaning between the words pioneer and settler. The term white-settler is in common use among academics and teachers interested in anti-oppressive education and postcolonial theory, and suggests invasion and dominance. However, should an average citizen of Saskatchewan exist, that person is apt to use the terms pioneers, homesteaders or settlers synonymously, speaking with pride and reverence, untainted by counter-narratives of race and invasion. A major grain elevator company in the west is called Pioneer; consequently, the word *pioneer* is literally part of the visual landscape, blazoned in red and yellow letters on inland grain terminals and elevators visible on the horizon for miles throughout the province. Yet for many, settlement remains a positive, if not neutral term.

European white-settlement is valorized in numerous formal and informal ways. Elementary school children participate in a very popular Heritage Fair competition each spring. Children select historical topics of local, provincial or national interest, conduct research with the guidance of their parents and teachers, prepare poster boards and rehearsed talks in order to compete locally for a chance to attend the National Heritage Fair. In the Heritage Fairs that I have attended, the heroism of early settlers is regularly celebrated, featuring the struggles resulting from crop failure, harsh climate and loneliness. On a larger scale but in similar ways, white-settlers were the focus of celebrations of the province of Saskatchewan's Centennial in 2005. First Nations people were featured in the promotional materials and public performances, often in historic traditional dress, as were many recent non-European immigrants. First-wave European immigrant heritage was also represented historically in the celebrations. For example, Ukrainian-Canadian dancers performed at the 2005 provincial gala in traditional national costumes of Ukraine. With the possible exception of Scottish highland dancers, British immigrants are not identified in comparable ways. Whereas the twirling ribbons of a Ukrainian headdress or the fringe of a plains Hoop dancer may be described as colorful or exotic, I have yet to hear a kilt described in that way. The Saskatchewan Centennial celebrated the creation of a political state which conforms to English legal and legislative structures. Despite the official inclusion of largely historic references to the First Nations people, the central theme of events made it clear that the story of Saskatchewan began with European settlement. How else might the references to the "next one hundred years" of growth and prosperity (or whatever other superlative might be cast upon the future) promised during the Centennial celebrations be explained?

In the 1950s and 60s the Government of Saskatchewan erected numerous historical monuments which tell the official story of settlement. They are liberally distributed throughout the country along the sides of roads and highways. Surprisingly durable, these monuments are composed of text etched on metal rectangular plaques that suggest the shape of the province, mounted on cement blocks or stone cairns. Sturdy and straightforward, the official historical record is an attempt to document the arrival of European settlers as the story of civilization in this area named the Great Plains of North America by Euro-Americans. There are individual markers devoted to First Nations and Métis history, many of which document the disappearance (and not the slaughter) of the bison. The destruction of a way of living that resulted from white-settler invasion, including the establishment of the reservations and residential schools, is submerged in the story of the relentless march of progress. Emberley (2007) explains that, "The rhetoric of aboriginality, however, has its own history, from its central position in nineteenth- and early twentieth-century preoccupations with Europe's infancy to its contemporary place as a sign of cultural difference, a Significant Other situated in a hierarchical opposition to the Enlightened Subject" (p. 27). A trope of the white-settler story is the introduction and development of civilization to less advanced cultures and people. The disappearance of evidence of other complex ways of life, such as stone medicine wheels and burial sites, resulting from the breaking of land for settlement is not a significant strand of the white-settler story. Similar to the official celebrations of Saskatchewan's Centennial, the markers focus on the collective pioneer provenance of the dominant white-settler class, and are part of the curriculum, the story of the past, in which citizens, including school children, are immersed. Indeed, education happens in informal and formal settings.

Figure 2. Heritage Horse-drawn Farm Machinery display at Davidson Saskatchewan

Another significant trope in the settlement story is transportation. The proliferation of Red River cart sculptures on the Saskatchewan landscape in recent years speaks to the role transportation plays in the perpetuation of white-settler imagination and history, but not to the extent of the story of the railroad. The haste to sign treaties with First Nations in the 1870s was due in large part to the anticipated completion of the Canadian railway which arrived in what is now Saskatchewan in 1882. The railway, not the wagon, brought the majority of white-settlers to Saskatchewan. As R. Douglas Francis (1989) explains,

> Many English-speaking Canadians saw a transcontinental nation as only a stepping-stone to something greater – imperial grandeur. They envisioned Canada, and particularly the West, as the last vital link in a continuous chain through British territory that would tie Britain to her Pacific imperial possessions – an "all-red route to the Orient." The Canadian West, therefore, would be the means to ensure the future greatness of the British Empire (p. 74).

The Dominion of Canada's immigration policy was designed to convince European farmers and labourers to emigrate from Europe to fulfill the federal government's goal to populate the North West territory and prevent the U.S. government from annexing the West. During the period between 1896 and 1914, the Liberal government led by Wilfrid Laurier commissioned artists and writers to produce propaganda that advanced a number of myths about the "last best west" that included land that did not require clearing, soil so rich farmers had no purpose for manure, and unfathomable economic opportunity for the hardworking (Francis, 1989). For Europeans motivated by the desire to escape poverty, avoid religious and political persecution, or start a new life, western Canada was branded as a utopia. Weather alone caused that story to be revised almost immediately.

The landscape is littered with museums, professional and amateur, state and privately funded. Small towns house remnants of white-settler life in a variety of formerly well-used public buildings such as schools, banks, post offices and grand houses. Specific cultural groups created museums to celebrate their traditions, an example being the Ukrainian Canadian Cultural Centre in Saskatoon. Continuing that impulse to preserve or create history, the provincially-funded system of Western Development Museums (WDM), found in four locations in Saskatchewan, North Battleford, Saskatoon, Yorkton and Moose Jaw, represent the state's effort to preserve white-settler history. Each site is devoted to a particular theme of the settlement-invasion of Europeans: in North Battleford, a heritage village and working farm; in Saskatoon, a 1910 boomtown; in Yorkton, European ethnicities are celebrated; and in Moose Jaw, transportation. These museums, formal and informal, are sites of knowledge production. They create and preserve white-settler identity and dominance.

For those who have traveled by rail or car across the southern half of the province of Saskatchewan, Don Kerr's (1988) description of the landscape in his poem "Editing the Prairie" will be familiar. He writes: "Well, it's too long for one thing/and very repetitive/Remove half the fields." The land is flat, the sky, limitless. The highway linking the province's two major cities, Regina and Saskatoon, has only two valleys to distract drivers during the two and a half hours required, roughly, to travel from the one city to the other. Blink or adjust the radio and it is possible to miss one of the valleys completely. The expanse of sky is interrupted by cloud formations, and the regularly spaced skylines of small prairie towns in the distance. At one time the highway passed through each hamlet, village and town, but for the last thirty years motorists have been able to zip by on the double-lane blacktop. Perhaps in an effort to seek the attention of passing travelers, or possibly in a collective effort to fill the epic spaces created by prairie sky, large pieces of folk art have proliferated on the outskirts of prairie settlements during this time period. A survey of the Large Canadian Roadside Attractions web-site (http://www.roadsideattractions.ca/sask.htm) devoted to these monuments shows that the major categories are Natural World, Emblems of Local Economy or Culture, and Historical subjects.

Should anyone dispute the lingering effects of British colonization on Saskatchewan we need only look to Highway 11, the province's major north-south corridor. Beginning in the south-east at the capital city Regina, named for Queen Victoria who reigned at the time of the signing of the major numbered treaties between First Nations people and the British Crown, the highway ends at Prince

Albert, at the geographic centre of the province, named for Victoria's husband and consort. Victoria and Albert's names also grace the two major thoroughfares in Regina, which in turn is called the Queen City. The city's logo features a Crown, and the colour purple. On June 20th, 2001 the Provincial Government renamed the 364 kilometres of highway Louis Riel Trail. Riel was tried for treason and hanged in Regina, shortly after the Riel Resistance (or Rebellion, depending on the political stance assumed). The press release issued on that day claimed to acknowledge the contributions of Métis people by honoring the leader of the Riel Resistance. Interestingly, the small blue government signs indicating the name change are infrequent and obscure.

Between Regina and Prince Albert, there are three local amateur museums and one pioneer village, a Western Development Museum, and over twenty white-settler historical markers and "roadside attractions" which I refer to as folk art. The local museums document the history of white-settlers in the area through collections of domestic and agriculture material culture from the first period of European immigration. The folk art ranges from the prosaic (tiger lilies, stalks of wheat), to the bizarre (giant coffee pot), to the ubiquitous (a mural of a man behind the plow at the Shell Station in Davidson, bison). Along Louis Riel Trail there are two major professionally-developed and provincial and federal government-funded historical sites devoted to First Nations and Métis history. Wanuskewin, a heritage site and museum devoted to First Nations located seven kilometers north of Saskatoon, includes an interpretive centre with a museum and art gallery, several walking trails where visitors may observe an archeological dig, a buffalo jump and medicine wheel. Further along the highway, the Duck Lake interpretive centre commemorates the Riel Resistance. North of Duck Lake is Fort Carleton, a provincial park which features a representation of a traditional fur trading post. It is arguable that the park has important components of First Nations and Métis history imbedded, given the role the forts played in colonization it is difficult not to associate the symbol of the fortress with regimes of oppression.

The most noticeable visual reference to Métis history along Highway 11 are a series of five folk art sculptures of Red River carts, bison and human figures created by Don Wilkins. On his website, Wilkins writes: "I've always had an interest in the history of the Métis people, especially the period between 1860 and 1905," explaining that he has two Métis grandchildren. "There is an important story to tell here, one that I don't think many people know about." (http://donwilkins.net/about.htm). Until I began taking photographs of historical markers and giant folk art in Saskatchewan, I did not recognize the figures as Métis. All are located on the outskirts of white-settler, not traditional Métis communities, along Highway 11. All are remarkably similar to the image of the pioneer discussed earlier: alone, at work, and male. I am convinced that the artist is motivated by the very best of intentions, and the work exhibits different intentions than the majority of roadside attractions which I think are designed to amuse or distract passers by. Knowing of his purpose, I see that Wilkins' work does create some tension between the competing stories of the Métis people and white-settlers.

Figure 3. Métis Fiddler, Red River Cart and a Giant Coffee Pot at Davidson, Saskatchewan

Wilkins' sculptures depict a variety of activities, including surveying, fiddling, and bone picking, described by brief passages of text written by a variety of amateur historians on permanent plaques. These captions are not to be confused with the official historic markers erected by the provincial government, however similar they are in terms of rhetoric and content. The description of the bone-picker at Dundurn is particularly useful for demonstrating the discursive production of white-settler identity and history I have been discussing in this chapter. A close reading of the language on the plaque reveals the spectrum of ambiguity, euphemism and amnesia that characterizes popular versions of white-settler history. Credited to Harvey Mawson, the plaques reads:

> DUNDURN
> HONORING THE PAST
> STRIVING TOGETHER FOR A BRIGHT FUTURE
>
> Dundurn, located in the heartland of the great north bison range, was known to buffalo hunters as "Round Prairie." Cree, Métis and Dakota Sioux chose the wooded hills of this historic land as a good place to stay. Cattle ranching was established here in 1886 and since then the growth and prosperity of our community has been, to a great extent, dependent on the agricultural sector.
>
> The horse drawn Red River Cart and "Bone Picker" are reminiscent of an era ending when the skeletal remains of approximately 2,000,000 buffalo were gathered in the vicinity of Dundurn and Hanley. The influx of homesteaders, beginning in 1903, marked a new chapter in our story of progress and continuity.

The language blithely reveals all. Events occur, eras pass and ways of life are eradicated. Progress and growth result in prosperity. In this version of history, those whose interests are served and privileges are protected are left to carry on as though nothing has happened.

CONCLUSION

On the same bright fall day that I visited the school described in the introduction, I had cause to make a road trip from Regina to Saskatoon, taking Highway 11, the Louis Riel Trail. I had visited the first school many times before, indeed had looked at the mural before, but beyond flinching at the clashing palette the muralist had used to paint the image of the pioneer man, had never considered its significance. I do not think the artist intentionally used jarring colours, or deliberately ignored colour theory, to create a dissonant image of the subject. Even I am not that filled with hope. It is more likely that the mural is a simple reproduction of a familiar image of the past that I have argued is part of the dominant discourse of Saskatchewan. White-settler discourses informed the curricula, formal and informal, that produced the student artist and by extension, the mural. The individual artist may be unconscious of the implications of the work, but the image is neither innocent nor neutral.

I was thinking about the image as I drove to Saskatoon, noticing again the sculptures, the giant pieces of folk art, until I reached Nutana Collegiate, originally Saskatoon Collegiate, the oldest high school in the city. Having an hour to wait before a meeting, I decided to visit a former student who was teaching there part-time. Nutana is "old school" with massive front doors and broad, dark hallways. As is my habit, I was examining the space adjacent to the main office when I spied what I thought was a James Henderson portrait of Chief Pemimotat around the corner. Sure enough, it was a Henderson, an artist famous for painting formal, traditional portraits of Indians, part of an effort in the last century to capture images of people whom at the time were assumed to be a dying race. The Pemimotat portrait is one of an impressive collection of paintings belonging to the school, which originated as a memorial to alumni who died in World War I. Noticing a curious stranger, the school librarian asked, "May I help you?" In this instance, the words are *schoolspeak* for "what is your business here?" I said I was intrigued by the collection of art. Delighted by my interest, and perhaps relieved that I was not going to be a problem, the librarian graciously provided a guided tour and I acquired a book published in 1995 documenting the story of the collection. The sophisticated benefactors responsible for the collection were not celebrating local amateurs; as funds allowed, they bought if not first-rate pictures by famous artists, then first-rate work by up-and-coming ones. They had an eye on the future. They were making a statement for subsequent generations: "We are educated people of substance. We know art." The collection grew until the fortunes of the community changed, and the affluent migrated to other areas of the city.

Now a community school, the Collegiate no longer serves the city's elite class as it did when the art collection was established. The students come from the Westside, across the river, where the social problems that accompany displacement and poverty abound. The majority of students are First Nations or Métis; the majority of teachers are not. The Collegiate is well-known in education circles in the province for innovative programming and has been successful in changing the experiences and outcomes of many students marginalized by racism and poverty. It tells a hopeful story. The physical space of the school would be commonplace in Saskatchewan were it not for the presence of the magnificent art collection.

Two large full-figure portraits hang in the library that are quintessential white-settler images, one of a young boy entitled "Spirit of Youth" and the other, "Pauline" the very essence of conventional female virtue of the last century. Both are dressed in ethnic costumes: the boy in short pants, white shirt and a tie, and Pauline in a style of sailor dress that I associate with the British upper-class. Let us say their costumes are English. As I imagine it, the expressions of the two figures, as they cast their eyes on the changing school life below them, reveal the past-present tension Bhabha describes as "the necessity not the nostalgia of living" (1994, p. 10) in a colonial state. The young boy's cheerful face brims with optimism and anticipation of boundless opportunity, perhaps even of entitlement. The more wistful expression of the girl denotes not only the demure gentility prescribed by her gender and social class, but to me betrays a sense of wonder at where the world they thought they were re-creating as white-settlers has gone.

Given the relatively brief period of white-settlement in Saskatchewan and its devastating effects on First Nations and Métis people in the province, who were displaced, oppressed and sometimes killed during the initial stages of colonization, it is not surprising that the versions of history validated by the dominant settler culture are notable for gaps and omissions. Francis (1989) writes: "The mythic region of the West, like all mythologies, has been a blending of fact and fiction, historical truth and literary creation, physical locale and mental perception ..." (p. 193). As encompassing, affirming and comforting as that view of the pioneer past, as perpetuated by public art and historical markers, formal and informal, official or folk art, can be for white-settlers, it is not adequate to understand the present. Not adequate, ethical, equitable or legal. My grandparents lived in, and had a part in creating, a settler society in Saskatchewan "where their descendants have remained politically dominant over indigenous peoples, and where a heterogeneous society has developed in class, ethnic, and racial terms" (Stasiulis & Yuval-Davis, 1995, p. 3). I now understand that the myth of the barren land (Wetherell & Potter, 1992) is part of a colonialist discourse that facilitated appropriation and exploitation of land inhabited by complex Aboriginal societies, whose own histories were demoted to static prehistory and supplanted by the heroic story of the European settler-invader.

Like me, many of the students I teach in the Faculty of Education at the University of Regina are great-grandchildren of white-settlers. Seeking what Kumashiro (2002) defines as repetition, many desire to see themselves represented in curriculum, making it difficult "to learn to think differently about their own lives or even to learn to use their lives to complicate theory" (p. 73). Disrupting the legacy of white-settler mythology in public education and society in general has significant implications for teacher education and for public discourse about education. In his 1966 essay "Curricular language and classroom meanings," Huebner wrote: "Today's curricular language seems filled with dangerous, non-recognized myths; dangerous note because they are myths, but because they remain unrecognized and unchallenged" (1999, p.102). I see a link between the warning and the challenge to engage in public discourse about education. To recognize and challenge the persistent story of Euro-American domination on the literal and curricular landscape is not beyond the intellectual and emotional powers of citizens. It is possible to recover from amnesia. As Huebner wrote: "knowledge and other cultural forms must be seen as vehicles for responsibility, conversation and promise" (1999, p.113).

As a white-settler, I have a responsibility to re-write the "the collective story we tell our children about our past, our present and our future" (Grumet as cited in Graham, 1991, p. 120). The public art and historical markers in schools and along public roadways inscribe a white-settler story on the imaginations of citizens and on the very landscape where we live. The framework for interpreting or reading the signs I have described provides a space to challenge the dominant discourse in Saskatchewan that privileges white-settlers and excludes First Nations and Métis peoples and recent non-European immigrants disenfranchised by the ongoing processes of colonization, whose stories are missing largely from formal and informal curricula. Perhaps we might aspire to a story that better serves us all.

REFERENCES

All sails set. (1948). Vancouver: Copp-Clark Publishing Co.

Bhabha, H. K. (1994). *The location of culture.* New York: Routledge.

Kerr, D. (1988). Editing the prairie. In L. Crozier & G. Hyland (Eds.), *A sudden radiance: Saskatchewan poetry* (p. 94). Regina: Coteau Books.

Dieter, C. (1999). *From our mother's arms: The intergenerational impact of residential schools in Saskatchewan.* Toronto, ON: United Church Publishing.

Emberley, J. V. (2007). *Defamiliarizing the aboriginal: Cultural practices and decolonization in Canada.* Toronto, ON: University of Toronto Press.

Francis, D. (1992). *The imaginary Indian: The image of the Indian in Canadian culture.* Vancouver: Arsenal Pulp Press.

Francis, R. D. (1989). *Images of the west: Responses to the Canadian prairies.* Saskatoon: Western Producer Prairie Books.

Graham, R. J. (1991). *Reading and writing the self: Autobiography in education and the curriculum.* New York: Teacher's College Press.

Huebner, D. (1999). Challenges bequeathed (1996). In V. Hillis (Ed.), *The lure of the transcendent, collected essays by Dwayne E. Huebner* (pp. 432–445). Mahwah, NJ: Lawrence Erlbaum Associates.

Huebner, D. (1999). Curricular language and classroom meanings (1966). In V. Hillis (Ed.), *The lure of the transcendent, collected essays by Dwayne E. Huebner* (pp. 101–117). Mahwah, NJ: Lawrence Erlbaum Associates.

Kumashiro, K. (2004). *Against common sense: Teaching and learning toward social justice.* New York: Routledge Falmer.

Monture-Angus, P. (1999). *Journeying forward: Dreaming of first nations independence.* Halifax, NS: Fernwood Publishing.

Murray, H. (1995, Fall). English studies in Canada and the case of postcolonial culture. *Essays on Canadian Writing, 56,* 51–77.

Said, E. (1993). *Culture and imperialism.* New York: Vintage Books.

Stasiulis, D., & Yuval-Davis, N. (Eds.). (1995). *Unsettling settler societies: Articulation of gender, race, ethnicity and class.* London: Sage Publications.

Saskatchewan Learning. (1999). *English language arts (ELA): A curriculum guide for the secondary level. ELA A10, B10, ELA 20, ELA A30, B30.*

Van Kirk, S. (1980). *Many tender ties: Women in the fur-trade society, 1670–1870.* Norman, OK: University of Oklahoma Press.

Viswanathan, G. (1989). *Masks of conquest: Literary study and British rule in India.* New York: Columbia University Press.

Wetherell, M., & Potter, J. (1992). *Mapping the language of racism: Discourse and the legitimation of exploitation.* New York: Columbia University Press.

Willinsky, J. (1998). *Learning to divide the world: Education at empire's end.* Minneapolis, MN: University of Minnesota Press.

JENNIFER A. TUPPER

DISRUPTING THE DISCOURSE OF PUBLIC EDUCATION: A CONVERSATION WITH DWAYNE HUEBNER

In his 1962 essay, "Politics and the Curriculum", Dwayne Huebner called for educators to consider what affects classroom actions in both positive and negative ways. He maintained that, "the existence of differing ideologies leads to public debate, and in some cases modification of classroom actions favouring the most powerful elite" (p. 20). In such an assertion, Huebner not only recognized the power of public discourse to alter educational practices, he also recognized that the act of educating must be considered in relation to political and ideologically systems of which students, teachers and parents are integral participants. These systems work in concert to determine (and privilege) not only what knowledge will be taught in schools, but also the officially sanctioned story of school. Mandated curriculum becomes a vehicle through which stories are told, both explicitly and implicitly (Tupper & Cappello, 2008). The reality for many students is that their storied lives remain outside of the official story of education told through curriculum, classroom practices, and educational procedures. Yet this trauma (for I believe that is the subtle effect on students whose stories remain silent in educational spaces) rarely if ever becomes the focus of public discourse of education.

While Huebner (1999) challenges educators to "master and participate in the public discourse about education" (p. 441), to do this well, we must first understand our own stories as schooled beings. Equally important, we must understand how our own stories are often in sharp relief to the way education is talked about and constructed in public spaces, especially as this talk effects what occurs in the classroom, classroom actions. In tending to the challenge of engaging in public discourse about education, I recognize that I must also attend to Huebner's (1999) other challenges; to affirm the significance of the imagination, speak up for children and youth, draw on the world's intellectual achievements and traditions, and surpass the technical foundations of education. These challenges do not exist in isolation of each other; rather they are inextricably linked in myriad ways. Each one of these challenges requires consideration of classroom spaces, the individuals who occupy these spaces, and how these spaces are influenced by external forces.

P. Lewis and J. Tupper (eds.), Challenges Bequeathed: Taking up the Challenges of Dwayne Huebner, 115–125.
© *2009 sense publishers. All rights reserved.*

With respect to engaging in public discourse about education, Huebner cautions educators to speak in language that may be understood by parents and students, and so I will endeavor to do so through a series of stories or vignettes that I hope begin to tell my story as a student, a teacher, an academic and a parent. I am also cognizant of Pinar's (2004) call to engage in complicated curriculum conversations which, by their very nature represent struggles to make sense of, to understand, to see anew, and may occasionally be muddled and messy. Perhaps, in some ways this is Caputo's (1987) appeal to "restore life to its original difficulty." And it is precisely why we need to engage in public discourse about education as storied beings, recognizing that the discourse as it is currently manifest, is too simple, takes too little account of multiple and conflicting stories, is very much in need of complicating beyond its technical rational foundations.

With this in mind, and drawing on the writing and thinking of Dwayne Huebner, this chapter represents my attempt to complicate, disrupt, interrupt, rupture the discourse of accountability that seems to permeate public narratives of education, shapes educational decision-making, and effects the lives of children & youth, parents, school administrators and teachers. The discourse of accountability certainly affects classroom acts in real and often political ways. To complicate, I offer a series of vignettes, my own stories as student, as teacher, as academic, and now as a parent of a school-aged child. To interrupt, I consider these stories in relation to the political nature of knowledge and school that Huebner has articulated since the early 1960s. And finally, throughout this chapter, as an act of disruption, I attempt to reframe public discourse about education by telling other stories that run counter to and complicate such discourse.

SOME PERSONAL STORIES OF SCHOOLING:
AS A STUDENT LEARNING TO READ

How we know and what we know is always within a context of who we are and where we are (Hurren, 2003, p. 120).

Very often, our personal stories, as complicated and messy as they may be, are not considered in school or curricular spaces. Rather, students are expected to either ignore or adapt their stories to 'fit' with curriculum, itself a product of political considerations that privilege certain stories at the expense of others (Tupper & Cappello, 2008). Cynthia Chambers (1999) recalls her own experiences of schooling in northern Canada at a time when the 'Dick and Jane' readers were found in classrooms throughout the country, tools to teach reading, but also to teach the value of a particular way of life, the value of a particular place. Chambers describes the dissonance she experienced when she realized that her own story was vastly different from the 'story' of Dick and Jane.

I too remember these readers in my early elementary years. I loved the shiny red, blue, green and yellow covers, which signaled each student's reading level. I was equally in love with Dick and Jane's mother. She seemed to always be baking cookies for the children, gazing at them with such affection and love, doing everything she could to ensure the happiness of her husband and children. Certainly there were some similarities between my home life and the home life depicted in these readers. My mother stayed at home with us. My mother prepared meals and tended to the upkeep of the house. But there were also significant differences. My mother struggled with mental illness. Her struggles often affected my brothers and me in ways that I am better able to understand now, but could make little sense of as a young girl. I have few recollections of my mother baking cookies or wearing an apron like Dick and Jane's mother, intended of course to protect the pretty dress she wore, so practical in tending to chores and children. I also do not recall my mother gazing upon my brothers and me with the same abject affection as Dick and Jane's mother, though I never doubted that she loved me. As a child, I understood that my mother was not quite like *Mother*, especially those days that her illness seemed to get the best of her. I have one memory of a Saturday morning when I was ten years old. In this memory my mother came home from the grocery store in an agitated state, certain that she had seen my grandparents (estranged from my family at the time); that they had come to take us children away from her. She insisted on loading us all into the car and driving to the church, a place she believed we would be safe. Once there, she insisted my father phone his parents in Nova Scotia to be sure that they were indeed still many provinces away, not a few blocks away with intentions of taking my brothers and I away. In moments such as this, I longed for the story depicted (and thus privileged) in and through the Readers. I wanted to be Jane. I wanted to lead her life which seemed so simple and straightforward and safe. My story did not fit with Jane's story, so I began retell it in my own head. I began to 'read' my life differently as I learned to 'read' Dick and Jane.

The Dick and Jane Readers at the time might be understood as representative of a public desire to focus on literacy skills in the classroom and a public desire to instill family values in students (whatever those might be). As literacy tools, the Readers had some utility for I and many other students used them to 'learn' to read. But these Readers also required that I re-read my own story in ways that made it simpler and more similar to the story of Dick and Jane. Jackson and Gee (2005), drawing on the work of Wason-Ellam (1997), argue that the pictures in school readers can "extend meaning beyond the written text or the reader's imagination or they can even recast the story" (p. 117). My experience of and with these readers involved "recasting" my story, the story that I needed to tell myself about my own family to mitigate the dissonance I experienced as I 'read' Dick and Jane.

So what might Huebner say about this? He might suggest that the use of the Readers reflected "a struggle for power and influence" in classroom spaces (1999, p. 95). He might also express concern that "knowledge is often separated from life" especially when the lives of students and teachers are in contrast to the knowledge advanced through officially sanctioned curriculum and mandated teaching resources, like the Dick and Jane Readers (p. 351). But do the readers reflect 'a struggle for power and influence' or do they reflect the result of that struggle? After all, the use of the Readers was widespread for many years, suggestive of the power of decision makers to shape classroom actions. Power is after all decision making (Huebner, 1999, p. 17). And what were the effects of using the Readers on students, beyond the obvious literacy outcomes they purported to achieve? I have already grappled with how my story bumped up against the story of Dick and Jane, and continue to for "[memory] is the one place you can never go home to but must always remember, because while the past is forever gone it is also always present" (Chambers, 2003, p. 107). Thus, my story of learning to read, of becoming 'literate' involves much more than just literacy skills and outcomes as written by ministries of education for curriculum documents and tested by teachers in classrooms.

Literacy remains central to public discourse about education even today. School boards and ministries of education throughout the country often cite literacy as a goal in continuous improvement frameworks (see for example Regina Public Schools Continuous Improvement Summary, 2007). Literacy outcomes are easily measured through the administration of standardized tests, with results of these tests becoming fodder for public discussion. Because of the pressure placed on schools and teachers to achieve mandated literacy goals, I am concerned conversations about literacy are too simple and that classroom actions are negatively influenced. While I believe literacy is an important goal, I also recognize the importance of complicating public notions of literacy as simply the ability to read a book or newspaper. Perhaps the conversation needs to return to the students, their stories, and how these often bump up against literacy goals and outcomes. Perhaps as a public concerned about education, we need to return to the "educational discourse of students and parents" as I have attempted to do in the telling of my own story (Huebner, 1999, p. 442).

SOME PERSONAL STORIES OF SCHOOLING:
AS A TEACHER LEARNING TO TEACH

When I was 23 years old, I graduated from a Bachelor of Education program, anxious to put into practice all the wonderful things I had learned in my teacher education classes. Having had a successful internship experience, I expected nothing less from my first 'real' classroom. I thought I knew a great deal about what it meant to teach, believing I was more than ready to teach. What I did know was how to 'have fun' in my classroom, entertain my students, and cover the curriculum content as prescribed by the ministry of education. It did not occur to me to consider the lived experiences of my students, their historically effected consciousness, or how they were situated by their race, class, gender, ability, etc. particularly in relation to prescribed learning objectives, a culture of exams, and an emphasis on technical approaches to teaching. I was unaware of my own educational story or of my students as storied beings (Huebner, 1999).

My first classroom was situated in an alternative high school for students who had not 'succeeded' in the mainstream system. They had either dropped out of school, been expelled from the physical space of school, or in a few cases, were there to improve their grades before going on to post-secondary education. Mostly they left the mainstream system not because they had failed in it, but because it had failed them, although I did not come to understand this until much later (the discourse of the school was one of 'failure'). On the first day when I walked into my classroom and met my students, I was not struck by the diversity that surrounded me. In fact I hardly even noticed it. Perhaps this was something to be proud of – color blindness. Not seeing the students as First Nations, or Asian, or Middle Eastern. Really not seeing them at all, not attending to them as storied beings. It allowed me to accept rather than challenge social studies content, corresponding knowledge objectives, and my own position of privilege as a white teacher.

Thus, I approached the officially sanctioned curriculum in a way that might have made the Ministry of Education proud. Each objective I wanted to accomplish appeared in the appropriate lesson plan and I always noted whether I felt the objectives were achieved. I was conscious of the need to evaluate student learning through testing their knowledge. My approach really could not have been more technical, more competency based, nor could it have better ignored the individual students in my class, each with their own unique stories that often were in tension with the official story of school and my own classroom actions. Yet I believed I was engaging in the practice of good teaching even though I did not "encourage each individual to grab hold of [curriculum] knowledge in a meaningful way (Huebner, 1999, p. 45). Huebner (1999) suggests that "the limits on what to teach, the domination of technical language, of behavioral objectives and evaluation cloud the understanding: understanding of self, of our work, of young people" (p. 381). This was certainly true for me.

When I shared the story of 'Canada' with my students in Social Studies 10, I was surprised to learn that it did not resonate with everyone in my class. As a student I had learned about the French and English as Nation Builders. In my Canadian History classes at university, this story was reinforced. Now it was my turn to tell it, so I did. If not for the voice of one student I might have continued telling this story.

Mariah:	Ms. Tupper
Me:	Yes Mariah
Mariah:	I'm just wondering about the First Nations perspective
Me (in my head):	There's a First Nations perspective?
	"What do you mean Mariah?"
Mariah:	You know, like we were here first and then the white man came. My people were this country. And then the white man came.
Me:	Oh, right. The First Nations perspective. That's not included in the curriculum.

This story is as much Mariah's story as it is my story, or perhaps even more her story and the story of The People. She had the courage to speak up and challenge my "passion for ignorance" (Britzman quoting Sedgwick, 2003). When she spoke it aloud, I had to hear it, reflect upon it, and begin unraveling my own sense of being a 'good' teacher, beyond the public discourse of 'good' teaching linked to exam scores, student achievement, and orderly classrooms. My teaching story was complicated by the student, not just because I got the story of Canada wrong, but because I embraced a particular story of school, of teaching, and of privilege. It happened because I was not a story listener, I did not attempt to recast the language of the institution and of the ideas that shape(d) it. My encounter with Mariah as a storied being created a space of tension for me to live with(in) amidst the competing stories (Aoki, 2003; 2004). Such spaces can be inherently productive as they allow us to consider anew our own sense of what we see, how we teach, and what stories we are telling.

Huebner (1999) reminds us "the educational task has become so strongly focused by the need for the teacher to teach and the student to learn, that neither has time to think about how that which is taught influences the life of the student" (p. 443). I would extend this further by suggesting that teachers and students have little time to reflect on the nature of knowledge itself, as socially constructed and as political. Knowledge serves a purpose, it is not and never has been neutral (Said, 2000). Why for example do students in Saskatchewan schools know almost nothing about the numbered treaties despite the fact that the province was entirely ceded through treaties with First Nations people (Cappello & Tupper, 2006; Tupper & Cappello, 2008)?

Like my experiences with the Dick and Jane Readers, Mariah's experience with the story of Canada stands in sharp relief to that which is told through the officially sanctioned curriculum. Yet, this is often not the stuff of public discourse about education. Instead, the discourse is concerned with gaps in students' knowledge of the official story (Tupper, 2008). We need only to consider media coverage of students' perceived ignorance of certain facts of Canadian history, usually in conjunction with Canada Day. Teachers are often targeted by the media as not doing their job, and students accused of knowing more about America than their own country.

This discourse needs disruption if we are to move beyond technical foundations of education as Huebner (1999) calls us to do. It also requires disruption if we are to move beyond an exam culture that measures what students 'know' by how well they do on a quiz or a test.

SOME PERSONAL STORIES OF SCHOOL:
AS A BEGINNING SCHOLAR

In Regina, where I live and work, the public school division has recently reorganized its planning and operations around four priority areas, including higher literacy and student achievement. Since I have already spent some time discussing literacy, I now turn my attention to complicating the discourse of achievement which I do not see as separate from the discourse of accountability, both preoccupations in public conversations about school. Accountability is not a new phenomenon in education, but it seems "the public has become [increasingly] alarmed that schools are not preparing students for the new millennium" (McEwan, 1995, p. 14). Calls for accountability (hidden behind concern for student achievement as measured through standardized tests) have significant implications for classroom actions. They often influence decisions teachers make in the classroom with respect to students and pedagogy. In educational contexts where exams are extensively used as tools of accountability, the exam often becomes the de facto curriculum, negating the stories and experiences students bring to the classroom.

This was certainly my experience, my story, teaching high school in Alberta. The pressure was on to teach to the test, to use old standardized exams as evaluative tools throughout the year, to ensure that students were well-equipped to write the exam, succeed, and move on. Pinar (2004) maintains that when curriculum is linked to student performance on standardized tests, "politicians have in effect, taken control of what is to be taught: the curriculum" (p. 2). He goes on to state that "examination driven curricula demote teachers from scholars and intellectuals to technicians in service to the state" (p. 2). This is precisely the concern that Huebner has been articulating for many, many years. "Rhetoric shaped by technical interests rather than educational interests" states Huebner, "influences public perception about the nature of education and thus grants undue power to people with technical interests who sway the minds and affections of young people" (p. 435). Such power influences classroom actions in very real and often harmful ways.

A number of years ago, when I was conducting my doctoral research in Edmonton, I had the opportunity to engage high school social studies teachers in conversations about a number of issues they encountered in teaching social studies, including the challenges posed by living and working within a culture of exams and high stakes testing (Tupper, 2004). For many years now, Alberta has mandated standardized tests at grade 3, 6, and 9 known as Provincial Achievement Tests. Each year, the two major newspapers in the province, The Calgary Herald, and The Edmonton Journal publish the results of the Tests and provide a ranking of all schools in the province based on Achievement Test Results. In grade 12, students in Alberta write Diploma exams in core subjects such as English, Social Studies, Biology, and Mathematics. These exams are worth fifty-percent of their grade in the course and are typically comprised of some multiple choice questions and some written responses. Diploma exams are often described as high stakes because of the percentage weight placed upon them and decisions made by post-secondary institutes as a result of them.

One of the teacher participants in my doctoral research, Carol, spoke about the realities she faced everyday in her teaching context with respect to student achievement. Over the course of the research, I came to know Carol quite well, listening to her story of teaching, her story of learning, and witnessing the tensions she was experiencing as her teaching story repeatedly bumped up against the discourse of accountability.

Carol believed in creating meaningful learning opportunities for the students in her class, connecting their stories to the story being told through officially sanctioned social studies curriculum. She wanted to find ways to help her students see themselves in curriculum. She also believed in the importance of including First

Nations issues and concerns in her teaching (despite their absence in official curriculum). However, Carol shared with me that she struggled to do these things in light of administrative pressure to ensure high scores on provincial exams. She told me that at her school, teachers participated in a practice she referred to as "unloading" whereby students who were thought to be weak, who might bring down class averages on exams, who might very well fail the exam, were 'unloaded' into lower level, non-academic classes. She confessed that she too had participated in this practice, despite her beliefs in fairness and equity, because she feared administrative sanction if her students fared poorly on standardized tests. Carol's story resonated for me as I too had experienced similar struggles in my teaching. My story of teaching and Carol's story of teaching were in common. Again, I must return to Huebner to help make sense of this, to complicate the discourse of accountability that can have such adverse affects on students (and teachers) without them even knowing it.

Huebner (1999) argues that students and teachers face evaluative practices because:

> they are the weakest politically, and most at the mercy of the principalities and powers. Students move on. Teachers can be replaced. Thus they are the scapegoats in the domination systems. The school's procedure, materials, and basic organization have longer lives (p. 413).

Such practices reflect the importance placed on the technical foundations of education by outside forces and those who have power within educational systems. In the public discourse about achievement, teachers are held accountable for low exam scores, not a system that privileges dominant knowledge systems, certain ways of knowing, and certain ways of representing knowledge (i.e.: multiple choice exams rather than learning portfolios). The public sees exam scores as tangible examples of teacher effectiveness or ineffectiveness. The discourse applauds schools who demonstrate excellence through their exam scores and punishes schools that fare poorly. Exams are one way to hold teachers accountable in the public discourse of education. Yet, in this complex web of politics and powers, what is at stake are the storied lives of students and teachers.

SOME PERSONAL STORIES OF SCHOOL: AS A PARENT OF A SCHOOL AGED CHILD

My oldest daughter is in grade one this year, and because I am home on maternity leave, I have had the opportunity to become more involved in her school, agreeing to serve as an executive member of the School Community Council (SCC). I attended my first official meeting in early September, determined to get the lay of the land, sort out personalities, learn about the workings of the school, and ultimately to get a sense of the politics. The meeting itself tended to focus on practical matters like budget and back to school barbecues, the less practical, more political matters occurred after the meeting, in brief conversations with other parents, questions about teachers, concerns expressed about school environment. I found myself standing with a group of three other parents outside the school after the meeting, enjoying the warm night. Two of the parents had children already in grade eight, and when they learned that I and the other parent had children in grade one, they wanted to share some of the collective wisdom they had procured having children in the school for the last eight years. They told us funny stories about their children's experiences, anecdotes about past school events, and 'advice' about certain teachers in the school. The exchange went something like this:

Parent 1: My son was in grade seven last year and his teacher stopped teaching math in November.

Jennifer: Why would she do that?

Parent 1: She doesn't like teaching math. She'd rather do other things.

Parent 2: I had to buy workbooks last year for my child so he could keep up with his math. Then they get to high school and they have no math skills, they struggle.

Parent 1: I was volunteering at a charity event on the weekend, and one of the grade eight kids helping out couldn't figure out how to make change from a twenty.

Parent 2: I know – it's terrible.

Parent 1: (lowering her voice) You know, there's no accountability for teachers in Saskatchewan.

Parent 3: What do you mean?

Parent 1: Well, there's no standardized tests so they can do whatever they want. Even the education students at the university learn they don't have to worry about being evaluated. I'm not saying that Alberta's got it right, but those tests make teachers accountable.

Parent 3: (as an aside to me) Is that true?

Jennifer: Hmmm....

The talk of parents, Huebner (1999) reminds us, "significantly influences the practices of and thinking about education (p. 441)." In the case of these parents, their talk was intended to 'alert' us to the lack of accountability in an educational system that has yet to wholeheartedly embrace standardized testing on a scale similar to other provinces in Canada. The educational story they told seems to reflect the present historical moment, described by Pinar (2004) as a "nightmare" (p. 3). Pinar argues that the school "has become a skill-and-knowledge factory...in the schools, millions live the nightmare each day, too few seem to realize they are even asleep" (p. 3). I suspect that the grade seven teacher's decision to spend less time on math is more complicated than a simple dislike of the subject. But I also understand that parents who are concerned about their children's success in school may embrace the discourse of accountability through their desire to see standardized tests implemented in Saskatchewan schools. Huebner (1999) challenges us to consider how "the fashion of using test scores [has] become so firmly embedded in public parlance about education" (p. 441). I believe it is because test scores are something we can 'sink our teeth' into more than the ambiguous love of learning or critical and creative thinking our children may embrace. A test score 'tells' us how our child is doing in relation to other children. A test score 'tells' us how well teachers are 'educating' our children, at least in a technical foundational sense. But test scores do little to help us understand the storied lives of children and teachers in schools.

Having lived and taught in such a system, the educational story I tell is in conflict with the narrative of school offered by these parents. I understand this (sometimes not as well as I would like) partly because I have taken some time to consider my storied self in relation to the official story of school; my storied self in relation to the students I teach, and; my storied self in relation to officially mandated curriculum. However, in conversation with these parents, I found myself struggling with what it means to be simultaneously parent, teacher and scholar. As a parent, I want my daughter to be proficient in math. As a teacher, I want her to love learning math (but I don't question that she should learn math). As a scholar, I want to find ways to surpass the technical foundations of education, the focus on mastery and skills that often constitutes the teaching of mathematics. So I find myself being always in tension (Aoki, 2004). This is not a bad thing; rather being in tension acknowledges the messiness of life, the complexity of being. It allows us to engage in Pinar's (2004) "complicated conversations" in ways that might not otherwise be possible. But how might such tension assist in disrupting public discourses of education so focused on accountability and achievement?

Let me return for a moment to the work of John Caputo (1987) who challenges us to move beyond facticity, a way of thinking and being in the world that he believes makes "light of the difficulty of existence (p.1)." The discourse of achievement and accountability in education might be understood as a discourse of facticity. Students cease to be storied beings as they write standardized exams. As I have already argued, these exams, the public discourse of accountability in education so pervasive in mainstream media simplifies and even ignores the lived experiences of students and teachers; the discourse ignores the messiness of life, allowing little if any room for productive tensions to inform our thinking about education. In turn, this influences the classroom actions that Huebner (1999) discusses in "Politics and the Curriculum". It influences the construction of curriculum, approaches to literacy, and ultimately our ability to engage in public discourse about education as storied beings. If we are to take up the challenge of engaging in public discourse about education that Huebner has bequeathed to us, we must do so critically and creatively. We must find ways to talk about education that "resonate with the experience of young people and their parents, that can be used in the mass media without being captured by ideological positions" (Huebner, 1999, p. 442). We must bring our storied selves to the conversation and in so doing disrupt, complicate the rhetoric of standards, test scores, accountability, the curriculum.

REFERENCES

Aoki, T. (2004). In W. Pinar & R. Irwin (Eds.), *Curriculum in a new key: The collected works of Ted T. Aoki*. New York: Routledge.
Aoki, T. (2003). Locating living pedagogy in teacher "research": Five metonymic moments. In E. Hasebe-Ludt & W. Hurren (Eds.), *Curriculum intertext: Place/language/pedagogy* (pp. 1–10). New York: Peter Lang.
Britzman, D. (2003). *After education: Anna Freud, Melanie Klein and psychoanalytic histories of learning*. New York: SUNY Press.
Cappello, M., & Tupper, J. (2006). *Aboriginal knowledge and perspectives: Identifying, delivering and assessing best practices with middle years students*. Regina: SIDRU.
Caputo, J. (1987). *Radical hermeneutics: Repetition, deconstruction and the hermeneutic project*. Bloomington, IN: University of Indiana Press.
Chambers, C. (1999). A topography of Canadian curriculum theory. *Canadian Journal of Education, 22*, 137–150.
Chambers, C. (2003). On being a disciple of memoir. In E. Hasebe-Ludt & W. Hurren (Eds.), *Curriculum intertext: Place/language/pedagogy* (pp. 103–110). New York: Peter Lang.
Hasebe-Ludt, E., & Hurren (Eds.). (2003). *Curriculum intertext: Place/language/pedagogy*. New York: Peter Lang.
Huebner, D. (1999). Challenges bequeathed (1996). In V. Hillis (Ed.), *The lure of the transcendent, collected essays by Dwayne E. Huebner* (pp. 432–445). Mahwah, NJ: Lawrence Erlbaum Associates.
Huebner, D. (1999). Politics and the curriculum (1962). In V. Hillis (Ed.), *The lure of the transcendent, collected essays by Dwayne E. Huebner* (pp. 15–22). Mahwah, NJ: Lawrence Erlbaum Associates.
Huebner, D. (1999). Politics and curriculum (1964). In V. Hillis (Ed.), *The lure of the transcendent, collected essays by Dwayne E. Huebner* (pp. 94–100). Mahwah, NJ: Lawrence Erlbaum Associates.
Huebner, D. (1999). Teaching as a vocation (1987). In V. Hillis (Ed.), *The lure of the transcendent, collected essays by Dwayne E. Huebner* (pp. 379–387). Mahwah, NJ: Lawrence Erlbaum Associates.
Huebner, D. (1999). Knowledge: An instrument of man (1962). In V. Hillis (Ed.), *The lure of the transcendent, collected essays by Dwayne E. Huebner* (pp. 36–43). Mahwah, NJ: Lawrence Erlbaum Associates.
Hurren, W. (2003). Auto'•geo'•carto'•graphia': A curricular collage. In E. Hasebe-Ludt & W. Hurren (Eds.), *Curriculum intertext: Place/language/pedagogy* (pp. 111–122). New York: Peter Lang.
Jackson, S., & Gee, S. (2005). 'Look Janet', 'no you look John': Constructions of gender in early school reader illustrations across 50 years. *Gender and Education, 17*, 115–128.
McEwan, N. (2005). Accountability in education in Canada. *Canadian Journal of Education, 20*, 1–13.
Pinar, W. (2004). *What is curriculum theory?* Mahwah, NJ: Lawrence Erlbaum Associates.
Said, E. (2000). *Reflections on exile and other essays*. Cambridge, MA: Harvard University Press.
Sedgwick, E. K. (1993). *Between men: English literature and male homosocial desire*. New York: Columbia University Press.
Tupper, J. (2008). Interrogating citizenship and democracy in education: The implications for disrupting universal values. In D. Lund & P. Carr (Eds.), *Doing democracy: Striving for political literacy and social justice* (pp. 71–84). New York: Peter Lang.
Tupper, J. (2004). *Searching citizenship. Social studies and the tensions of teaching*. Unpublished Doctoral Dissertation, University of Alberta, Edmonton.
Tupper, J., & Cappello, M. (2008). Teaching treaties as (un)usual narratives: Disrupting the curricular commonsense. *Curriculum Inquiry, 38*, 560–578.
Wason-Ellam, L. (1997). If only I was like Barbie. *Language Arts, 74*, 430–437.

LACE MARIE BROGDEN

A SOMEWHERE MIDDLE

Undoing Illusions of the Discrete in Times of Curricular Contradictions

When coming to this reading, please note the countenance is not even; there is sometimes (perhaps most times) an infrequent or irregular beat. When coming to this reading, it may be useful to think techno-pop – syncopation, or maybe jazz – improvisation. In coming to this reading, please read as I have written, in pieces/peaces.

This reading (and its writing) reflects some of the challenges of theorizing and enacting curriculum in a post-cetera era, where 'linear' objectives and 'progressive' learning outcomes give way to syncopated curricular (f)acts, where "*The Order of* [schooling] *Things*" (Foucault, 1973) gives way to teachers and learners in an improvised curricular dance.

This reading, like the reading of curriculum itself, calls up uncertainty, where uncertainty leads to possibility, and possibility leads to curriculum.

So it is, still and again, that this reading, like the reading of curriculum itself, places us – reader and writer, writer and reader – fully within circles of meaning making (the term 'spiralling curriculum' might also come to mind), fully within hermeneutic spaces of understanding that both speak to and generate curricular challenges. Within and through these readings of curriculum, this chapter addresses Huebner's call for attention to educational domains and phenomena and his assertion, widely echoed in poststructural theory (Baudrillard, 2000/2003; Britzman, 2000; hooks, 1990; de Certeau, 1984), that "knowledge is a social construction, not an individual construction" (Huebner, as cited in Casey, 1995, p. 200). Within and through these readings of curriculum is curriculum itself.

A FEW ASSUMPTIONS (THE TERM 'PRIOR UNDERSTANDINGS' MIGHT ALSO COME TO MIND)

For here, "for now" ("Vintage Laurel," Ellis, 2004, p. 179)...

teaching is not (only, not usually) a positivist endeavour;
   e x t e n s i o n... curriculum is not a fixed commodity.

learning happens in complex, non-linear patterns and ruptures;
   e x t e n s i o n... curriculum is fluid and emergent.

P. Lewis and J. Tupper (eds.), Challenges Bequeathed: Taking up the Challenges of Dwayne Huebner, 127–141.
© *2009 sense publishers. All rights reserved.*

teachers produce (and in producing are also produced by) professional, pedagogical and intellectual possibilities of learning;

e x t e n s i o n... curriculum is a socially-constructed, generative process.

learners bring primordial, limiting, malleable, mutating needs and complex, limiting, malleable, mutating understandings to contexts of learning and being;

e x t e n s i o n... curriculum is context specific.

and, by e x t e n s i o n, curriculum is enacted by and acts upon teachers and learners, (re)producing itself as it produces acts of teaching and learning.

STILL AND AGAIN: HISTORICITY AND RE:ITERATIONS OF AND IN CURRICULUM THEORIZING

In his closing remarks for *Contemporary Curriculum Discourses: Twenty Years of JCT*, William Pinar (1999) argues that Reconceptualism has become, in its myriad forms, part of mainstream curriculum theorizing. Pinar declares "the Tylerian dominance has passed. Like a disappearing star in another galaxy, however, it takes some years for everyone, depending upon his or her location, to see this" (p. 490). This observation emerges from his reflections on 20 years of curriculum theorizing, and although the Tylerian dominance may appear to have passed in the field of curriculum theorizing proper, such a shift is not so apparent in the continued dominance of modern, technical discourses in many lived curricular spaces throughout North America, curricular spaces where teaching and learning happen in the day-to-day.

In 1989, arguing in favour of continued attention to Dwayne Huebner's work (his 1966 essay "Curricular Language and Classroom Meanings" in this case), Kathleen Casey (1995) wrote, "in the contemporary United States, technical demands for efficiency, standardization, and rationalization continue to crowd out political concerns about the exercise of power and control in education" (p. 200). Indeed, I maintain Casey's observations from 1989 – themselves 20 years old by the time this writing finds its way to press – could have been written today, especially in the continuing climate of high-stakes standardized testing and ever-increasing demands for 'accountability' prominent in many North American jurisdictions:

> Today's fix is to make educational research scientific, and the federal government [of the United States] has taken the lead in this project by mandating scientific method into law.... The fundamental idea is that rigorous science will make better schools, that quality science will enable us to finally reengineer schools so they work. (Freeman, deMarrais, Preissle, Roulston and St. Pierre, 2007, p. 25)

In this approach to paying attention to (and not knowing[1]) the historicity from both within and beyond the field, I do not mean to imply curricular landscapes have remained unchanged. As Janet L. Miller (2005) notes, "the US field, its conditions, and its contemporary constructions are not and cannot ever be 'the same' as during the reconceptualist movement" (p. 10). Indeed, in the United States and in Canada, curriculum theorizing feels imperatives of the millenium – with September 11, 2001 being a marker of particular import (Miller, 2005; Chambers, 2006) to both contexts. As Cynthia Chambers observes, "since the fallout from September 11, 2001, curriculum studies in Canada has become more concerned with education and empire, and pedagogy in times of war" (p. 27). From a "post"colonial perspective, however, it may also be useful to note that these imperatives, while contextually contemporary, are not necessarily "new." Chambers explains,

> ...without memory, without history we might imagine that empire and education, pedagogy and war are only now linked. We might imagine that living in a time of war is somehow new, particularly for Canadians. And yet even a cursory glance at Canadian history, even a tentative scraping through the layered palimpsest of national memories reveals that in Canada— education has always served empire—and parts of the nation have always been at war with each other—or others. (p. 27)

It is in view of these contested spaces of both educational research and curriculum theorizing that I re:turn my musings about context and historicity. I agree with Casey's (1995) assertion that political concerns about power and control in education continue to be overshadowed by dominant discourses of the technical, particularly efficiency (the term 'economic' might also come to mind) and standardization (the term 'normative' might also come to mind). I reiterate, therefore, my argument for the ongoing relevance of Casey's concern over the continued dominance of technicality (however unfortunate such an ongoing relevance might be deemed to be). As I take up Huebner's (1999) challenge of using the world's intellectual traditions and achievements, I call first on these past intellectual traditions of curriculum theory itself. In so doing, I acknowledge Miller's (2005) reluctance to fall into either "insulated nostalgia [...of] exhilarating times" or "despair about current conditions" (p. 10), and recognize my own vulnerability in relation to possibilities of the same. Simultaneously, I acknowledge a nagging feeling that the field of curriculum theorizing – and the educational arena it professes to inform – are still, and perhaps now more than ever, susceptible to "the politics of evidence" (Denzin, 2008, p. 319).

At the risk of committing curricular career suicide[2], I find myself left with a strong suspicion that the Tylerian influences – the very same influences Pinar would have us watch fade past the stars – are still omnipresent in contemporary spaces of curriculum as lived. Further, I find myself left wondering about the extent to which the field of curriculum theorizing itself ought to claim to have wriggled free from these same discursive pressures. As Patti Lather (2004) reminds me, "this is [still] your father's paradigm" (p. 15); perhaps, in curriculum theory as in education research more generally, "we need to put our critical theory to work in this moment of our now" (p. 22). Indeed, this imperative may be at the heart of Huebner's call.

TAKING UP THE CHALLENGE

Teachers, Huebner (1999) observes, "must act in an imperfect world. To postpone action until the makers of knowledge and technique establish the educational millennium is sheer irresponsibility, based upon illusions of progress. We have no choice but to risk ourselves" (p. 385). In issuing his third challenge, Use the world's intellectual traditions and achievements, Huebner calls on the University, and on curriculum theorists in particular, to take a similar risk. "We [curriculum theorists] are left," asserts Huebner, "with the task of asking how the great diversity of intellectual systems of critique and imagination can be related to the human enterprise of education" (p. 440). Thus, through his third challenge, Huebner (1999) asks what insights the educator might offer the philosopher.

In accepting Huebner's call for attention to intellectual spaces that may inform and be informed by curriculum theory, a useful question surfaces:

How might we, as curriculum theorists, adopt critical and imaginative intellectual positions as we conceive the work we have yet to do?

I propose one possibility for such critical imaginings is the que(e)rying of curricular (f)acts, where que(e)rying calls for a repositioning or questioning of prior conceptions and of tacit understandings of the everyday (de Certeau, 1984).

In the remainder of this chapter, I offer, by way of example, two altered readings of curricular artifacts – the first is a re:reading of 'curriculum objectives,' the second, a re:writing of 'lesson plan.' Using these two art/if/acts[3] (Brogden, 2008) as places of both curriculum theorizing and philosophical musing, my intent is to create spaces where "otherness is present yes, but with a debt and duty to the historicity of what has gone before" (Trifonas, 2005, p. 206). My hope is that these two examples might encourage our re:apprehending of some of the philosophical presence/presents (Melnyk, 2003; Heidegger, 2002/1969) of/in the teacher/learner relationship that happen with, in and through curriculum and curriculum theorizing.

DISRUPTING CURRIUCLUAR (F)ACTS
THE GLOBAL: RE:READING 'CURRICULUM OBJECTIVES'

The structures of learning (the term 'framework' might also come to mind) in many formal learning environments, particularly those whose governance is mandated by the State, commonly take shape in the form of curriculum objectives (the term 'learning outcomes' might also come to mind). Often appearing in official governance documents (those issued by governments and school boards, for example) or in official institutional documents (those issued by institutions such as universities with Teacher Education programs, for example), curriculum objectives explicate the goals, aims and philosophy of the governing bodies by which they are produced.

When examining the 'objectives' found in curriculum documents, a common pattern emerges: 'general' notions and ideologies are translated and transmutated into 'specific' directives about teaching and learning. Varying degrees of specificity are employed to describe and prescribe the activities of teaching and learning through (and for) the 'attainment' of objectives. However, these transcriptions may be fatally flawed if, as I suspect is the case, James Haywood Rolling (2006) is right in his assertion that "planned learning outcomes do not construct minds; children [and other learners] figure themselves out" (p. 41).

The first altered reading I propose takes the form of a set of three juxtapositions, placed together in an attempt to disrupt some of the (f)acts of curriculum, to disrupt (in sometimes small, almost imperceptible ways) notions of the discrete with/in curriculum; placed together also in an attempt to dwell in a somewhere middle. This move to the in-between does not 'just happen'; indeed, as Wang (2006) cautions, "a third space can not be assumed; it must be created" (p. 111).

Adopting an emergent, unfixed paradigm for curriculum making, this altered reading[4] focuses on a middle space (Wang, 2004; Aoki, 2003; Robbins, 1999). Each juxtaposition offers a philosophical dwelling in a somewhere middle between two citations of curricular artifacts (one from a K-12 setting, one from a postsecondary setting), and each is followed by a commentary on the somewhere middle, even though, and sometimes especially because, "a third space does not stay with itself" (Wang, 2006, p. 115).

Juxtaposition no. 1 of 3: (Curricular) Naming

Excerpt from a Government Mandated Curriculum Guide	a somewhere middle	Excerpt from a Graduate Course Syllabus
"**English Language Arts - A Curriculum Guide for the Elementary Level (2002)**" (Saskatchewan Education, 2002)	where to name is to re:position a claim categorize legitimize occupy spaces of curricular (un)certainties	EC&I 808 – INSTRUCTION: THEORY & PRACTICE

Calling into question the name of a thing need not be seen as an argument against the thing itself; rather questioning the names we give (the term 'curriculum development' might also come to mind), and then adopt (the term 'curriculum implementation' might also come to mind), and then reproduce (the term 'curriculum actualization' might also come to mind), could be seen as a way of repositioning ourselves (as curricular agents) and our teaching. Indeed, questioning our curricular acts of naming could lead to spaces where altered forms of legitimized learning – and perhaps more importantly, legitimized knowing – might reside.

Juxtaposition no. 2 of 3: (Purported) Purposes

Excerpt from a Government Mandated Curriculum Guide	a somewhere middle	Excerpt from a Graduate Course Syllabus
Aim and Goals The language arts are central to all learning. The purpose of the English language arts curriculum is to guide the continuous growth and development of students' thinking and language abilities from kindergarten to grade 12. The study of English language arts enables students to understand and appreciate language, and to use it in a variety of situations for communication, personal satisfaction, and learning." (Saskatchewan Education, 2002)	"Repositioning is the postmodern processing of thought by revisiting discourse-bound knowledge structures even after they have been shaped into a coherent form in consciousness, with the ultimate effect of disrupting the certainty of those forms" (Rolling, 2004, p. 49). in spaces of a somewhere middle theory dwells time re:c(o)urses the 'stuff and nonsense' of teaching emerges	**COURSE DESCRIPTION** This course explores instruction as socially constructed practice shaped by teacher biography, social contexts and best [sic] practices. Students engage in inquiry and critique to better understand and improve [sic] their instructional practices.[5]

There is sometimes an illusion of fixity in the claiming of some specific goals, purposes or intent of a given curriculum. From this illusion of fixity, dwelling in the in-between might enable a loosening, an opening up of that which curriculum is purported to intend. As with the previous juxtaposition of naming, this pushing against fixity is not intended to dismiss nor deny. As Wang (2006) observes, "without engagement with the original two spaces nothing new can be generated" (p. 121). One of the calls of the somewhere middle, therefore, is to (re)examine the oft taken-for-granted assumptions residing within curriculum, both written and enacted. This call beckons because, as Wang further cautions, "being immersed in any one space uncritically merely leads to the reproduction of the existent" (p. 121).

Huebner challenges us to move towards extra-disciplinary (the term 'extra-curricular' might come to mind) networking; he challenges us to move towards spaces where education and philosophy merge, co-mingle, and mutually inform one another. Poets have long heeded this call of mutuality, distilling words in an attempt to push our understandings and question our (in)actions: "What are the roots that clutch, what branches grow, out of this stony rubbish?" (Elliot, 1936/1963, p. 63) Indeed, how might we – educational researchers "working the ruins" (St. Pierre & Pillow, 2000), curriculum scholars theorizing "an engaged and provocative pedagogy in a third space" (Wang, 2006, p. 124), and philosophers questioning degrees of belief, "even the delirium of non-knowledge" (Deleuze, 2001, p. 44) – how might we work in ways that allow our disciplines to coalesce through juxtaposition, complexifying understandings within and between both education and philosophy? Perhaps juxtaposition is itself one of curriculum's global possibilities. After all, when "juxtaposed, the meaning of a constellation is our interpretation of its organizational structure and relationships and cannot be condensed to a single essence or placed in a particular hierarchical order" (Fleener, 2005, p. 10).

Juxtaposition no. 3 of 3: (Theorizing) Theoretical Positionings

Excerpt from a Government Mandated Curriculum Guide	a somewhere middle	Excerpt from a Graduate Course Syllabus
"Philosophy This curriculum recognizes that language is basic to thinking and learning in all cultures, just as thinking is central to all modes of language use. An effective English language arts program… fosters a positive attitude about language, language learning, and the self as a language learner. It is important for teachers to provide interesting and meaningful listening, speaking, reading, writing, viewing, and representing activities that engage and enable all students to become confident and competent language users… Language arts teachers should strive to develop a caring language community in which all students feel accepted and	"Such an interpretation suggests that absolute translation is an impossibility, that translation is always incomplete and partial, and further that ongoing translation is always ongoing transformation, generating newness in life's movements" (Aoki, 2003, p. 7). in these spaces of in-between negotiations engender (and are gendered[6] by) negotiation "A key aspect of language is recursivity… our abilities to self-reference – that is, to cleave our individual selves from one another and from our contexts – is clearly amplified by, if not rooted in, our language" (Davis, 2004, p. 154).	**THEORETICAL POSITIONS** This course promotes the use of critical, postcolonial, postmodern, poststructural and social justice perspectives, engaging educational professionals in decentring and re:politicizing instructional practices. This course will privilege a lens of language and power in Canadian schools to question and disrupt some of the quotidian (De Certeau, 1990) practice and praxis that invoke instruction. Participants will be encouraged to take an informed, critical position when engaging in class assignments and activities, to share their "small stories" (Moissiac & Bamberg,

| confident that they will be supported by others in language learning and in taking risks. The respectful relationship that teachers establish with their students and the environment that teachers create affect the learning of all students in positive ways" (Saskatchewan Education, 2002). | between language and languaging a somewhere middle of complicity, complacency, criticality collectivity, agency and intersubjectivity emergent moments of our now que(e)rying moments of how historicity and possibility attention to tension(s) dwelling re:writing being | 2005), and to work towards new and/or altered conceptions of instruction and/in education. |

THE LOCAL: RE:WRITING THE 'LESSON PLAN'

A commonplace (the term 'foundational' might also come to mind) tool of teaching and learning is the 'lesson plan.' Teacher educators tell how to construct it, preservice teachers learn how to produce it (and be produced by it in both their understanding and performing acts of teaching), teachers write it, students 'follow' it, and administrators 'supervise' and 'evaluate' it. But how does the lesson plan operate? What might this tool – pervasive in the lived curriculum of classrooms – have to offer us? And further, what might we – the scholars who theorize it and the teachers who implement it – have to offer the lesson plan (and by extension, offer ourselves)?

Instructions for writing a lesson plan
    (and, *Altered readings through curriculum theorizing*)
        (as well as, M USINGS ON PEDAGOGICAL UNCERTAINTY)
            (and also with, **Companion Readings in Philosophy**)

The lesson plan should be coherently structured
    "As a student of teaching, one of my earliest lessons was how to develop a lesson plan. A good plan, I was told, would not only state the objectives to be attained, it would also anticipate the conditions under which the plan itself would falter" (De Fabrizio, 2004, p. 4).
        SOMETIMES, PERHAPS MOST TIMES (NOW), I PLAN IN SUCH A WAY THAT MY PLAN CAN COME UNDONE; INDEED, I CELEBRATE THOSE PEDAGOGICAL MOMENTS WHERE UNDONENESS REIGNS.
            "*First, différance* refers to the (active *and* passive) movement that consists in deferring by means of

delay, delegation, reprieve, referral, detour, postponement, reserving" (Derrida, 1972/2002, p. 8).

Curriculum objectives should be clearly stated

"The plan was an articulation of the desire to direct, not only what will be learned and how it will be learned, but also who will learn and who will teach" (De Fabrizio, 2004, p. 4).

SOMETIMES, PERHAPS MOST TIMES (NOW), I AM MAGPIE; I SWEEP IN ON TEACHABLE MOMENTS, FILTCH UNEXPECTED LEARNINGS, REVEL IN THE AHA, RECAST TIME.

"It has almost been assumed that if the educator can clearly specify his [*sic*] goals, then he has fulfilled his responsibility as an historical being. But historical responsibility is much too complex to be so easily dismissed" (Huebner, as cited in Slattery, 1995, p. 613).

Instructional strategies should be delineated

"...a good plan was a dynamic cartography, one that planned for its own difficulties and prepared alternative strategies for the recuperation of its designed trajectory" (De Fabrizio, 2004, p. 4).

SOMETIMES, PERHAPS MOST TIMES (NOW), I EMPLOY STRATEGIES WITH WHICH I AM MOST COMFORTABLE SO AS TO ANTICIPATE MORE (ALAS, NEVER ALL) OF THE INEVITABLE WAYS THEY COULD (ALAS, OFTEN DO) DERAIL.

"Mistrust no one who offers you water from a well, a songbird's feather, something that's been mended twice" (Crozier, 1999, p. 37).

The lesson plan should include adaptations for differentiated instruction

"Although the plan was aimed directly at embodied students, it simultaneously presumed that they did not exist. Its success and closure depended upon the absence of that unpredictable disruption definitive of real life and personified by the 'difficult' student" (De Fabrizio, 2004, p. 4).

SOMETIMES, PERHAPS MOST TIMES (NOW), I AM REMINDED OF THE COMPLEX, CONTRADICTORY AND CREATIVE WAYS OF LEARNING AND BEING IN THE WORLD.

"This realization does not free me from the responsibility to be attentive to who said what when – in fact, it seems to amplify the need to be familiar with what has come before – but it is liberating in that it highlights the importance of a repetition. Not a mindful mimicking, but a mindful reiteration" (Davis, 2005, p. 132).

Evaluation should reflect intended learning outcomes (evaluation procedures should be described in detail)

> *"The plan, by incarnating the excess it forecloses, teaches one thing above all: that containment is an impossible, if irresistible, scenario" (De Fabrizio, 2004, p. 4).*
>
> HOW WILL I KNOW WHAT THEY KNOW, WHEN I (STILL) DON'T KNOW WHAT I (DON'T) KNOW?
>
>> **"I ought to have said: a pound, or a kilo. More or less. A big book or a little kilo of dreams. Consider the weight of each dream; or of a thought; or of a kiss; or of a squeeze of a left hand" (Cixous, 2003/2006, p. 11).**

In many ways (but perhaps not yet most ways now), proposing altered readings of curricular art/if/acts such as the lesson plan is not a "new" idea. James Haywood Rolling, Jr. (2006), for example, promotes the notion of "the curriculum learning sketch rather than the curriculum lesson plan… [where] a learning sketch tends to mitigate around the constraints of predictability and measurement… [and] includes a field for multiple outcome possibilities, as those possibilities come to mind" (p. 41). In a similar vein, Marilyn Cochran-Smith and Susan Lytle (2006) propose the following complex, emergent definition of teaching:

> teaching requires the intentional forming and re-forming of frameworks for understanding practice. It is about how students and their teachers construct the curriculum, co-mingling their experiences, their cultural and linguistic resources, and their interpretive frameworks. Teaching also entails how teachers' actions are infused with complex and multilayered understandings of learners, culture, class, gender, literacies, social issues, institutions, "herstories" and histories, communities, materials, texts, and curricula. (p. 691)

So, if the idea is not new, why replay it here? The intent of this altered/pedagogical/ philosophical reading of these curricular art/if/acts is that of complexifying ways in which objectives (and other "goals" of curriculum), and the lesson plan (and other "tools" of curriculum) can be re:apprehended by theory. My hope is that in these alterations we may find altered ways of using theory – altered ways of using the world's intellectual traditions and achievements (Huebner, 1999) – to inform the practices within which and through which curriculum comes to be enacted.

IN:CONCLUSIONS

Huebner's (as cited in Miller, 2005) long-ago accusation of "moribund" has, indeed, rippled through the field of curriculum theorizing for many years. And yet, even Huebner has succumbed to a continued interest in the possibilities of curriculum – his five challenges provide evidence of his ongoing engagement in spite of what may have seemed, at times, a resignation. As for his third challenge, that of using the world's intellectual traditions and achievements, the words of Miller (2005) appear cogent: "we have to re-make the field every day, in relation to particular worldly events, issues, people and in tension with our desires for recognition and our simultaneous irreducibility to a collective local and/or global 'we'" (p. 16).

Re:production need not equal sameness; reproducing discourses within academic spaces of curriculum theorizing and pedagogical spaces of curriculum making need not succumb to a repetitive sameness. Rather, we might continue to alter ways of theorizing curriculum with a view to pushing the edges of the field, asking ourselves the following question:

How might we dwell in a somewhere middle, and invite others to join in the uncertainty?

Perhaps, in disrupting curricular (f)acts, in displacing the normative, in que(e)rying iterations and in re:producing attention, curriculum and the intellectual scholars who make it their life's work, will encounter generative possiblities of time and space where "the educator has something unique to say" (Huebner, 1999b, p. 440), to which philosophers, scholars and practitioners will listen. And, perhaps altering our philosophical endeavours within and beyond the field will generate altered habits of mind (Turner, 1996), altered ways of coming to terms with the terms that 'come to mind' when theorizing and enacting curriculum.

In calling for a re-engagement in the "paradigm dialogs" of qualitative inquiry, Norman K. Denzin (2008) argues "it is time to think through how we got to this place, time to ask where do we go next" (p. 315)? Denzin's assertions for contemporary qualitative inquiry capture the salience of Huebner's third challenge. Engaging in re:interpretations of curriculum theory, using the interdisciplinary wealth of the academy, and que(e)rying our ways of knowing and doing curriculum work are indeed important tasks of this place, and the University, with its Departments of Curriculum and Teacher Education programs, ought to be leading the way.

Curriculum theory both produces and is produced by intellectual traditions of the University; like the University, its historicity is its presence. And, also like the University, within curriculum theory lie possibilities "to resist effectively... to organize an inventive resistance, through its oeuvres, its works [and to resist] all attempts at reappropriation" (Derrida, 2005, p. 24). Or, stated another way,

> it is our hope that a pedagogy of place, to bring students in proximity to the past, that to stand where thirty to sixty million bison once grazed, and to know that only 1300 remain, is to face the precariousness of life and our responsibility to ensure that it may go on. (Chambers, 2006, p. 36)

This is in:conclusion
Digging around curriculum theory's *Fields of Play*[7]
"The artifacts sign so loudly"[8]
Words more than words can say

Dear Philosopher/Scholar/Teacher
  kindly listen
  we are one and o/Other the same
  but for *différance*[9]
  producing and produced
  our work to un-name[10]

Still and again
"We have no choice but to risk ourselves" (Huebner, 1999, p. 385)

POSTSCRIPT: MUSINGS FROM AN AND-GENERATION CURRICULUM SCHOLAR (FOR NOW)

I think I am perhaps, as Reynolds (2003) suggests, part of "the 'next generation' of curriculum scholars... the generation that understands the **AND**" (p. 95). Understanding the AND AND communicating the AND, however, do not just happen. Replaying (and altering) Wang (2006), the "AND" "can not be assumed; it must be created" (p. 111). In this chapter, I have played within curricular spaces, calling attention to ANDs... written objectives AND socioconstructivist learning-in-action, lesson plans AND philosophical musings, pragmatics of the now AND post-cetera positionings of the how, AND, repositioning the possible to dwell with AND in a somewhere – perhaps virtual – middle.

"What we call virtual," Deleuze (2001) argues, "is not something that lacks reality but something that is engaged in a process of actualization following the plane that gives it its particular reality" (p. 31). Enacting curriculum, that is, engaging in teaching and learning with teachers and learners, is AND does actualize curriculum. What the educator might offer the philosopher, therefore, AND, what the philosopher might re:turn to the educator, is theory and/for practice, theory that is, in the words of Hays (2002) "ready to travel."

> Theory is ready to travel. Although at its best, theory will stay close to the historicity of its material, mediating between specific historical contexts, theoretical constructions also possess an uncanny capacity to cross over, drift, and expand across disciplines, however much authors, institutions, and orthodoxies try to confine them. (p. ix)

Negotiating spaces where theory is ready to travel AND where practice is ready to dwell in a somewhere middle can perhaps bring us closer to curricular ruptures and their ensuing possibilities of risk AND – Huebner might smile – of hope. "Becoming, new ways of thinking, always proceed from the 'in-between'" (Reynolds, 2003, p. 94). Thus, looking for spaces of a somewhere middle is one more way to renew and review the work we do, as educators and as philosophers, in the name of, AND for, curriculum.

NOTES

[1] The phrase "paying attention and not knowing" is invoked here as an intentional echo of the work of Antoinette Oberg (2003), where paying attention and not knowing is "characterized as suspending expectations and delaying the desire to conceptualize" (p. 124).

[2] As Baudrillard (2001/2004) cautions, "quotation is never innocent" (p. 13). Intertextual meaning making with/in the research process is both a solitary and social performance, subject to the rules – and the risks – of the genre. Readers who are versed in curriculum studies, and who have been paying attention to the dominant discourses cited in this opening section – Pinar, Miller, Casey, Chambers – as well as the less than unanimous way in which I have *sighted* these well known scholars will have perhaps noted the precarious precipice of 'truth' and meaning (Melnyk, 2003), upon which I have perched my words. My intent is not to criticize, nor negate, rather to push, to question, and to re:iterate ways in which we produce curriculum theory and are produced by it.

[3] "using art/if/acts of practice… autoethnography can be used to sift through and over archaeological digs of curriculum as lived, using artful writing for critical reflection. In pedagogical terms, we can use acts of teaching and learning to write out our art" (Brogden, 2008, p. 860).

[4] I draw here on the definition of altered reading proposed by Jill Robbins' (1999) work on Emmanuel Levinas. Robbins states, "my goal is to explore the ways in which reading alters – or interrupts – the very economy of the same that the other interrupts" (p. xxiv), recognizing, as does Robbins, the Derridean paradox therein: "it is an irrefutable logic that pure alterity should not be compatible with the logic of alteration" (Derrida, as cited in Robbins, 1999, p. xxiv). One implication of alterity for curriculum theorizing then becomes the impossible possible (Derrida, 2005) of reinscribing curriculum through alteration.

[5] The excerpt from a course outline includes a course description (as published in the University of Regina Graduate Calendar) and is reprinted here as it appeared in the Summer 2008 version of the University of Regina course EC&I 808; the remainder of the excerpt is attributed to the course instructor, and author of the present chapter, L.M. Brogden (with her recognition of those who wrote and taught the same course in previous iterations). Its inclusion is employed as both 'evidence of practice' (the term 'curriculum making' might also come to mind) and as autoethnographic positioning.

[6] I have used gender here in the interests of pushing the play of language. Along with sexism, the invocation of other –isms and –ities also applies: racism, class-ism, able-ism, heteronormativity, *et j'en passe…*

[7] After Richardson (1997)

[8] After Kaufmann (2005) and Brogden (2008)

[9] After Derrida (1972/2002)

[10] After Rolling (2008), where "to unname is to undermine purported origins, to burrow between the archaeologies that constrain, to initiate and inaugurate anomalous genealogies that thrive and proliferate and die and leach new life between the layers" (p. 934).

REFERENCES

Aoki, T. T. (2003). Locating living pedagogy in teacher "research": Five metonymic moments. In E. Hasebe-Ludt & W. Hurren (Eds.), *Curriculum intertext* (pp. 1–9). New York: Peter Lang.

Baudrillard, J. (2004). *Fragments* (C. Turner, Trans.). London: Routledge. (Original work published 2001)

Baudrillard, J. (2003). *Passwords* (C. Turner, Trans.). London: Verso. (Original work published 2000)

Britzman, D. P. (2000). If the story cannot end: Deferred action, ambivalence, and difficult knowledge. In R. Simon, S. Rosenberg, & C. Eppert (Eds.), *Between hope and despair: Pedagogy and the remembrance of historical trauma* (pp. 27–57). Oxford, England: Rowman & Littlefield.

Brogden, L. M. (2008). Art·l/f/act·ology: Curricular artifacts in autoethnographic research. *Qualitative Inquiry, 14*(6), 851–864.
Casey, K. (1995). Teachers and values: The progressive use of religion in education. In W. Pinar (Ed.), *Contemporary curriculum discourses: Twenty years of JCT* (pp. 199–232). New York: Peter Lang.
Chambers, C. (2006). "The land is the best teacher I have ever had": Places as pedagogy for precarious times. *JCT: Journal of Curriculum Theorizing, 22*(3), 27–37.
Cixous, H. (2006). *Dream I tell you* (B. B. Brahic, Trans.). New York: Columbia University Press. (Original work published 2003)
Crozier, L. (1999). *What the living won't let go*. Toronto, ON: McClelland & Stewart.
Certeau de, M. (1984). *The practice of everyday life*. Berkeley, CA: University of California Press.
De Fabrizio, L. (2004). Transgressing the curricular body. *JCT: Journal of Curriculum Theorizing, 20*(2), 3–6.
Davis, B. (2005). Interrupting frameworks: Interpreting geometries of epistemology and curriculum. In W. E. Doll, M. J. Fleener, D. Trueit, & J. St. Julien (Eds.), *Chaos, complexity, curriculum and culture: A conversation* (pp. 119–132). New York: Peter Lang.
Davis, B. (2004). *Inventions of teaching*. Mahwah, NJ: Lawrence Erlbaum.
Deleuze, G. (2001). *Pure immanence: Essays on a life* (A. Boymand, Trans.). New York: Zone Books. (Original work published 1995)
Denzin, N. K. (2008). The new paradigm dialogs and qualitative inquiry. *International Journal of Qualitative Studies in Education, 21*(4), 315–325.
Derrida, J. (2005). The future of the profession or the unconditional University (Thanks to the "Humanities," what could take place tomorrow) (P. Kamuf, Trans.). In M. A. Peters & P. P. Trifonas (Eds.), *Deconstructing Derrida: Tasks for the new humanities* (pp. 11–24). New York: Palgrave MacMillan.
Derrida, J. (2002). *Positions* (A. Bass, Trans. 2nd English ed.). New York: Continuum. (Original work published 1972)
Eliot, T. S. (1963). The burial of the dead. In *T.S. Eliot collected poems: 1909–1962*. London: Faber and Faber. (Original work published 1936)
Ellis, C. (2004). *The ethnographic I: A methodological novel about autoethnography*. Walnut Creek, CA: AltaMira Press.
Fleener, M. J. (2005). Introduction: Chaos, complexity, curriculum, and culture: Setting up the conversation. In W. E. Doll, M. J. Fleener, D. Trueit, & J. St. Julien (Eds.), *Chaos, complexity, curriculum and culture: A conversation* (pp. 1–17). New York: Peter Lang.
Freeman, M., deMarrais, K., Preissle, J., Roulston, K., & St. Pierre, E. A. (2007). Standards of evidence in qualitative research: An incitement to discourse. *Educational Researcher, 36*(1), 25–32.
Foucault, M. (1973). *The order of things*. New York: Random House.
Hays, K. M. (2002). Introduction. In J. Baudrillard & J. Nouvel (Eds.), *The singular objects of architecture* (R. Bononno, Trans., pp. vii–xiii). Minneapolis, MN: University of Minnesota Press. (Original work published 2000)
Heidegger, M. (2002). *On time and being* (J. Stambaugh, Trans.). Chicago: University of Chicago Press. (Original work published 1969)
hooks, b. (1990). Postmodern blackness [Electronic version]. *Postmodern Culture, 1*(1).
Huebner, D. (1999a). Teaching as a vocation (1987). In V. Hillis (Ed.), *The lure of the transcendent: Collected essays by Dwayne E. Huebner* (pp. 379–387). Mahwah, NJ: Lawrence Erlbaum Associates.
Huebner, D. (1999b). Challenges bequeathed (1996). In V. Hillis (Ed.), *The lure of the transcendent: Collected essays by Dwayne E. Huebner* (pp. 432–444). Mahwah, NJ: Lawrence Erlbaum Associates.
Kaufmann, J. (2005). Autotheory: An autoethnographic reading of Foucault. *Qualitative Inquiry, 11*(4), 576–587.
Lather, P. (2004). This is your father's paradigm: Government intrusion and the case of qualitative research in education. *Qualitative Inquiry, 10*(1), 15–34.

Melnyk, G. (2003). *Poetics of naming*. Edmonton, AB: University of Alberta Press.

Miller, J. L. (2005). The American curriculum field and its worldly encounters. *JCT: Journal of Curriculum Theorizing, 21*(2), 9–24.

Moissinac, L., & Bamberg, M. (2005). "It's weird, I was so mad": Developing discursive identity defenses in conversational "small" stories of adolescent boys [Electronic version]. *Texas Speech Communication Journal, 29*(2), 142–156.

Oberg, A. (2003). Paying attention and not knowing. In E. Hasebe-Ludt & W. Hurren (Eds.), *Curriculum intertext* (pp. 123–129). New York: Peter Lang.

Pinar, W. F. (Ed.). (1999). *Contemporary curriculum discourses: 20 years of JCT*. New York: Peter Lang.

Reynolds, W. M. (2003). *Curriculum: A river runs through it*. New York: Peter Lang.

Richardson, L. (1997). *Fields of play: Constructing an academic life*. New Brunswick, NJ: Rutgers University Press.

Rolling, J. H. (2004). Figuring myself out: Certainty, injury, and the poststructuralist repositioning of bodies of identity. *The Journal of Aesthetic Education, 38*(4), 46–58.

Rolling, J. H. (2006). Who is at the city gates? A surreptitious approach to curriculum-making in art education. *Art Education, 59*(6), 40–46.

Rolling, J. H. (2008). Secular blasphemy: Utter(ed) transgressions against names and fathers in the postmodern era. *Qualitative Inquiry, 14*(6), 926–948.

Saskatchewan Education. (2002). *English language arts - A curriculum guide for the elementary level (2002)* [Online]. Retrieved July 17, 2008, from http://www.sasked.gov.sk.ca/docs/ela/introduction.html

Slattery, P. (1995). A postmodern vision of time and learning. *Harvard Educational Review, 65*(4), 612–633.

St. Pierre, E. A., & Pillow, W. (Eds.). (2000). *Working the ruins: Feminist poststructural theory and methods in education*. New York: Routledge.

Trifonas, P. P. (2005). Ourselves as another: Cosmopolitical humanities. In M. A. Peters & P. P. Trifonas (Eds.), *Deconstructing Derrida: Tasks for the new humanities* (pp. 205–220). New York: Palgrave MacMillan.

Turner, M. (1996). *The literary mind: The origins of thought and language*. Oxford, UK: Oxford University Press.

Wang, H. (2006). Speaking as an alien: Is a curriculum in a third space possible? *JCT: Journal of Curriculum Theorizing, 22*(1), 111–126.

Wang, H. (2004). *The call from the stranger on a journey home: Curriculum in a third space*. New York: Peter Lang.

DOUGLAS BROWN

FOUCAULT AND THE LURE OF THE TRANSCENDENT: CURRICULUM KNOWLEDGE, SCHOOLING, AND THE PUBLIC WORLD

POWER AND THE CURRICULUM: A CHALLENGE TO EDUCATIONAL CURRICULUM THEORISTS

Huebner and Reconceptualization

The reconceptualization of educational theory and practice has garnered widespread attention in recent decades eliciting a restive acknowledgment if not recognition from a significant corpus of educational stakeholders. Common to the reconceptualization movement has been a growing criticism of forms of "scientific reductionism" with its focus upon instrumentalist pedagogical and curricular practices (both in design and practice) promoting schooling (and in turn curriculum management) as answerable to a series of objectified practices utilizing structure and technique. The reconceptualization movement has engendered to replace narrow instrumentally reductionalist approaches to education with perspectives emphasizing the social and political complexities presented in teaching and learning situations – a move then toward the dynamic and the integration of both societal processes and lived experience (Lysaker & Goodman, 2000, p. 249).

Dwayne Huebner is credited with being one of the shaping influences in the reconceptualist movement. Huebner's earlier writings question the legitimacy of curricular decisions predicated strictly upon behavioural and so-called "scientific" rationales. Examples here are Huebner's articles "Politics and Curriculum," and "Knowledge and Curriculum". In Huebner's literature the reader is confronted with an approach linking curriculum production and dissemination to demonstrable elements of power. That is, the claim is made that curriculum by nature is political.

By the mid seventies Huebner's growing attention to power results in a more radical formulation engaging both Marx and Piaget in what he calls "genetic Marxism" (Huebner, 1981, p. 127). Again here the identification and conceptualization of power in curriculum is promoted, for "if we remember that education is a political activity… and that the school is one way to organize that power and influence, then we can try to share the control of the school and use it for our political purposes" (Huebner, 1999, p. 232). There is then a connection for Huebner between power and agency; one might argue that one invokes the other. Huebner, in "Poetry and Power," calls for action claiming, "a struggle to remake the school is a struggle to make a more just public world" (p. 232). Fear endorses inaction, for we are

P. Lewis and J. Tupper (eds.), Challenges Bequeathed: Taking up the Challenges of Dwayne Huebner, 143–160.
© 2009 sense publishers. All rights reserved.

inactive when "we are afraid to acknowledge that power makes up our centre – a power that necessarily comes up against the power of others: principals, parents, kids, board members, text writers" (p. 232). Arguably, then, discussions engaging Huebner and curriculum are discussions on power – politicized discussions – the prescripts of (Huebner) reconceptualization rejecting the claim that curriculum, and in turn learning, can be proffered on purely scientific grounds. Decades of curricular analysis and critique by the venerated author substantiates this claim, and although the specific texture and colour of that critique can and does vary (given particulars of theme as well as the point in Huebner's career when the material is produced) the power/political dynamic remains a constant.

Huebner reminds us that institutions do not have memories, humans do – that is we struggle to overcome our doubts (i.e., the fear of commitment, the risk of compromising our sense of importance, and significantly, the fear of further liability). Drawing upon Marx, Huebner introduces us to the alienation that attenuates the omnipresent disjunction between our private forms of self-identification and our public lives as educators. We are not producing a commodity. If we accept that education is a political activity, and that schools are sites of personal power, then we are less susceptible to performing functions merely as extensions of that institution (another's will to power). Huebner warns against the misinterpretation of our responsibilities as educators, to not just reinforce the call to individualism and liberal education technologies but to heed our larger public responsibilities in combating public inequities and abuses of state. (p. 233) The world of the school, of curriculum, is a public world. For power is disabling as well as enabling, with the political/agency, the requisite wisdom needed in distinguishing the difference. Thus we act to engage, and at times, alter those curricular spaces in terms of what we teach as well as why and how we teach it.

Foucault, and the Poststructural Challenge to Reconceptualization: The Question of Agency

There are, however, challenges made to reconceptualization, challenges specific to both the function and historical role of the school, and from this, the "principled" approach to educational reform. The general thrust behind a critique such as Huebner's demands we become acquainted with the function of education and the role of schooling on two fronts. One, that authentic engagement is required (to know and remake schooling in an image of our self involvement with a public world), and secondly, that we need to hold to a principle or ethic by which method and content can be remade. Systems that fail to do this (systems that answer to some internally guided initiative or prescriptive structures) are said to be "instrumental, technocratic, or managerialist." This is so as these methods, or approaches, in some way inhibit the self-reflexive road to personal development that is deemed desirable by more democratic/emancipatory understandings (Hunter, 1996, p. 146). Reformation or reconceptualization then hints of a principled response to education and schooling, in combating totalizing forces or structures (e.g., isolating aggressive market forces, state power, or some overarching narrative or value structure [e.g., positivism] that works to block democratic engagement).

Hunter, reviewing Foucault's genealogies, cautions against assumptions of higher principle (Hunter, 1996, p. 146). Hunter identifies this reciprocal relationship between power and control as contrived, questioning the notion that the modern school is or should be governed by a so called "principled approach," or even that theorists in the name of the modern school can "conduct themselves as principled persons" (p.146). For the school is not and never was the product of political struggle, democratic policies, or self-realizing classes, but rather comprises "contingent assemblages" coming together under "blind historical circumstances" (p. 146). This is based upon Foucault's assertion that both the "formation of the person" and the social uses of modern education in and of themselves are inseparable from the historical configurations of the modern school as a society construction (p. 148), as the modern school system did not assume its mass bureaucratic and disciplinary composition out of common neglect, abuses in state power, or market influences. The bureaucratization of the modern system rather integrated the prevailing exigencies of social governance and pastoral discipline (Christianity) as placed upon the post-enlightenment modern state. The modern school system then did not evolve out of a cultural current antithetical to the climate of democracy and self-realization; to the contrary in adapting "pastoral guidance" to its own uses, state schooling rendered self-realization into a disciplinary objective (p. 147). Hunter cautions us not to misinterpret the evolution of mass education under a post-enlightenment climate. Censured are both liberal and Marxist traditions relying upon a principled politic of agency and amelioration, (i.e., Huebner's primary focus upon enlightenment and action). Foucault would caution that the school has neither failed nor succeeded in this regard.

However Foucault is not finished yet. For in accepting Foucault's genealogical interpretation of Post-enlightenment schooling we accept his critique of modern power. Post-enlightenment combined the need to produce a well-tempered population (in tune with the larger security and prosperity of the new nation states) with the existing social technologies of the Christian school systems of the day.[1] Individual citizenship was thereby exchanged for compliance as highly normalized, and for the most part voluntary, subjects upheld the demands of the evolving modern state. Therefore, in issuing citizenship and a self-realized status to the modern the post-enlightenment school also retained the collective attachment of that subject. The state then looked after the "interests of the totality" while at the same time "individualizing the subject" as an extension of that totality (Corlett, 1994, p. 213). As Corlett writes in *Community Without Unity*:

> Just as the Roman Catholic church concocts pastoral power by allowing people to discover souls (which gives the church access to their innermost lives), so the modern state exercises pastoral power by allowing people to develop an individuality (which requires state interference for protection). In devising this "tricky combination" of being "both an individualizing and a totalizing form of power" the state has accomplished a most subtle domination.

And, according to Foucault, the practice of everyday life unknowingly conspires." (Corlett, 1994, p. 213)

The modern then (living, working, speaking, a sexual being) remains an object to his/herself. With Foucault the disciplinary society (facilitated through institutions like the school) comes to pass through this subtle control of the subject. What is significant here, in terms of reconceptualization, is that one should not expect the school or its agents to work in the direction of some greater humanity (or against it) when both historical purpose and function would empirically bar it from this context. The critique then is that we, as modern subject, are accustomed to identifying the state (whether through critiques on rigid curriculum structures or standardization) as a threat to self-realization and personal liberty, when in effect individual liberty and self-realization are inextricably tied to the evolution of the modern subject – the school a participating institution to this passive form of subjugation.

Thus with Foucault's understanding of genealogical power it is difficult to justify the moral accuracy, never mind ascendancy, of any reconceptualization or general principle predicated upon personal efficacy and agency. It becomes even impractical to assume that a principled response is of itself possible, as that principle is a product, historically, of, and affixed to, modern power. We then field a discussion on curriculum power, as initiated by Foucault, with no incendiary initiative, no reason to question Huebner's status quo (at least in adhering strictly to Foucault's genealogy).[2]

But if Foucault is correct and the historical development of the bureaucratic and disciplinary function of the school through modern education remains antithetical to the instruments of principled educational theory and agency, then where does that leave theorists like Huebner assuming the critical separation between the theorists and the object of critique.[3] There are two courses for action here. One is to dispel any application of absorbing Foucault's genealogy into Huebner's power/agency debate. Certainly a more tried/conventional understanding of power as it applies to schooling, in general, and curriculum in particular, will allow Huebner the social and strategic space for political action. However, there is another alternative. The so-titled poststructural critique of Foucault has something to add to the power/agency curricular debate,[4] at the very least in formulating a critique. This outcome may well be more compelling in terms of what it offers both theorist and educator. For Huebner may have more in common with Foucault than seems theoretically, or strategically, possible.

POWER AND AGENCY – THE POSTSTRUCTURAL STRUCTURAL IMPASSE AND THE CURRICULUM AS POLITICAL

Hunter admits that Foucault's work has had a limited impact on the field of educational research; arguably Foucault is a poststructuralist theorist and a substantial body of theoretical engagement has evolved within the modernist/ structuralist academic tradition. With Hunter, the educational field has been historically divided between educational psychological views that find potential dialogue and critique "functionally" integrated within the larger system itself,[5] and elements of a more "progressive," arguably better-adapted school denoting a sociological application characterized through a predilection to censure these underwriting educational practices as ill-equipped. For the sociological approach sets out to effectively identify and describe the societal imprint of schooling, particularly in explaining institutional manifestations of politics and power (1996, p. 143).

Within this sociological field of critique a further distinction highlights liberal and critical elements of theoretical engagement. Liberal approaches brandish compliance and support for an in place system (although demanding a particular vigilance in understanding and critiquing these processes), while critical approaches promise a more general disavowal of the products and processes of modern schooling – as is the case with the American-based critical pedagogy movement.

Huebner's appeal (particularly with his later writings) issues a challenge to both educator, and community, to ascribe a more critical educational path (the critical approach), and to sanction and endorse a more reflexive curricular model.[6] Thus directives in critical pedagogy, as well as British born educational phenomenology, have garnered support by curriculum theorists like Huebner intent upon seeking to better understand the alleged reproduction of oppressive social relations as fielded through patriarchy, class hegemony and racism, and it is also within this critical movement that Foucault has rendered his greatest influence on modernist theory. So, arguably, there exists the potential to reconcile these theorists. For Hunter, when Foucault has been "taken up' it is often within the critical sociological movement and by theorists like McLaren, Giroux and Kincheloe (p. 144).

While Foucault has also found a home within these fields of ethical activism, the product is not, however, without some distortion, not only in the circumscribed formulations of human capacities, but importantly, in remaining true to Foucault's contribution towards the productivity of disciplinary power.[7] It is, however, Foucault's production of disciplinary power, his emphasis upon the technical nature of the administration of schooling (independent of state and corporate power) that should prove of interest to us here. Arguably, Foucault has something to offer the curriculum theorist, as well as those whom hold a stake in the process of schooling.

Huebner asks us to consider our own ethical and political responsibilities in addressing the project of schooling, particularly where curricular interests are concerned. Foucault might well ask of us the same, although eschewing the standard emancipatory agenda instantiating the progressive elements of critique, consciousness raising, and agency.[8] For Foucault does not provide an adequate theory for either the formation of the subject within a social context, or that societal context (society).[9]

The postructural world of Foucault marks a significant departure from critical approaches (e.g. critical pedagogy) that historically centre the modern subject within a given societal context. This muddies the water somewhat (in terms of seeking a compromise) particularly given Huebner's invitation to recognizable actors (university teachers, administrators, teachers) within the educational community, focusing importance on both the role of the political, and of power in curriculum production and dissemination. Drawing on the imperative of the political Huebner (above) is said to invoke two things. The first, authentic engagement, begs the necessity of human agency (so prevalent in the emancipatory narratives of critical pedagogies), or the desire to act on the world and enact change. This assumes both a conscious self and the capacity to act. The second entails a moral imperative, or principle, from which to act; a foundational conception of morality, truth, or justice upon which such actions are predicated (Francis, 2001, p. 68).

However, many poststructuralists, and Foucault is no exception here, call into question both the fixity of self – or subject agency – and the accompanying knowledge networks by which we derive value (principled response) – or our contentions of right and wrong, inclusive of notions of personal or self-efficacy.[10] But to read something as political implies a presence or power of enacting that relationship. Foucault decries any understanding of power that of itself connotes or furthers the so-called role or hierarchy of a reason employed as agent in opposing or curbing the power of the modern state (so influential in the project of modern schooling). As Corlett writes:

> Relying on Enlightenment philosophy to curb the modern state is like putting reason in charge of itself—trusting its capacity to reach for the truth. Foucault asks: "Shall we try reason? To my mind, nothing would be more sterile." (Corlett, 1993, p. 210)

Western reason/rationality has dominated from the period of Enlightenment, articulating knowledge formats in subjugating and normalizing ways. The issue of control and domination then is not marketed in the excess and abuse of the state but rather is associated with the growth and alignment of specific knowledge forms, as that knowledge industry penetrates the lives of a population. For Foucault, control means something significantly different on the body of the modern. Traditional placements under the sovereign leadership of the king or lord sustained autocratic forms of top-down control. Recalling Hunter's objection to historical approaches that invoke some transcendental source or moral principle, we balk. For the modern, visible, hierarchical control has been usurped by a post-enlightenment "discipline" which allows us to be critical, separate, autonomous, individual, while at the same time self-regulated through facets of self-recognition and an individualizing protocol (Corlett, 1993, 210). The modern state exercises pastoral power in enabling our role as rational individuals. Certainly, for the school the task of understanding abusive power just got that much harder:

> The modern school system is not the historical creation of democratic politics or of popular political struggle. Neither, on the other hand, can it be understood as the instrument through which the aspirations of rational individuals or self realizing classes have been defeated, through the cold calculations of the state acting on behalf of an inhuman economic system. Empirically ... the school system can be neither as good as its critics wish it were, or as bad as they think it is (Hunter, 1996, p. 147).

Power then becomes relational, rationality a facet of discourse dominating Western thought and in turn "inscribed" upon the bodies of the modern with an almost moral force negotiating the polarity of chaos and order, reason and irrationality (Paechter, 2001, p. 43). Power for Foucault "is not something that is acquired, seized, or shared, something that one holds on to or allows to slip away; power is exercised from innumerable points, in the interplay of nonegalitarian and mobile relations' (Foucault 1978: 94).

But is there room for this brand of Foucault in an analysis such as Huebner's, one that endeavours to track curriculum in all its political devices in the wake of claims by the author to seek out more progressive "concepts of power" (Huebner, 1999, p. 99). For some theorist like Jurgen Habermas and Nancy Fraser, Foucault's stark and pessimistic view of the modern landscape provides little, if anything, to a debate which should be formulated, respectively, around modernist notions of communicative action, or individual need (Fraser, 1989; Hunter, 1996, p. 144). Arguably, any vision based upon such a negotiated terrain (Foucault) can only end in relativism, or worse, epistemologies underwriting political insensitivity and indifference, and thus derailing a more politically responsive and accountable curriculum.

However, these criticisms undersell the alternative, an understanding of power founded on the need for greater analytical sophistication, yes, but acknowledging the utility in ascribing to agreed upon constructs of value and/or agency required by those assembled at Huebner's "control points" of engagement. Arguably Huebner is progressively seeking such a compromise, hardly rejecting the complexity of analysis Foucault is offering, just the predetermining effects of modern power. Huebner is searching.

Recontextualizing Power

Pinar notes that, early on, Huebner is calling for an understanding of curriculum "as historical and biographical/autobiographical text," some twenty years before "other sectors of contemporary curriculum scholarship" (Pinar, 1999, p. xvii). And certainly, as reviewed above, Huebner begins a meaningful discussion of power years before it becomes fashionably employed in critical pedagogical use – structural or poststructural. In a discussion on democracy Huebner writes that "the prevailing democratic conception never quite realizes the dimensions of a political ideology, for it fails to deal with conflict and struggle and the phenomenon which resolves both – power" (Huebner, 1999, p. 16). Here there is a presence of (as Pinar notes) a power that moves beyond traditional hierarchies of interpretation moving towards a more circular and capillary presence (p. 16).

In "Politics and the Curriculum," an article released well over a decade before "Towards a Political Economy of Curriculum," Huebner is actively searching for the latency of power in curricular production and text. Searching for the implications of curricular politics in the classroom, Huebner warns against the instrumental nature of power effectively blocking meaningful contact between groups, and inhibiting classroom action. Huebner here suggests a closer examination of "action, elites, and ideologies" (p. 20). Ideologies for Huebner underwrite specified foci and concerns as the classroom assumes a political tension admitting the omnipresence of coexistent ideologies or politicized currents. For example, the ideology of a "managerial level" carries as concern the performance capacity of "the community." "Hence, in curriculum several conflicting ideologies could well exist side by side as different elites are united by, and push, different ideologies... and it behoves the educator to manoeuvre in the political arena more skilfully" (p. 20).

While much of Huebner's writing at this juncture resembled Parsons more than Foucault, one may argue for the undercurrents of a multiple power dynamic,[11] if not an embryonic cry for a theory of discourse. This sensibility, that power and knowledge are somehow more, an appeal for a greater analytic complexity, remains with Huebner as his texts evolve - the tenor becoming more prominently political in the 1970s.

Certainly, recontextualizing Huebner's appeal is not without its fascinations, despite the author's placement firmly, historically, within the modernist tradition (if for no other reason than to accommodate the theorist's desire to better understand and articulate the power/politic). And arguably an effective exposition of power is at the heart of any meaningful curriculum review – modernist or not. Here it might serve to more closely examine Huebner's understanding of power in comparison to that as generally promoted by both Marxist and liberal understandings.

Under the more conventionalized version we see power as something that can be quantified, a commodity possessed by one to be imposed or used against another. In a classroom situation this power can then accommodate the will of another, can be used in both legitimate and illegitimate/repressive formats and in turn alter or in other cases suspend the formation of student beliefs. Here the power of the institution is turned outwards away from the specifics of the everyday towards a wider agency. For traditional liberal approaches, then, one may extol some form of contract theory (Marshall, 1989, p. 101), for more critical schools, predicated on neo-Marxist, or post-Marxist prescripts, there might be some mention of a prevailing overriding structure and an accompanying ideological or hegemonic network.

Huebner, consistently in his later writings, applauds vigilance in tracking and decoding hierarchical power regimes, or what is deemed the "controlling functions inherent in institutionalized educational structures" (Huebner, 1981, p. 126). For Huebner the task of these macroanalyses is to "point out the masking function of much past and present curricular language that proclaims the school's presumed role in "self-realization" and a more perfect "democratic" society. Arguably such criticism is engaged with the quest of exposing historical abuses of curricular power at the hands of those most privileged in sequestering, designing and disseminating classroom knowledge.

However, as alluded to above, Huebner's writings also indicate a willingness to follow these configurations back inward to the location of the teacher and/or student, in terms of how localized power is unpacked, and how curriculum is received and employed at the micro level. Huebner's interest with the local can engender a reading that credits the theorist with the desire to advance conventional understandings of curriculum, society, and state past the macro, past a straight materialist critique. Huebner in "Towards a Political Economy of Curriculum and Human Development" quotes Joel Kovel, noting that Marxism generally has not been used to explore the "micro aspects of education – the interpersonal or intersubjective." This is so principally because Marx found it necessary to bracket the subjective in the task to explain objective phenomena while unveiling a concern "with only those aspects of human life that could be objectified and hence become a commodity" (Huebner, 1981, p. 126). While there is sufficient controversy here to dedicate further discussion,[12] Huebner's purpose, it seems, is to draw attention to the "micro aspects" of education, or what he deems the interpersonal and intersubjective (p. 127).[13] Huebner identifies Piaget and the "different definitions of knowledge structures" claiming we can no longer see knowledge as a finished form.

Despite the theorist's intention of adhering to specific interpretations of subject and society that are relatively fixed, in fact prescriptive,[14] Huebner advocates a need to examine the micro-networking of power, particularly as it affects the production and assimilation of knowledge. It is not as if Huebner rejects macroanalyses predicated upon a critique of political economy, but rather finds a need to put a finer point on that analysis. Censure is extended to schools of thought, such as behaviourism, scientific management and positivism, which do not effectively do either, schools that subscribe to a fixed and totalizing underwriting curriculum ethic (at the expense of more than the personal). For it remains imperative to not only question the role of the state/educational apparatus and its role in reproducing or underwriting a specific version of the world around us, but the procedural requirements of teaching and learning itself, that is what structure or discipline is required for a student or teacher to formulate a true or acceptable proposition under the teacher/learner relationship. We have here a demand, and analyses, on power that moves beyond the macro, past society as structure, moving towards a use and interpretation that stresses the importance of culture, of the intersubjective. However is this far enough, that is, what are our options if we wish to reconcile Huebner with Foucault? A closer examination of Foucault's understanding of power/knowledge, language, and ultimately, discourse, will help.

Power/Knowledge and the Role of Discourse

In the development of poststructural thought Foucault stands apart from many others in that he anchors facets of his epistemology in the world of structural relations. That is, Foucault does not talk about an "extra-discursive" order as primary, that is where discourse bankrolls a system through which meaning and momentary order is brought to the world. For Foucault, both "discourses and institutions are fixed by the power relations inherent to them" (Craib, 1992, p. 186). Taking leadership from Nietzsche, power becomes knowledge, knowledge itself inseparable from power while concomitantly issuing a power over others – the power to define others. Our worlds are thus contrived, products "of a myriad of power relations" (p. 186), while at the same time engendering resistance and the ensuing struggle over that power/knowledge configuration.

Arguably Foucault's treatment stands in historic opposition to conventional understandings of knowledge (that is the use of knowledge as a commodity) of itself allowing us to do things we could not do in its absence – or a truth.[15] For Foucault:

> Truth is a thing of this world: it is produced only by virtue of multiple forms of constraint. And it induces regular effects of power. Each society has its regime of truth, its 'general politics' of truth: that is, the types of discourse which it accepts and makes function as true; the mechanisms and instances which enable one to distinguish true and false statements, the means by which each is sanctioned; the techniques and procedures accorded value in the acquisition of truth; the status of those who are charged with saying what counts as true. (Foucault, 1980, p. 131)

Truths then are carried through discourses and discourses wield power by constructing ideas, and objects in different ways (Francis, 2001, p. 67). The self, or what we would call a self, is positioned in discourse. Therefore we can be positioned in differing ways at differing times as we simultaneously exercise and undergo power. Power is capillary, not hierarchical. Power is relational and benign, it is not insidious or autocratic; we all exercise and feel the effects of it. For Foucault, the internal discipline we exercise is underwritten by the institutions we build around ourselves; reinforced by the knowledge that gives those institutions legitimacy and identity.

With Foucault, disciplines are both knowledge regimes and physical spaces by which we alter, in time, power relationships, communication, and individual capacities and abilities (Marshall, 1989, p. 105).[16] The initiation of specific disciplines however requires some form of control or power, and here we are directed to the function of knowledge as an instrument of power. In Foucault's case we are talking about a subtle and relatively unobtrusive mechanism, or the post-enlightenment imposition of the human sciences (knowledge and process) discussed above. Knowledge of this type both legitimates and underwrites power networks. The power may be our own to change it, or at least our part of it, but it requires questioning our own notions of truth.[17] In the formal educational setting students and faculties exist within physical structures penetrated by modern discourse as specific skills and abilities are fashioned.

Think of a shift away from coercive measures in schools to disciplines that reinforce the more liberalized methodology of modern schooling and the emergent focus upon normalization and rehabilitation.[18] Power in this fashion is not overt and punishing in violent ways, that is compliance is not initiated through force or intimidation.[19] Power does not act upon a belief or ideology, but upon our action. Activities and timetable are constructed and citizens are formed. Our social sensibilities, or deeper reflective impulses on justice, the environment, and human value, inform subject constructs that are modern, critical, and empathetic. The result is a subject type carved out of the processes of modern power – the modern – a kind and politically astute individual that engages a plethora of issues and causes because it is the right, the rational, thing to do. This form of power maintains the so-called humanity of the other as that individual is always recognized and maintained to the very end as a person who acts – a citizen (Marshall, 1989, p. 104). Moreover power is used and distributed by agents whom are often quite unaware of its use and presence. We draw on networks of knowledge that legitimate our profession, and more importantly, initiate regimes that draw on forms of self-regulation, with justification (legitimating) provided through post-enlightenment reason (in the form of the human sciences). These regimes are both narrow and broad and although they are not dominant in any hierarchical form (knowledge/power regimes can always be contradicted and contested by other discourses) discourses are intimately embedded in power relations, as some discourses are more powerful than others; one is not free simply to choose which discourse one wishes to operate in.[20]

The body can therefore function as a battleground as the effects of discourse are palpable as well as linguistic. For Paechter the discourses by which we operate register at visceral levels. "For example, the discourse of the good quiet girl, instantiated for example in the widely held belief that girls are less boisterous than boys from birth, actively constrains the ways in which young girls are able to use their bodies" (Paechter, 2001, p. 43). For Foucault this social technology (technology of power) is used in conjunction with historical criteria – but make no mistake - modern power is employable and effective because it works. Any caveat Huebner has regarding the political nature of school curriculum is supported here, as knowledge/power networks are both insidious and totalizing.[21] Thus day-to-day curriculum and pedagogies often avoid critical review and critique given the insidious nature of the mechanisms of power going uncontested, even at individualized sites.[22] Schools of intellectual thought reject alternative visions, some a vision at all. We regulate ourselves. For Paechter:

> Foucauldian poststructuralism, because of its emphasis on the distributed and resisted nature of power, also forces us to focus on the ways in which power operates, and in particular on the ways in which we are ourselves seduced into accepting what are in some respects oppressive power relations. (Paechter, 2001, p. 46)

Power as it acts upon our bodies is not to be understood as something negative or even oppressive; some aspects of power are "profoundly pleasurable;" we are caught in its networks precisely because some aspects of the exercise and experience of power are pleasurable (Foucault, 1980).

Discourse then is inextricably tied in with the processes of schooling, as both student and teacher alike conforms to power's normalizing influences. Gore notes that as teachers we regulate and condition students through the very "progressive" practices we employ in the classroom (Gore, 1993, p. 57).[23] That is when we test a student we do more than either may know or understand. We firstly normalize this individual, rearranging environments into techniques s/he will acquire as discipline in the future, as that person is enroute to becoming a self-governed individual. By assigning a person a mark you objectify that person – as belonging to that mark – offering a subject role to the owner of that mark. For Foucault, subjectivity is created in this manner, as the body assumes layers of disciplinary power. Addressing the science classroom Paechter (2001) notes that:

> It is not enough to say that science is a set of procedures by which propositions may be falsified, errors demonstrated, myths demystified, etc. Science also exercises power: it is, literally, a power that forces you to say certain things, if you are not to be disqualified not only as being wrong, but, more seriously than that, as being a charlatan. (2001, p. 42).

The game of critique and reflexivity then may be more complicated than we originally thought. Certainly Foucault does offer us something here, although, at times his approach may be somewhat formulaic.[24] However, for Foucault (Foucault's epistemology) there exists an uncertainty concerning agency, that is, our ability to act independently of the social mechanisms that surround us. We are positioned in discourse, self-regulating, our claim to subjectivity, to independence and critical insight, historically carved out of the very substance that we serve to control. Then is the analytical sophistication of Foucault at odds with the general ethic of criticism, remaining cognizant of Huebner's mission to open-up, to reveal, to critically appraise the process of curriculum production and administration? That is, can we at most, use Foucault as critique or method by which to deconstruct and reposition the curriculum debate? I have argued above that Huebner has much to offer both theorist and educator. However, there remains the substantive issue surrounding the matter of reconceptualization, that is agency, or the process by which educators/students may become empowered – issue of the authentic and principled response. Foucault calls into question specific assumptions on modern power. The poststructural criticism (e.g., Gore, Ellsworth) criticism of "critical action" in general, and ultimately of agency, resides visibly in the background compromising what is left over. That is the charge that "emancipatory" theories consistently address issues of empowerment in "ahistorical and depoliticized abstractions." "For how can I unproblematically bring subjugated knowledge to light when I am not free of my own" (Ellsworth, 1992, p. 99). The issue of the political, of agency, remains just that.

REVISITING THE QUESTION OF AGENCY

Huebner acknowledges the importance in recognizing that power/knowledge configurations incorporate both macro and micro dimensionality. For curriculum is not just something done to learners via the forces of state through bureaucratically complicit components, but something learners engage in, at capillary levels, building and articulating meaning about their sense of self and the world around them. The author's attempt to meld elements of Piaget to Marx signifies this seriousness. With Huebner, we have to learn to interpret curriculum as a politicized component in schooling. We need to act in deconstructing the multitude of ways that power permeates the process of schooling. Huebner notes that it is a lack of clarity about our public world, the world around us that engenders a lack of clarity and vision about the school (Huebner, 1999, p. 232). We have to understand who we are and how we got that way. Arguably neither Foucault nor Marx would deny the importance of these historical antecedents. For Huebner, "progressive concept of power suggests that because teachers, administrators, college and university teachers, and non-professionals have different control points or different types of decisions and sanctions, they might also need quite different ideologies" (p.99). For whether we find ourselves suspended within discourse or foundationally embedded and interpolated through our material surroundings, there exists a need for vigilance. As Gore asserts empowerment must occur in sites of practice (Gore, 1992, p. 66).

With Foucault, liberating power denotes an ethical commitment to breaking down the disciplinary practices of regulation and surveillance. Thus curriculum planning and implementation or critique, as the case may be, represents an act on the part of teacher and student to question. To question "regimes of truth," method of valuing, ways of thinking and acting that are downloaded and engaged at the level of the body. For Marxist inspired critical pedagogies the call is to identify and clarify systems of abuse while acting to end the contributory structures in that oppression. We must work towards material change through culturally inspired and articulated challenges.

However, these are dramatically different methodologies. Poststructuralists point towards the need for critical pedagogy to overcome the relative fixity of the truth discourse (truth claim). Grand narratives, or forms of transcendental signification that engender a confidence in the inborn rightness of an act or belief culturally impose subject positions and social technologies (ways of being and doing) upon administrators, curriculum writers, teachers and student. This can result in misinterpretation, reification, and cultural rigidity. Oversignification can also contribute to forms of oppression. For example, Francis points out that feminists may be in possession of their own power yet the movement may actually act in ways that oppresses others, as:

> It means little to thread a discourse on empowerment in sweeping maxims. By couching student empowerment in broad humanistic terms we fail to focus upon identifiable events, situations or groups in "contortions" of rhetoric (as highlighted above) which are dictorial and paternalistic. (Francis, 2001, p. 67)

For Foucault the challenge lies elsewhere, viz., in overcoming the totalizing effects of post-enlightenment power. For how can we set out to change something when our actions themselves are subject to review? Unfortunately, as indicated above, the failure to identify and isolate institutions of abuse or oppression, as existing within a given context, can lead to forms of relativism and inaction (e.g., on what basis can one formulate a class analysis or gender critique, or even justify the impulse for social change).

So can we resolve the disenfranchising tendencies of a postructural approach like Foucault's with Huebner's call for action, the diktat that curriculum decisions are ostensibly political decisions? Certainly Foucault's understanding of the complex networking of power could prove invaluable in reviewing power/knowledge configurations at micro-levels, or explaining multiple power positioning (Francis, 2001, p. 69). To accomplish this, some advocate that discourse be weighed, in terms of residual dominance and effect, a method of microanalytical accounting so to speak. The advantage of identifying the more dominant and destructive discourses then is couched in an expectation that these discourses are potentially reformable (for example by introducing a fairer curriculum thrust in a program dramatically driven by Eurocentric values). However the residing assumption here is that we are still somehow capable of standing back and ascribing value, or principle, within the flow of modern discourse.

Rorty argues that Foucault is not so different than Dewey only that his take on resistance (and in turn effective action) is more pessimistic (as cited in Marshall, 1989, p. 108). But this is problematic, as Dewey's remedies take place within the post-enlightenment rational/liberal framework (as above), a framework that we must escape (and yet cannot) to mount a serious attack on the power/knowledge nexus. Gore entertains a compromise; that although post-enlightenment power/knowledge is totalizing, we can chip away – through self-engagement and review of the self – at the "cracks and gaps" of our own (e.g., as teachers), arguably oppressive, "regimes of truth" (Gore, 1993, p. 135). Foucault agrees, stressing vigilance in combating the crippling effects of modern discourse while adding, if "everything is dangerous then we always have something to do" (as cited in Gore, 1993, p. 136).

For Foucault makes it clear that he is not attempting to supplant other approaches to the politics of the everyday (e.g., the broader theories of social control, legitimization and state power). It is defensible to accept the notion of micro-power, of modern power as carried through the disciplines of the human sciences, without subscribing to their totalizing influence or pre-eminence.

Mentioned above, Foucault anchors his understanding of post-renaissance power in his own genealogy, in turn marking specific historical or material events and relationships. Hunter articulates this. Thus Foucault argues for a power/knowledge nexus, an understanding that moves away (in kind) from the crippling influences of hierarchical, top-down, coercive power systems – although he is willing to make exceptions. However, we might question the totalizing effect of a modern power in a Western world still heavily under the influence of material/economic regimes, relations of production, class legitimating and social domination. As is achieved in Jameson's text *Postmodernism,* one can argue that the material continues to play a contributory role in the modern cultural architecture, and we can do so effectively without surrendering up Foucault's larger epistemology or ethical framework (Jameson, 1997, p. 50). If 9-11 has taught us anything, as theorists, it is that modernism is not dead, and that coercive power can still relegate, displace and violate at the level of the everyday – in school and out.

FOUCAULT AND THE LURE OF THE TRANSCENDENT

Francis notes that, undeniably, outstanding issues of class, gender, and race impact us at micro-levels, even given an understanding that these issues are not of themselves an evil and that, arguably, there remains little reason as to why these influences should be ignored. Foucault notes that capillary power is also the power to resist. Francis adds that, it seems entirely plausible to assume that human power relations might be as equally "complex and contradictory" as the discourses that employ them (Francis, 2001, p. 71). It is contentious to suggest that modern educational critique must engage only one theoretical schematic at the expense of another. Certainly, Huebner has not avoided multiple perspectives in the past. After all, it is Huebner's richly variegated criticism of overtly proprietary/managerial forms of curriculum coordination that initiates this discussion. Arguably, Foucault has something to add to any debate that serves to inform public reason in conflating social mechanisms of predictability and control. The application of Foucault (particularly his understandings of power/knowledge) offers the curriculum theorist something else – another contributory conceptual set of tools in a growing tapestry of educational political engagement and critique.[25] In doing so we adhere to Huebner's desire for a more sophisticated mechanism of appraisal. Emphasizing a dedication to vision and clarity, Huebner might argue, the curricular theorist is left little choice but to stay the course.

NOTES

[1] Foucault is primarily addressing Western or European genealogies here, an approach of itself problematic to some.

[2] Is a narrative emancipatory if a theorist cannot find an epistemological platform independent of modernizing power from which to launch never mind substantiate a moral principle? Theorists would argue that Foucault himself provides the space for such a critique through the "ethics of the self" and this possibility will be taken up later.

[3] Foucault emphasizes that we have no life of our own outside this hegemonic order. Our understanding of culture, our social practices are the products of various technologies of power inclusive of dialectical positions and habits of mind.

[4] It is important to remember that a large body of Huebner's work was drafted in advance of the poststructural/postmodernist challenge to structuralism.

[5] Included here are many of the behavioural and positivist approaches Huebner calls into question as being overtly reductionist

[6] Early on in his writing Huebner may well have been associated with the liberal camp noting that both theory and theorists evolve or adapt to theoretical challenges.

[7] Hunter notes that it is at Foucault's criticism of an emancipatory discourse that, ironically, is incorporated into the critical theorist's emancipatory project. It is Foucault's critique of the "interdependency of power and knowledge" then that is used to critique the primacy of capitalism, patriarchy and racism.

[8] Redress, then, is forthcoming in resistance to class disparity, racism or patriarchy - products of top-down state sanctioned institutions of social domination.

[9] Specific modernist interpretations like psychoanalysis, phenomenology, or historical materialism endorse an understanding of self and society that avail detailed examinations of both self and society. That is these theories recognize the inherency of personhood as a formulated self and by extension a society composed of those actors (Hunter, 1996, p. 144).

[10] The ideals underpinning "Grand Narratives" denote a power relationship that assumes the right and wrong of specific acts. But these foundational concepts of morality require deconstruction as claims to right are predicated upon prior assumptions (discourses), for example, the primacy of reason.

[11] Talcott Parsons, an American Sociologist is perhaps best known for his production of a general theoretical system known as Structural Functionalism. An advocate of "grand theory" Parsons attempted to integrate the social sciences, as well as the output of many of his predecessors, in an explanatory approach of categorization and predictability.

[12] For Morrow, Marxist inspired critiques like critical theory attempt to move beyond strict economist interpretations acknowledging the importance of culturally inspired readings. Critical theory then stresses "the increasing superstructural dominance characteristic of late capitalism as a crucial aspect of the incorporation of the working class," as it furthers the partial abandonment of more extreme theses regarding the 'one—dimensionality—' of modern culture. With Morrow, structuralist Marxism has effectively "popularized hyperfunctionalist theories of cultural reproduction" while theorists working out of the Frankfurt tradition (e.g. Frederick Jameson, Stanley Aronowitz, Alvin Gouldner, Habermas, etc.) have focused upon various tensions existing at the level of culture (i.e., cultural production and methods of resistance or emancipatory processes). Comparable developments have evolved in the British tradition of cultural Marxism (Raymond Williams, E.P. Thompson), Gramscian inspired projects of cultural theory, and Goldmann's genetic structuralism. (Morrow, 1985, p. 16).

[13] Unfortunately the focus remains upon the relative indelibility and at times transparency of self and society.

[14] Walkerdine in her deconstruction of Piaget and his theories in developmental psychology examines the "discursive positioning" of females (teachers and students) in schools. Walkerdine notes that the genetic epistemology of Piaget is incomplete in addressing significant issues of power and identity (e.g., as played out in the formation and the regulation of female sexuality). (Lather, 1992, p. 123)

[15] Foucault's work tends to be focused in three domains – a genealogy of power, an archaeology of knowledge, and an ethics of the self.

[16] The modern classroom might be a nice fit here.

[17] Including beliefs in emancipatory power. Remember these are not principled truths but discourses suspended in post-enlightenment relations of power/knowledge.

[18] The education of the whole child introduces dimensions of health, sexuality, and moral education; foci usually supported by school faculty and staff.

[19] Marshall notes that power here must be distinguished from violence in that violence merely breaks, closing the door to all possibility. (Marshall, 1989, p. 104)

[20] Foucault understands discourse as an organized complex of statements, terms, categories and beliefs structured in relation to historical, social and institutional specificities (Scott, 1988, p. *35*). Discourses appear and affect the nature of the body, mind and the emotional life of subjects.

[21] Although a differing form of politic.

[22] This includes school programs on social justice and radical pedagogy.

[23] Is a circular seating arrangement superior to alternative configurations or merely a preference of method, particularly if students through the process sacrifice privacy as opened up to the gaze of the other. (Gore, 1993, p. 57)

[24] Dreyfus and Rabinow never hesitate to call Foucault a structuralist, claiming his Archaeology of the Human Sciences conformed well "under the influence of structuralist enthusiasm sweeping Paris" at the time. (Dreyfus and Rabinow, 1983, p. 16)

[25] This is not to validate the "pick and choose" approach so prevalent in many critical pedagogical applications.

REFERENCES

Brown, D. (2004). *A review of the role of culture and cultural identity in the new Alberta social studies curriculum*. Unpublished Doctoral Dissertation, University of Alberta, Edmonton, Alberta, Canada.

Corlett, W. (1993). *Community without unity*. Durham, NC: Duke University Press.

Craib, I. (1992). *Modern social theory: From Parsons to Habermas* (2nd ed). New York: St. Martin's Press.

Dei, G., et al. (2000). *Removing the margins: The challenges and possibilities of inclusive schooling*. Toronto, ON: Canadian Scholar's Press.

Dreyfus, H., & Rabinow, P. (1983). *Michel Foucault beyond structuralism and hermeneutics*. Chicago: University of Chicago Press.

Ellsworth, E. (1992). Why doesn't this feel empowering? Working through the repressive myths of critical pedagogy. In C. Luke, & J. Gore (Eds.), *Feminisms and critical pedagogy* (pp. 90–119). New York: Routledge.

Foucault, M. (1978). *The history of sexuality, volume one*. Harmondsworth: Penguin.

Foucault, M. (1979). *Discipline & punishment: The birth of the prison*. New York: Vintage Books.

Foucault, M.(1980). *Power/knowledge*. New York: Pantheon Books.

Francis, B. (2001). Beyond postmodernism: Feminist agency in educational research. In B. Francis & C. Skelton (Eds.), *Investigating gender: Contemporary perspectives in education* (pp. 65–76). Philadelphia: Open University Press.

Gore, J. (1992). What we can do for you! What can 'we' do for 'you'? Struggling over empowerment in critical and feminist pedagogy. In C. Luke, & J. Gore (Eds.), *Feminisms and critical pedagogy* (pp. 54-73). New York: Routledge.

Gore, J. (1993). *The struggle for pedagogies*. New York: Routledge, Chapman and Hall.

Huebner, D. (1981). Towards a political economy of curriculum and human development. In H. Giroux, A. Penna, & W. Pinar (Eds.), *Curriculum & instruction: Alternatives in education* (pp. 125–138). Berkeley, CA: MrCutchan Publishing.

Huebner, D. (1999). *The lure of the transcendent: Collected essays by Dwayne E. Huebner* (V. Hillis, Ed.). Mahwah, NJ: Lawence Erlbaum Associates.

Hunter, I. (1996). Assembling the school. In A. Barry, T. Osborne, & N. Rose (Eds.), *Foucault and political reason* (pp. 143–166). Chicago: University of Chicago Press.

Jameson, F. (1997). *Postmodernism*. Durham, NC: Duke University Press.

Lather, P. (1992). Post-critical pedagogies: A feminist reading. In C. Luke, & J. Gore (Eds.), *Feminisms and critical pedagogy* (pp. 120–137). New York: Routledge.

Lysaker, J., & Goodman, J. (2000). Conceptualizing reconceptualist theory and practice in literacy teacher education. *Curriculum Inquiry, 30*(2), 249–260.

Marshall, J. (1989). Foucault and education. *Australian Journal of Education, 33*, 2.

McLaren, P. (2003). *Life in schools: An introduction to critical pedagogy in the foundations of education*. Toronto: Irwin, ISBN 0-582-28683-2, 258 p., pp. 25–70.

Misgeld, D. (1988). Education and cultural invasion: Critical social theory, education as instruction, and the 'Pedagogy of the Oppressed'. In J. Forester (Ed.), *Critical Theory and public life*. Cambridge: MIT Press.

Morrow, R. (1985). Critical theory and critical sociology. *Canadian Review of Sociology & Anthropology, 22*, 5.

Nietzsche, F. (1990). *The birth of tragedy & the genealogy of morals*. New York: Anchor Books.

O'Neill, J. (1988). Decolonozation and the ideal speech community. In J. Forester (Ed.), *Critical theory and public life* (pp. 57–76). Cambridge: MIT Press.

Paechter, C. (2001). Using poststructuralist ideas in gender theory and research. In B. Francis & C. Skelton (Eds.), *Investigating gender: Contemporary perspectives in education* (pp. 41–51). Philadelphia: Open University Press.

Payne, M. (1997). *Reading knowledge: An introduction to Barthes, Foucault, and Althusser.* Oxford: Blackwell.

Ransom, J. (1997). *Foucault's discipline.* London: Duke University Press.

Scott, J. (1988). Deconstructing equality-versus difference: Or, the uses of poststructuralist theory for feminism. *Feminist Studies, 14*(1), 33–50.

Smart, B. (1995). *Michel Foucault.* New York: Routledge.

HEATHER RITENBURG

ENCOUNTERING HOPE – TEN MEDITATIONS TOWARDS UTOPIA IN A PHD PROGRAM

This chapter is written as a series of meditations through which I offer you the opportunity to heed Huebner's (1996/1999) call to affirm the significance of the imagination. The meditations are grounded in my vision of hope emerging as curricular spaces are opened to arts-based imaginings.

I invite you to engage with the meditations to create an evocative knowing as opposed to simply reading them for declarative knowledge. Meditations 1 to 4 will move us into exile as we encounter Huebner's (1975/1997) questioning cry, "Why do we move around so frantically?" (p. 130). Meditations 5 and 6 will encourage us to consider a myriad of dreams and imaginings. It is here that I encourage you to pause in your reading to contemplate any educational dreams or imagined utopias the meditations may evoke. In meditations 7 and 8, I share my vision of hope imagined – where it is that I feel held and hopeful in shaping an educational future. And as we ground and connect our hopes in meditations 9 and 10, I trust that my vision will hold a place alongside your vision in, as Huebner (1975/1997) says, "the conscious shaping of the future" (p. 132).

> We lack an educational poetry which stirs the imagination and harnesses our power. (Huebner, 1975/1997, p. 132)

I felt as though I was weighed down at the bottom of the deep end of a pool, near enough to the surface to see light and murky human shapes, but far enough away to feel a growing panic that I might not make it back to the surface.

I peered around the seminar table. I was surrounded by disembodied, muffled voices discussing issues in curriculum studies. I struggled to hear what was being said. I was overcome by feelings of despair at the painful tensions and pulls I was experiencing as the course confronted me – as I confronted myself – as I encountered curriculum through complicated and complicating discourses of gender, culture, race and colonialism.

I wonder why I am here. Why now.

> "Why do we move around so frantically...? Why do we not comport ourselves in such a manner that our center – our sense of who we are and what we are about – can be restored and reformed? Why do we not pause to feel the painful tensions and pulls in us, which are reflections of the tensions and pulls of our society?" (Huebner, 1975/1997, p. 130)

Huebner's questions resonate deep with/in me – spiritually, intellectually, philosophically through my being. As a first-year doctoral student in education curriculum studies, I feel painful tensions and pulls. Tensions pulled me to doctoral studies. Yet I move frantically between classes – pulled between assignments and commitments and expectations and . . . posts. Painful pullings between posts – post modernisms, post structuralisms, post feminisms, post colonialisms. . . .

I hear Huebner's (1996/1999) call for the affirmation of the significance of the imagination and heed it as a simultaneous call *to* imagine – to invoke an 'educational poetry' of a future reimagined and imagined into being.

I catch a lull in the conversation.

I lift my eyes and meet those of my colleagues.

I begin to cry.

MEDITATION #1: TEARS TO STILLNESS

The moments we live either are instants in a process previously inaugurated, or else they inaugurate a new process referring in some way to something in the past. (Freire, 1994, p. 27)

My tears mark the moments that Freire honours as inaugural moments in life – those moments that beckon and whisper - *look . . . listen . . . feel . . . breathe.*

To Freire, every moment holds possibility as forever connected and forever connecting.

Look now, I remind myself. *Listen with the future. Feel into the past.*

Remember to breathe.

Remember to breathe.

Remember to breathe.

I struggle in the inbetweens,[1] and my tears mark the moments that bring me to a standstill - to a still/stand.

Stay. ( ) Stay. ( ) Stay. ( )

Stay in your body.

Stay in your body.

In damp staying I return to myself. The tears welcome me when in the searching out are no . . . more . . . answers. In wetness they slide me to a stop placing the brakes on action, momentum, the exhausting ongoing that directs (my) (me) life.

"*No one goes anywhere alone,*" Freire continues, "*least of all into exile.*"[2] We go with our whole self: passion, longing, sadness, hope, desire, dreams in smithereens but not abandoned, knowledge stored in the countless fabrics of living experience, availability for life, fears and terrors, doubts, a will to live and love. Hope, especially.[3]

MEDITATION #2: TO A STILL/STAND

This course will consider issues central to the [under/standing] of curriculum as it relates to current educational settings. (Tupper, 2007)

Egan	**Pinar**
Aoki	**Huebner**
Chambers	**Hasebe-Ludt**
Hurren	**Fowler**
Ellis	**Said**
Kanu	**Donald**
Tang	**Jardine**
Cajete	**Ermine**
Gazeta	**Kafala**
Cary	**Sumara**
Davis	**Laidlaw**
Grumet	**Stone**
Miller	**O Donoghue**
Tupper	**Johnston**
Schick	**St. Denis**
Cappello	**Britzman**
Kinsman	**Davis**
Loutzenheiser	

I
UU
IIIIII
UUUU
IIIIII
UU
I U
IUIUIUIUIUIUIUIUIUIUIUI's

MEDITATION #3: INTO EXILE

(in movement)

*Pull Slice
Recover*

*Pull Slice
Recover*

*Pull Slice
Recover*

*Sudden open long
Sudden focus L
Sudden focus recover R*

*Close L up
Focus forward*

*Sustained L
AST hand nears*

*Sustained fwd
AST hand rotates parallel*

Sustained R to chest

*Sudden pulse
into
Vibration*

*Side with fists,
Back resume pulse,
Side with fists,
Front opening hands*

Inhale

Exhale

Inhale

Exhale

(relax arms/drop head/relax body))

MEDITATION #4: IN EXILE

Stay.

( )

*If we ask where and what kind of place is the place of hope,
then one answer might be utopia.*[4]

Stay.

( )

Utopias encourage us to ask and answer the question, "for what may I hope?"[5]

Stay.

( )

*What follows is a tentative course outline
tentative because we can never predict those unexpected moments
that arise, causing us to detour on our journey.
Very often these detours present opportunities for learning and reflection
that might not have emerged had we stuck rigidly to the schedule.*[6]

Stay.

( )

MEDITATION #5: PERCHANCE TO DREAM

Utopia has literary, religious, political, scientific, technological and economic meanings as well as historical and cultural resonances.[7]

Consider *Plato's Republic*, Francis Bacon's *The New Atlantis*, Huxley's *Brave New World*, and Hilton's Shangri-La in *Lost Horizon*. Consider John Lennon's *Imagine* and Lois Lowry's *The Giver*.[8]

Consider the utopian social movement of the early nineteenth century triggered by the development of commercialism and capitalism. Consider capitalist utopias based on imagined market economies. Consider the dreams underpinning the utopia lived out as dictatorship. Consider the dreams nurturing the utopia of global world peace.[9]

Consider the Christian, Jewish and Muslim ideas of the Garden of Eden. And Heaven. And Hell. Consider the Buddhist concept of Nirvana. Consider the Shaker movement. Consider the utopian dreams of a better life driving science and technology such as the absence of death and suffering, reproductive imaginings, and unending Jetson-like leisure.[10]

Consider cultural utopias based on constructed memories of a distant past of instinctive harmony between humankind and nature – the Greek Golden Age, the Biblical Garden of Eden, indigenous traditional ways and cultures.[11]

Consider the Simple Living movement. Consider urban planning. Consider learning environments. Consider curriculum reform. Curriculum development. Curriculum bandwagons.[12] Consider curriculum . . . curriculum spaces[13]. . . curriculum intertext.[14]

Curriculum IntoText
Place & Space/Colonial Discourse/
Ecological and Indigenous Perspectives/Postmodernism /
Gendered Discourse/Cultural and Racial Discourse /
Queer Theory/Autobiography[15]

MEDITATION #6: PERCHANCE TO HOPE

There is no change without dream, as there is no dream without hope. (Freire, 1994, p. 91)

A society's education entails (in all senses) its future. To allow the utopian imagination to become so stunted that the practices and contents of its teaching carry no message to the future about its emancipation, nor hold out . . . a promise of happiness, is only to ensure that the future society will be an awful one. (Inglis as cited in Sawyer, Singh, Woodrow, Downes, Johnston and Whitton, 2007, p. 227)

Utopia has social, psychological, spiritual, aesthetic, educational and curricular meanings as well as ecological, radical, courageous and playful possibilities.

Consider utopianism as "a distinctive vocabulary of hope."[16]

Consider utopianism as "a distinctive vocabulary of hope [that] teaches us that society . . . [is] both imagined and made and that we can accordingly believe [it] can be reimagined and remade."[17]

Consider hope as characterized by a sense of time as open.[18]

Consider "a robust hope [that] recognizes and acknowledges obstacles and provides a context for meeting and dealing with them."[19]

Consider "Richard Kearney's suggestion that the different meanings ascribed to the imagination can be understood to bear what Wittgenstein describes as 'family resemblances'. . . . that [unite] each type of imagining [as] the ability of the imagining body to offer possibilities of existence."[20]

Consider possibilities of existence "once we do away with habitual separations of the subjective from the objective, the inside from the outside, appearances from reality, [when] we might be able to give imagination its proper importance and grasp what it means to place imagination at the core of understanding."[21]

I consider how utopian possibilities might be subverted by a "currently fashionable pragmatism . . . which insists that 'good' utopias must be realistic and practical"[22] thereby implying a utopian function that provides alternatives that can be mined for short term change.[23] I consider how Huebner must have despaired the pragmatic as he admonished any re-imagination of education if it entailed the creation of new language, new practice, new resources or new buildings[24] "as if they were the given's with which we have to work."[25]

I imagine utopia as less a form of representation and more a journey in which time is open and ordering is suspended.[26]

I close my eyes and I/eye imagine.

My I's/eyes open.

MEDITATION #7: IN HOPE PERCHANCE TO IMAGINE

Hope can arrive only when you recognize that there are real options and that you have genuine choices. (Groopman as cited in Sawyer et al, 2007, p. 230)

The imagination "works surreptitiously and quietly" (p. 162), and it is in the silent recollection and contemplation of what has been learnt or experienced that the imagination goes most effectively to work. (Warnock as cited in Egan, 1992, p. 158)

Lisa Cary holds me when she states, "*The way we know what we know* is a curriculum issue – a Curriculum Space."[27]

I am held in the philosophy of the Arts Education curriculum developed in Saskatchewan, Canada in the early 1980s.[28] And in the philosophy and practice of the Arts Education Program at the University of Regina.[29] [30] Imagined, emergent curriculum spaces.

Of the many things I know and believe the arts to be, they are ways of knowing. With, in, through and as the arts, I come to know myself, and you, and the world in ways that are possible only of the arts. The arts are for everyone, they are of everyone, we all are arts.

In these early days of doctoral studies I imagine into possibility. I unbind and deframe historic and cultural constructions in the arts. I set aside for a time the western world's obsession with pedestals and boundaries. I disregard the power-hungry questions of "what is art" and "who is an artist." I am more interested in what is possible as I imagine myself in(to) curricular spaces where people "[do] not split the artistic from the functional, the sacred from the secular, art from everyday life."[31]

It is life. It/art/life.

I feel held.

I feel hopeful.

MEDITATION #8: IMAGINE ANEW

Hope can flourish only when you believe that what you can do can make a difference, that your actions can bring a future different from the present. To have hope, then, is to acquire a belief in your ability to have some control over your circumstances. You are no longer entirely at the mercy of forces outside yourself. (Groopman as cited in Sawyer et al, 2007, pp. 230–231)

Whenever the future is considered as a pregiven – whether this be as the pure, mechanical repetition of the present, or simply because it "is what it has to be" – there is no room for utopia, nor therefore for the dream, the option, the decision, or expectancy in the struggle, which is the only way hope exists. There is no room for education. (Freire, 1994, p. 91)

Cradled by Cary, I am nourished by Maxine Greene's urging that "informed engagements with the ... arts is the most likely mode of releasing our students' ... imaginative capacity."[32] I am strengthened by Huebner's belief that imagination "undergirds everything that the educator thinks and does."[33] I am encouraged as Greene impresses that "imagination is as important in the lives of teachers as it is in the lives of [our] students."[34]

In hope imagined I find why I am here. I press through renewed in my experience – renewed in my knowing – that arts-encouraged imaginings can tease open the (im)possibilities of separating curriculum, pedagogy and our humanness.

I find myself held.

I find myself hopeful.

I find my/self.

ENCOUNTERING HOPE – TEN MEDITATIONS

MEDITATION #9: GROUNDING HOPE

Tears speak of something that is written in a space hovering above this page. In a place around this book, but not in it . . . All that really is genuine about this is taking up a space around this book . . . around me . . . Inside me. (Kuiack, 2004, p. 131)

My tears ground me in hope reminding me of "the 'kinship' among times lived"[35] – that I am complicated and complex; that I am rich with experience and naïve in my knowing. And if I continue ever outward, ever forward, ever onward, I risk missing living the kinships among these parts of my being. Forever connected and forever connecting. I risk missing dwelling faithfully in the world.[36]

MEDITATION #10: TEACHING AS SITES OF MY BEING

In the spaces above this page (me) and in the places around this chapter (me), reside historic collisions of sites of certainty – colonialism, patriarchy, heterosexism, racism, modernism, postmodernism, and/in me.

Teaching as sites of my being – sites of uncertainty, of possibility, of hope.

Being as sites of my teaching – sites reimagined and imagined in(to) hope.

AFTER MEDITATION: BEING AS SITES OF MY TEACHING

The scent of oranges.[37]

[1] (Smith, 2003)
[2] (Freire, 1994, p. 31)
[3] (Freire, 1994)
[4] (Halpin, 2007, p. 244)
[5] (Halpin, 2007, p. 244)
[6] (Tupper, 2007)
[7] (Utopia, 2008)
[8] (Utopia, 2008)
[9] (Utopia, 2008)
[10] (Utopia, 2008)
[11] (Utopia, 2008)
[12] (Huebner, 1975/1997, p. 130)
[13] (Cary, 2006)
[14] (Hasebe-Ludt and Hurren, 2003)
[15] (Tupper, 2007)
[16] (Halpin, 2007, abstract)
[17] (Halpin, 2007, abstract)
[18] (Godfrey, 1987, p. 106)
[19] (Sawyer et al, 2007, p. 234)
[20] (Steeves, 2004, p. 5–6)
[21] (Greene, 1995, p. 140)
[22] (Levitas, 2004, abstract)
[23] (Levitas, 2004, p. 271)
[24] (Huebner, 1995/1999, p. 402)
[25] (Huebner, 1995/1999, p. 401)

[26] (Marin in Halpin, 2003, p. 35)
[27] (Cary, 2006, p. 134–135)
[28] (Saskatchewan Ministry of Education, n.d.)
[29] (Ritenburg, 2001)
[30] (Ritenburg, 2006)
[31] (Brunner, 1994, p. xiv)
[32] (Greene, 1995, p. 125)
[33] (Huebner, 1996/1999, p. 436)
[34] (Greene, 1995, p. 36)
[35] (Freire, 1994, p. 27)
[36] (Huebner, 1995/1999, p. 403)
[37] Oranges carry meaning for me of connection to the earth through the (re)generation of organic matter. The scent of oranges is the scent of time, of imagination, of hope.

REFERENCES

Brunner, D. (1994). *Inquiry and reflection: Framing narrative practice in education*. Albany, NY: State University of New York Press.

Cary, L. (2006). *Curriculum spaces: Discourse, postmodern theory and educational research*. New York: Peter Lang.

Egan, K. (1992). *Imagination in teaching and learning: The middle school years*. London: Althouse Press.

Freire, P. (1994). *Pedagogy of hope*. New York: Continuum Publishing Company.

Godfrey, J. (1987). *A philosophy of human hope*. Boston: Martinus Nijhoff.

Greene, M. (1995). *Releasing the imagination: Essays on education, the arts and social change*. San Francisco: Jossey-Bass.

Halpin, D. (2003). *Hope and education: The role of the utopian imagination*. London: RoutledgeFalmer.

Halpin, D. (2007). Utopian spaces of "Robust Hope": The architecture and nature of progressive learning environments [Electronic version]. *Asia-Pacific Journal of Teacher Education, 35*(3), 243–255.

Hasebe-Ludt, E. and Hurren, W. (2003). *Curriculum intertext: Place/language/pedagogy*. New York: Peter Lang.

Huebner, D. (1997). Poetry and power: The politics of curricular development. In D. J. Flinders & S. J. Thornton (Eds.), *The curriculum studies reader* (pp. 130–136). New York: Routledge.

Huebner, D. (1999). Challenges bequeathed (1996). In V. Hillis (Ed.), *The lure of the transcendent, collected essays by Dwayne E. Huebner* (pp. 432-445). Mahwah, NJ: Lawrence Erlbaum Associates.

Huebner, D. (1999). Education and spirituality (1993). In V. Hillis (Ed.), *The lure of the transcendent, collected essays by Dwayne E. Huebner* (pp. 401–416). Mahwah, NJ: Lawrence Erlbaum Associates.

Kuiack, M. (2004). Embracing 'Fields of Influence' while exploring alternative paths of knowledge. *Canadian Journal of Environmental Education, 9*, 123–135.

Levitas, R. (2004). Hope and education. [Review of the book *Hope and education: The role of the utopian imagination*]. *Journal of Philosophy of Education, 38*(2), 269–273.

Ritenburg, H. (2001). Relationships in learning: Arts education at the University of Regina – an interview with Dr. Norman C. Yakel. *McGill Journal of Education, 36*(3), 261–270.

Ritenburg, H. (2006). *A good place to be: An arts-based exploration of my experience as a mature student in the Arts Education Program at the University of Regina*. Unpublished Master's Thesis, University of Regina, Regina, Saskatchewan, Canada.

Saskatchewan Ministry of Education. (n.d.). *Arts education (K-1): Introduction - philosophy*. [Online]. Retrieved June 27, 2008 from http://www.sasked.gov.sk.ca/docs/artsed/g1arts_ed/introduction.html#philosophy

Sawyer, W., Singh, M., Woodrow, C., Downes, T., Johnston, C., & Whitton, D. (2007). Robust hope and teacher education policy [Electronic version]. *Asia-Pacific Journal of Teacher Education, 35*(3), 227–242.

Smith, D. (2003). Preface: Some thoughts on living in-between. In E. Hasebe-Ludt & W. Hurren (Eds.), *Curriculum intertext: Place/language/pedagogy* (pp. xv-xvii). New York: Peter Lang.

Steeves, J. (2004). *Imagining bodies: Merleau-Ponty's philosophy of imagination.* Pittsburgh, PA: Duquesne University Press.

Tupper, J. (2007). *EC&I 924, Issues in curriculum theory, course outline.* Available from Dr. Jennifer Tupper, Faculty of Education, University of Regina, Regina, SK, Canada, S4S 0A2.

Utopia. (2008). In *Wikipedia, the free encyclopedia.* Retrieved June 27, 2008, from http://en.wikipedia.org/wiki/Utopia

WENDY DONAWA

SURPASSING THE TECHNICAL: A FRIENDLIER DISCOURSE

INTRODUCTION

Does anyone else remember Dick Tracy's amazing two-way wrist-radio? Before television entered our lives, my brothers and I would lie on our stomachs on the living room floor devouring the Sunday funnies and speculating—how amazing it would be to see and talk to someone all the way across town! What power: to spy, to have all that illicit information. And how might we use it to embarrass or coerce, to persuade, to subdue the bully, to get the right answers to the next test? We have moved, of course, beyond children's fantasies, beyond the speculative realms of *Brave New World* and *1984*, beyond even the ability to be surprised by cloning, nanotechnology, or the fractal technological potential of the future.

A TECHNICAL LINEAGE

Dwayne Huebner's challenge to surpass the technical foundations of education calls to me because this technical hegemony so infuses the ethos and delivery of contemporary pedagogy. And not just in educational realms: The technical (and increasingly technological) ground of almost every conceivable social activity permeates our daily lives so that it is the air we breathe; it is normalized into invisibility, and we attend to it no more than a fish reflects upon the water it swims in. We use our debit cards, book a flight, vote, donate to a charity, receive medical care, shop at the supermarket: Our mode of access to these activities, the choices we make, and the protocols we follow are observed, recorded, and regulated; they are promoted or restrained by information empires so science-fiction-vast that they are difficult to conjure, and by the commercial and ideological interests these empires serve.

Our technical world is the air we bipeds breathe, and though we revel in the marvels it offers, we tend not to dwell on the implications of its construction, nor the consequences of its unfolding. So dizzying is the pace of change and increase in complexity that Dick Tracy's two-way wrist radio may as well be a bison on the walls of the Lascaux Caves. And our young are socialized at this breakneck pace, with a cognitive overload of data, multi-tasking, and information that submerges the short-term memory and short circuits "the kind of focused reflective attention that might have made this information useful in the first place" (Lorinc, 2007, p. 51).

P. Lewis and J. Tupper (eds.), *Challenges Bequeathed: Taking up the Challenges of Dwayne Huebner, 173–186.*
© 2009 sense publishers. All rights reserved.

The challenge to surpass the technical is thus entwined with Huebner's other four challenges. How is our affirmation of the imagination (his second challenge) constrained if what can be imagined is to be conveyed only in technical modalities? The generous support that institutions offer information technology and competency-based learning may be the prudent fostering of a future workforce. But this support is generally accompanied by diminished support for the "frills" of art, music, physical and liberal education, which in turn restricts the nurturing of creative, original, bodily, spiritual, and poetic paths to understanding.

It is difficult to celebrate the world's traditions and achievements (Huebner's third challenge) amidst an ethos of the technical. Intellectual complexity is pruned into binary tidiness, new processes and ideas are reduced to what is programmable, and attention need not be brought to anything longer or more demanding than a sound-byte. Moreover, institutional memory itself is technologically amputated as libraries wonder what to do with oceans of microfiche, or as entire memory banks, unless translated into new media, become as obsolete as wax cuneiform tablets. The gilded magnificence and intricate calligraphy of the 9th century Book of Kells can still open up that age of faith and make possible its repetition as a horizon of meaning. But a 1998 dissertation written in WordPerfect is already lost and inaccessible.

As for the challenges of public educational discourse and youth advocacy, the fourth and fifth challenges, these too are constrained if the house of being that is language is to be constructed through evidence-based logic and categorizing, and if their openness to the ambiguous, the spiritual, and the creative are effaced by technological priorities.

This is not a judgment on technical advances themselves, but on their place in thinking about knowledge, and in shaping and ascribing its worth. No one wants to put the genie back in the bottle; however, we do want to direct the genie's energies to generative ends. Technical discourses need not be blamed for labeling and categorizing, for positivistic and binary modes of thought; one might as well blame a dull pencil for a dull essay. Technical processes are valuable servants; they are deplorable masters; they are means, not ends. The technical offers wonderful tools to enhance the construction of curriculum; but it is neither the pedagogical architect nor the building. As Huebner puts it, "The technical must become a subsidiary language for educators" (1999, p. 434).

Jon Kabat-Zinn (2005) speaks of those whose knowledge he seeks to surpass as *lineage*: "If we are wise, we will make every effort to read their maps, explore their methods, confirm their findings, so that we may know where to begin and what we might make our own...and where...potential innovations lie" (p. 93). He compares the intelligent incorporation of what has gone before to *autopoesis*, the process by which cellular growth adds to itself while retaining its organizational integrity:

> Life is utterly historical...at every level—from the biological to the psychological to the social to the cultural—there is a fundamental need...for scaffolding. We depend on instructions, guidelines, a context, a relationship...to venture meaningfully into the wilds of our own minds....we need to contextualize our

efforts, yet without getting caught in the narratives that having such a framework and context usually entails (pp. 95–97).

But unless the technical does become Huebner's "subsidiary" language, in all likelihood schools will continue to "lack the qualities that permit morally gratifying relationships" (Huebner, 1999, p. 434). And the tasks of educators may continue to be seen in terms of Hannah Arendt's (1958) separation of *work* from *labour*. Arendt saw work in terms of worldly accomplishment, with durable products that bear witness to our endeavours, that offer us an identity, and that may outlive us. Labour, on the other hand, involves the "monotonous performance of daily repeated chores" (p. 100), and leaves nothing behind. This conceptual division may explain why tenure is often the outcome of a CV with an impressive list of publications; it seldom results from the repetitive, nurturing attentiveness of teaching and mentorship. In contemporary terms, Arendt's *labour* would probably include the technological tedium of vast call centres and the service industries. And it would also include the huge misappropriation of teachers' time and resources servicing the Provincial Achievement Tests, or the Procrustean curriculum of No Child Left Behind. The nurturing, imaginative, and spiritual work of education that would foster Huebner's "morally gratifying relationships" exists within relations of power that "render invisible, unspeakable or trivial the routine moral activities that we sense…are essential to goodness" (Calhoun, 1992, p. 117), and that erase the mediating caring for the other's moral wellbeing that is at the heart of education.

Technical foundations in contemporary education, then, have inverted the old dictum that form follows function. When form truly follows function, its byproduct is a mysterious and authentic beauty of shape and proportion and being. It is here we find the exquisite asymmetry of the nautilus shell, the clavicle's subtle curve, the ribbed sand beneath the outgoing tide, the branching tributaries of rivers, and of our own arterial and nervous systems. The Greek search for the Golden Mean is early evidence of the human need to understand the nature of beauty, whether subsequently expressed through a portrait mask of an Egyptian god-king, the attuned functionality of a Stradivarius violin, or a work of contemporary architecture possessing the symbolic and aesthetic qualities Huebner speaks to (pp. 434–45). It is also present in the work of educators who invite the startling, the expressive, the ambiguous, and the lovely into their classrooms, who encourage open-ended inquiry and sustained reflection, who acknowledge multiple paths to understanding, and who make of their teaching a *poesis*.

If, however, the technical cart is before the linguistic horse, then function follows form, so that ideas and institutions evolve entirely within the boundaries of a pre-determined technical structures and strictures. Teachers, students, and course content are developed and evaluated in terms of what can be measured, quantified, and validated, for the positivistic woof and warp of our communal fabric also informs the ways we think about education and its functions. And it excludes, diminishes, distorts, or marginalizes what cannot be thought about in this way. "What we don't talk about, bring into existence by our articulation of it, is relegated to the realm of madness", says Sharon Butala (1994, p. 116).

And yet, and yet...even if there were a choice, who really would advocate a nostalgic return to good old days that weren't? We have come to expect an unlimited choice of information and communication as a norm and a right, a technical lineage that we can enjoy ourselves and that we can share with our students. Who would surrender the delight of chatting with a student in Indonesia, or the Arctic, of communicating with like-minded colleagues across the globe? Who does not love someone who is alive only because of marvelous technological advances in medicine?

So, how might we make visible those realms of experience excluded (and therefore made invisible) by binary and positivistic forms, and how might we at the same time acknowledge our debt to technical accomplishments and their "...power to fabricate educational environments [that Huebner finds] ...wonderful and significant" (p. 434)?

A relationally based model may help us re/vision education. Relational models for thought and action that integrate the thinking, feeling, and relational intelligences have, in the past, been dismissed as "soft" (read: lacking rigor and validity) research. But thinking has shifted amongst some developmental psychologists and neurobiologists, and Daniel Siegel (2007) points out the "interconnection among brain, mind, and relationship [that constitute] a triangle of reality...[R]elationships among people...involve the [neural] flow of energy and information...relationships shape energy and information flow—as is happening now by these words in your mind" (p. 49).

> An interpersonal neurobiology approach to the ways our social lives help promote well-being views neural integration as the outcome of attuned relationships (p. 39).... *Interpersonal integration* becomes a vital way in which our brains' hardwiring to connect enables us to feel grounded in the world....Attunement is not a luxury; it is a requirement of the individual to survive and thrive....secure interpersonal attunements likely create states of integration that promote internal attunement and mindfulness (p. 317).

Attunement-based relationships (parental, pedagogical) have always structured human experience, although they have not always been the focus of academic research. I have chosen, for the remainder of this chapter, to explore the attunements of friendship, and to suggest ways in which they integrate our intellectual, moral, creative, and social lives, ways in which they surpass the technical.

AN EPISTMEOLOGY OF FRIENDSHIP

Where are we going?
What are the bindings?
What behooves us?
      Adrienne Rich (1991), *An Atlas of the Difficult World*, p. 23.

I suggest a theory and practice of friendship that offer a template for both self-understanding and academic inquiry. In the following discussion I lay out my understanding of four qualities that I have found to characterize friendship, and which provide conditions for its practice: imaginative empathy, trust, reflexivity, and narrative connection.

The etymological roots of *practice* signify doing and action. I suggest that we are friends to the degree that we are committed to the work, the practice, of friendship. Moreover, I contend that those qualities that shape the practice of friendship also encourage an epistemologically friendly framing of inquiry into pedagogy and other discourses. When we theorize–observe, perceive, envision, discern–what are we subsequently bound to do and how are we bound to act? What practices behoove us?

Rather than weigh and assess differing educational discourses as contending contradictions, why not "enlarge the boundaries of discourse" (Antoinette Oberg, personal communication, 1998) and invite in multiple voices? It is possible to embrace contraries if our aim is to disclose meaning and enhance understanding rather than to "prove" a truth. A dialectic of poetry–the integration of the inner voice and the voice of reason, what Buddhists call the *heart-mind*—can drive the search for insight and understanding, create opportunities for new connections, and reconstruct our conception of critical thought. Paths to knowledge are not immutable, and need not exclude one another. "A person does not 'know' irrespective of the object of knowledge or the practices in which she is engaged", claims Ruddick (1996, p. 254). And I have found this to be so; even in daily life my cognitive activities continually shift as I silently follow a challenging line of thought, as I consult a mechanic about my car, as I banter with a friend about which film to see, as I try to make a decision about my health, as I write this chapter.

Moreover, it is possible to transfer habitual, relational ways of thinking to varied and seemingly unrelated contexts, as a number of feminist scholars propose: Sara Ruddick has outlined how "maternal thinking, as a whole, might affect even models of theoretical science" (1996, p. 254). Mary Catherine Bateson builds on this capacity to transfer productive habits to other domains: "We must transform our attitude towards all productive work and toward the planet into expressions of homemaking, where we create and sustain the possibility of life" (1990, p. 136). Similarly, Elizabeth Abel (1981) has found that the relational ties of affection and intimacy create an imaginative identification with others that is "the essence of literature and of moral growth" (p. 422). And Dwayne Huebner seeks an educational environment that encourages "qualities that permit morally gratifying relationships among people" (p. 434).

These thinkers suggest that it can be both possible and desirable to transfer one habitual kind of meaning-making to other, expanded contexts. This pattern resonates for me, and it is the one I follow below, contending that the phenomenon of friendship provides a template for self-understanding, for teaching, and for academic inquiry. How might understanding through friendship surpass the technical foundations of education?

Waste. Waste. The watcher's eye put out, hands of the builder severed,
brain of the maker starved
those who could bind, join, reweave, cohere, replenish
now at risk in this segregate republic
locked away out of sight and hearing, out of mind, shunted aside
those needed to teach, advise, persuade, weigh arguments
those urgently needed for the work of perception
work of the poet, the astronomer, the historian, the architect of new streets
work of the speaker who also listens
meticulous delicate work of reaching the heart of the desperate woman, the desperate man
– never to be finished, still unbegun work of repair – it cannot be done without them
And where are they now?
        Adrienne Rich (1991), *An Atlas of the Difficult World*, p. 11

Surpassing the Technical with Empathy

The imaginative empathy of friendship speaks to knowledge of another that is inseparable from self-knowledge, and, conversely, to self-knowledge that is foundational to knowledge of others. Friendship's dual empathy is equally central to the mindful educator's task; the capacity to preserve the other's distinctiveness, and to perceive herself from the other's perspective, makes responsible action and moral agency possible.

The imaginative intelligence implicit in the reciprocity of friendship is ballast and anchor to the responsible educator. Attending to the contrasting perspectives of self and other can interrupt those otherwise habitual patterns of perception and interpretation that foster obtuseness and thoughtlessness. This attentiveness is the antithesis of *thoughtlessness*, the careless and willful ignorance of self and other that prevents empathy.

Thoughtlessness encourages the laziness and entropy of Jane Hirshfield's "ordinary mind" (1997b, p. 6); it enables much evil and accounts for evil's astonishing banality. Regarding the other without empathy, seeing arrogantly, is not only wrong, but harmful; it incorrectly constructs another being. Racism, misogyny, homophobia, pornography, all are harmful, sometimes lethal "seeing". This carelessness enables a neglect of relation that reverberates along a spectrum from a friend's betrayal or a teacher's wounding comments, to political catastrophes to genocide. Writing *Eichman in Jerusalem*, Hannah Arendt was struck by Eichman's "manifest shallowness...insensitiveness, opacity, inability to make connections...something entirely negative: it was not stupidity but *thoughtlessness*" (as cited in Brightman, 1995, p. xxii).

Moral imperatives are relational, not technical. Self-discipline, self-knowledge, the empathic ability to distinguish one's own interests from those of the other create a new reality. No one, says Mary Catherine Bateson, "is independent of the actions and imaginations of other...No legal definition can free us from the need to bring one another into being" (1994, p. 63). Neither a mere contradiction of the symbolic order nor yet another binary, this dual vision embodies the creative tensions between a necessary sense of realism and the simultaneous visionary power of the potential, the possible, the imagined.

Empathy illuminates friendship's voluntary nature; our friends and the aims of our friendships are freely chosen, not inherited or socially ascribed. And the voluntariness is not contractual, but mutual, reciprocal, shaped by shared confidence, trust, disclosure, and *care*.

Here the contexts of friend and educator diverge, for the educator's vocation *has* contractual and legal dimensions, and carries the added dimension of working within unequal relations of power. Empathy's work here is to ensure that its dark shadow, charisma, does not predominate. Relational skills can be used for good or ill, as any politician may attest; the charismatic educator may compel trust that draws forth a longing akin to love, a longing that may manifest itself as the urge to emulate, to excel, to obey, to self-denigrate. The charismatic herself remains invulnerable, absorbing the trusting vulnerability of others. The charisma may be a gift or a burden, but it certainly is a responsibility, as is all power.

To return to the initial suggestion that friendship offers a template for academic inquiry: How does the friendly practice of empathy answer the challenge to surpass the technical? An enlarged capacity for empathy invites metaphor and narrative. It illuminates meaning-making; it constructs relational ties that link private and public discourse.

The empathic insight so necessary to friendship is also crucial to the emotionally literate scientist, scholar, teacher, or administrator. Empathy is relational, not contractual; it opens up for us standpoints that permit multiplicity, and offers autonomy of choice. Empathy encourages evocative experimental forms of research, and engages emotional and bodily modes of understanding. It nurtures ways of knowing that encourage praxis; it encourages discourse that is accessible, appropriate, and reliable, and language that makes possible reflective and theoretical places of dwelling (Huebner, 1999, pp. 143–158). It is in the empathic, thoughtful, and poetic use of language "that truth establishes itself. Truth is the bringing forth of what is into unconcealment" (Huebner, p. 148). Or, as Jane Hirshfield says, "Poetry's work is the clarification and magnification of being" (1997b, p. vii). "Only the presence of many possibilities allows a writer to see which may lead toward the new. Plenitude calls forth plenitude, of the world and of the mind." (p. 43)

Despite the plenitude of an Oxford Ph.D. in anthropology and a promising academic career within her grasp, Camilla Gibb found herself increasingly unable to reconcile the conflict between her passion for writing fiction and the call to a far more prestigious academic life. Although postmodern anthropology seems less rooted in scientific detachment and objectivity than its previous, traditional mode, Gibb found it to be still defined by its rigor, its intellectual authority and its superiority to "mere" artists. Yet that authority resided in "the absolute effacement of the speaking and experiencing subject" (Pratt, as cited in Gibb, 2008, p. 10).

But, says Gibb, "My field was, if I'm honest about it, much less defined by...the more formal aspects of my research than by my relationships with people in the field (p. 10). And her professional stance meant "I was forced to dispense with...people. I had to put people I cared about—people whose place and culture I was writing about—at a distance" (p. 11). Her empathic instincts and her professional stance were incompatible.

Gibb chose to follow the call of her writing: "People naturally assumed I must be having some kind of breakdown" (p. 9). Bringing her talents, her empathy, her emotional and spiritual responses to bear on her year of fieldwork living with a Muslim family in the eastern highlands of Ethiopia, she wrote *Sweetness in the Belly* (2005). Gibb writes not only from an incisive intelligence and extensive lived experience, but also from a wise heart. This compassionate, visceral narrative with its richly detailed social tapestry and compelling characters is set against the devastating Ethiopian famines and revolutions of the 70s, and, in Huebner's terms, "lays out" (p. 151) the conditions of exile and belonging, of grace in the face of unbearable loss. As one reviewer put it, "Empathy rises like the fumes of incense (Lindner, 2006). Camilla Gibbs had cherished "the proud [scholarly] tradition that I had inherited" (p. 9). But through her empathic and humane living in the house of being that is language, she found she needed to surpass her discipline's technical discourse: its "profound conformity, ... rigidity,... conservatism and an internalization of the hierarchy of [the academic] universe" (Gibb, 2008, p. 9).

Nor is the impulse to protest form and surpass the technical confined to educational or literary discourses (although Camilla Gibb's and Gabor Maté's writing is, in the deepest sense, educational). Gabor Maté, who practices medicine among the despairing and addicted of Vancouver's East Side, speaks to the mind-body separation of our culture, and to the need to surpass our technological, neurological, and chemical understanding of healing. He finds the excessive emphasis on genetics as an answer-all is "an impediment to our understanding" (2008, p. 181), and notes that much valuable brain research is dismissed, not widely taught in medical schools, and "virtually unfamiliar to the medical community" (p. 180). But the transformation necessary to healing requires understanding that

> we have something in or about us that transcends the firing and wiring of neurons and the actions of chemicals. The mind may reside mostly in the brain, but it is much more than the sum total of the automatic neurological programs rooted in our pasts. And there is something else in us and about us: it is called by many names, "spirit" being the most democratic and least denominational or divisive" (p. 200).

"The golden rule may be inscribed in our brain circuits" he muses, "not as a commandment, but as an essential part of who we are.... It seems that we are wired to be in tune with one another's needs, which is one of the roots of empathy" (p. 391).

And it is empathy that makes possible a practice of trust.

Surpassing the Technical with Trust

Trust, like empathy, is of a voluntary, non-contractual nature, and is fraught with inevitable risks and vulnerabilities. Trust is not a product, but an empathic *procedure* that guides our actions and interactions. To a large extent, trust directs how we can know and therefore what we can know. The trust or distrust a child feels for a teacher, a voter for a politician, a lover for a partner, a reader for a writer, will markedly affect the kind and degree of attention brought to the details of what she is told, what is sufficiently significant to be remembered and integrated with lived experience. Trust affects how one person connects with another person, text, or discourse, and the meaning she makes of it.

Yet trust, so important a constituent of relationship, eludes definition. Nor is its practice reducible to guidelines or principles of regulation. Annette Baier (1994) notes that we rely on the good will of those we choose to trust, and often we only recognize what trust involves when we have been injured by its unexpected absence.

When we trust someone, we trust them to use without malice the discretionary powers our trust gives them; we trust them to be attentive, observant, and discriminating in the expression of their good will, of their *trustworthiness* toward us. This is why principles cannot regulate trust. This is why mortgages and pre-nuptial agreements and contracts like those required by Human Research Ethics Committees (which rightly attempt to protect the subjects of research from exploitation), cannot really guard against betrayals of trust and intimacy.

It is problematic that openness, vulnerability and the longing to trust go with a surrender of the soul's defenses. But parents and educators and those in positions of relative power will recognize that Baier points to "the expected gain in security which comes from a climate of trust...In trusting we are always giving up security to get greater security, exposing our throats so that others become accustomed to not biting" (1994, p. 15).

How does trust help us live in the world as it is while maintaining a vision of the world as it might be? With trust, hope is possible; the manifestation of spirit is possible. Dwayne Huebner, too, sees hope as a manifestation of spirit in an uncertain world. "Love and care provide not certainty, but hope"(p. 350). There are grounds for hope in the recognition that life is too complicated and multifarious to grasp, that there is more to us than can be known, that we can transcend the "given-ness" of the world. He warns us to guard against "easy interpretation" (recalling Arendt's "manifest shallowness," Hirshfield's "laziness and entropy of ordinary mind," and the dominance of purely technical and instrumental discourse). Trust affirms its presence in hope. Trust in scholarly inquiry enables researcher and researched to "affirm the critical but refuse the cynical and establish hope as central to a critical, pedagogical and political practice" (Mourad, 1997, p. x).

> I know that
> hope is the hardest
> love we carry.
> Hirshfield, (1997a), *Lives of the heart*, p. 39

Surpassing the Technical with Reflexivity

"Being online," says John Lorinc, "has become a state of being" (2007, p. 59). The chronic distractions of the 'technological miasma" (p. 50) he documents, and of their implications for learning, are the very antithesis of the mindful reflexive practices that bring us to the manifestation of spirit so crucial in cultural, educational, and political life, and so central in how we can teach and learn. "It may be that our hyper-connected world has quite simply made it difficult for us to think" (p. 50).

The digital impact on the educational world has, on the one hand, made possible enriched resources, almost infinite modes of communication, and an expanded understanding of what *literacy* means. On the other hand, its service to the realm of the technical is less benign. The computer's capacity to process information lends itself seamlessly to the educational rhetoric of values and ends, and to the subsequent tests, scores, ratings, and evidence-base evaluation that validate this rhetoric. The curricular tail wags the dog, as, for instance, the structure and intent of online courses are structured by the technological discourse of instructional designers. This discourse erases language that reinforces our being-in-the-world as teachers, language that "lives, grows, and projects possibilities for being." (Huebner, p. 145) that encourages curiosity, ambiguity and openness, and that allows the possibility of transcendence. It is surely not a coincidence that the dominant tropes of scientific and positivistic discourse in education have coincided with diminished support for the humanities, especially for literature, and in some cases, the elimination of literature from courses of educational studies (personal communications and observations). And this cultural domination "cannot be confronted by people who remain unaware of how their imagination—the foundation of their knowing, acting, valuing, and freedom—has been and is being shaped or formed" (Huebner, 1999, p. 436).

Lorinc reminds us that *multi-tasking* is a phrase initially used to describe the capability of the computer, not of the human brain (p. 59). There are limits to our mental capacities to adapt to digital ones. Our brains need time to focus, sort, scaffold and encode the information that bombards us in such quantities and with such speed and disruptive frequency. And there are psychic costs to the brain fatigued by ceaseless digital demands that replace human interaction or inner contemplative and cognitive activity. The diminished ability to process and retain information accompanies compulsiveness, lack of discernment, and diminished interpretive ability. Consciousness is fragmented in a digital world that is, quite literally, addictive.

But it is our critical thoughtfulness, our reflexivity, our capacity for critique, that determines the meaning we make of the discourses available to us, that gives us agency and enables our interpretive ability. Reflexivity is the third of friendship's practices to be considered here as an alternative to the dominance of the technical. Friendship constructs a counterculture that supports critical reflection; a friend's perspective offers "discontinuity in a habitual pattern of perception and interpretation" (Stanley, 1994, p. 202). "Thinking is the theory; thoughtfulness is the practice [of friendship]" says Janice Raymond (1986, p. 218). The contrasting perspectives offered and reflected upon in the trust of friendship enlarge our own subjectivity. In the untidiness, complexity and incommensurability of life, friendship offers a discourse that (as Huebner says of transcendent educational language) "opens up a world" and makes possible a reflective place of dwelling, "a place within which that which is can shine forth"(1999, p. 153). The empathy and trustworthiness discussed earlier in this chapter arise from attentive, self-conscious critical reflection, but they also, in a circular recursive process, nurture further reflection.

However, for many, for those who are unaware that they are unaware, the only available discourses may be those habitual, ideological discourses subject to easy interpretation; and their responses will very likely be automatic, unmindful, limited to prior frames of reference, responses Buddhists would call *unskillful*. Unknowing, they proceed "unthinkingly down the paths laid out by others....unaware of the source of these paths, and thus ...unable to return to the freedom of the original decision points" (Huebner, p. 145).

Here is the crux of the teacher's task: cultured in language "as agar medium is the culture of microorganisms"(Huebner, p.145), the educator may unfold for students the double possibilities of discourse: "Language...hides man [sic.] from his world and from himself. As it opens up some possibilities it covers others. The veil torn from some aspects of the world conceals others"(p. 145). The fully conscious teacher knows language, like thought, must be unfolded with care; words must be chosen with heedfulness and attunement, with poetizing.

The reflexive, recursive cycling of attentiveness, insight, and understanding also shows mindful educators the deep interconnections between their academic interests and the circumstances of their lives. Our own lived experience is discourse, is text, is a cultural product, like anything else "created as a result of human action and reflection" (McEwan, as cited in Pinar, Reynolds, Slattery, and Taubman, 1995, p. 49). When, through reflection, we understand how and where we are located in our own discourse, we do dis/cover our own ideological agendas, and can call into question the assumptions that lock us into narrow, rigid ways of being. We can bring into the light of awareness our hidden curricula of political texts and impulses: embodied, post-colonial, racialized, gendered.

What Jane Hirshfield calls *concentration* is what I understand by reflexivity: "A wholeheartedness [in which] world and self begin to cohere. With that state comes an enlarging; of what may be known, what may be felt, what may be done" (1997b, p. 4). Hirshfield suggests that, just as geological pressure turns ocean sediment to limestone, so the writer's concentration transforms the subject of discourse. She outlines three modalities of concentration: a *drawing inward*, towards a common centre of integrity and coherence; a *focusing outward*, to enable clarity and exactitude; and an *increase in strength and density* that is an altered meaning-making state of mind, that opposes "ordinary mind" (pp. 5–7) and "easy interpretation" (Huebner, 1999, p. 154).

> The heart alone
> is voiceless. By itself it knows
> but cannot think, and so
> it cannot close the door to fear.
>
> It is thought
> that pulls the bright gut of the heart
> to speech.
>   Jan Zwicky, (2004), *Robinson's Crossing,* p. 24

Surpassing the Technical with Narrative Connection

> An inability to fit events together…to make the narrative connection, is a radical incompetence at being human. So seen, stupidity can be defined as a failure to make enough connections, and insanity as severe repeated error in making connections. (Le Guin, 1989, p. 43)

At this point, I want to gather up the strands of friendly theory and practice I have unfolded and speak to their narrative dimensions. Empathy is a narrative project, calling into question the predictable, the banal, the thoughtless. It demands responsiveness, an attentive reading of the other's narrative. It prompts relational ties that link our personal and public worlds, and opens up standpoints that are other than our own. The empathic imagination that widens our experiential base makes possible moral growth and transcendence; it also makes possible a methodology of trust. Trust, too, affects the tales we tell; it directs what we attend to, what we find significant, what we integrate into our life story. Reflexivity enriches the meanings of the narratives we encounter, or that we generate. Empathy and trust in turn make possible a reflexive attentiveness that allows insight and understanding. Reflection shows us that narrative is always a process, connecting the individual to the environment she is shaped by. It is in the confluence of these qualities that the narrative connection of theory and practice is manifested.

Events and experiences of the myriad world flow around and past us: what we notice and remember of them, and the meaning we make, are the stories we tell. To perceive the material conditions and relational networks that shape our lives (and our students' lives) is to interpret our (and their) experience. To make connections between our critical intelligence and our lived experience is to narrate, to theorize our own lives. To understand the interests of the dominant is to understand *their* [gendered, racialized, political] narratives. And to write one's own narrative is to name and empower the self.

Narrative identity is, among other things, a moral process. Empathy and insight determine the peculiarities and congruence of our friends' and students' stories. To "read" the narratives of self and other involves "an epistemological and moral lean toward an other" (Schweickart, 1996, p. 320), and the caring intersubjectivity that "reads" another into being also defines the self. As a friend of mine wrote amidst the difficulties of caring for terminally ailing parents, "caring for others and caring for the self became in my mind inextricably linked....my identity...was tied up with my ability to take care of them when they were vulnerable" (personal communication, Nan Peacocke, 1999).

The knowing self begins in attachment, in relational context, it arises from and constitutes the intelligence that links, compares, finds cause, deduces, projects outcomes (Kerby, 1991, p. 87). Narrative enables us to enlarge habitual ways of knowing and transfer them to other discourses. And I have done exactly that in my use of friendship as a template for being-in-the-world as a teacher, writer, researcher.

And where does truth lie? How are things, "really?" Narrative truth does not reside in its correspondence to prior meanings: the truth *is* the narrative meaning; its authenticity. A different story is possible, always, it is partial in both senses of the word. And to understand a story is to understand the metanarrative in which it is embedded. To understand Gibb's (2005) young protagonist teaching the Qu'ran in a Harare slum is to comprehend the dynamics of Thatcher's Britain, the politics of famine, the forces that would topple a 2000 year old dynasty, the complexity of identity, and the way gender plays out in vastly differing cultures. To understand the defiant/agitated/anxious student who takes the back seat in our class may be to recognize the political priorities behind the budget cuts in social supports, and their effects on vulnerable families. And to understand the decline of the humanities and of curricula that "foster morally gratifying relationships" (Huebner, 1999, p. 434), is to comprehend the hegemonic power of the technical.

And it is humane narrative connection that brings me, in the end, to Ruddick's (1996) understanding: "I look for ways of knowing and counting knowledge that would judge...in the light of the pleasures they offer, the love they make possible, the care they provide, and the justice they observe" (p. 267).

REFERENCES

Abel, E. (1981). (E)Merging identities: The dynamics of female friendship in contemporary fiction by women. *Signs, 6*, 413–434.
Arendt, H. (1958). *The human condition.* Chicago: University of Chicago Press.
Baier, A. (1994). *Moral prejudices: Essays on ethics.* Cambridge, MA: Harvard University Press.
Bateson, M. C. (1990). *Composing a life.* New York: Plume.
Brightman, C. (Ed.). (1995). *Between friends: The correspondence of Hannah Arendt and Mary McCarthy 1949–1975.* San Diego, CA: Harcourt Brace.
Butala, S. (2008). *The girl from Saskatoon: A meditation on friendship, memory, and murder.* Toronto, ON: HarperCollins.
Calhoun, C. (1992). Emotional work. In E. B. Cole & S. Coultrap-McQuin (Eds.), *Exploration in feminist ethics: Theory and practice* (pp. 117–129). Bloomington, IN: Indiana University Press.
Gibb, C. (2005). *Sweetness in the belly.* Scarborough, ON: Doubleday Canada.
Gibb, C. (2008, February). Lured by fiction. *Academic matters*, 8–11.
Hirshfield, J. (1997a). *The lives of the heart.* New York: HarperCollins.
Hirshfield, J. (1997b). *Nine gates: Entering the mind of poetry.* New York: HarperCollins.
Huebner, D. (1999). Language and teaching: Reflections in the light of Heidegger's writing about language (1969). In V. Hillis (Ed.), *The lure of the transcendent: Collected essays by Dwayne E. Huebner* (pp. 143–158). Mahwah, NJ: Lawrence Erlbaum.

Huebner, D. (1999). Spirituality and knowing (1985). In V. Hillis (Ed.), *The lure of the transcendent: Collected essays by Dwayne E. Huebner* (pp. 340–352). Mahwah, NJ: Lawrence Erlbaum.

Huebner, D. (1999). Education and spirituality (1993). In V. Hillis (Ed.), *The lure of the transcendent: Collected essays by Dwayne E. Huebner* (pp. 401–416). Mahwah, NJ: Lawrence Erlbaum.

Huebner, D. (1999). Challenges bequeathed (1996). In V. Hillis (Ed.), *The lure of the transcendent: Collected essays by Dwayne E. Huebner* (pp. 432–446). Mahwah, NJ: Lawrence Erlbaum.

Kabat-Zinn, J. (2005). *Coming to our senses*. New York: Hyperion.

Kerby, A. P. (1991). *Narrative and the self*. Bloomingdale, IN: Indiana University Press.

Le Guin, U. (1989). Some thoughts on narrative. In U. Le Guin (Ed.), *Dancing at the edge of the world: Thoughts on words, women, places* (pp. 37–45). New York: Grove Press.

Lindner, E. (March 19, 2006). An empathetic 'farenji' torn between worlds. *Miami Herald*. Miami, FL.

Lourinc, J. (2007, April). Driven to distraction. *The Walrus, 4*, 50–59.

Maté, G. (2008). *In the realm of hungry ghosts*. Toronto, ON: Alfred A. Knopf Canada.

Mourad, R. (1997). *Postmodern philosophical critique and the pursuit of knowledge in higher education*. Westport, CN: Bergin & Garvey.

Pinar, W. F., Reynolds, W. M., Slattery, P., & Taubman, P. M. (1995). *Understanding curriculum: An introduction to the study of historical and contemporary curriculum discourses*. New York: Peter Lang.

Raymond, J. G. (1986). A vision of female friendship. In J. G. Raymond (Ed.), *A passion for friends: Toward a philosophy of female affection* (pp. 205–241). Boston: Beacon Press.

Rich, A. (1991). *An atlas of the difficult world: Poems 1988–1991*. New York: W.W. Norton.

Ruddick, S. (1996). Reason's "femininity": A case for connected knowing. In N. Goldberger, J. M. Tarule, B. M. Clinchy, & M. F. Belenky (Eds.), *Knowledge, difference and power: Essays inspired by Women's' Ways of Knowing* (pp. 248–273). New York: Basic Books.

Schweikart, P. (1998). Reading ourselves: Toward a feminist theory of reading. In R. C. Davis & R. Schleiffer (Eds.), *Contemporary literary criticism: Literary and cultural studies* (pp. 197–219). New York: Longman.

Siegel, D. J. (2007). *The mindful brain: Reflection and attunement in the cultivation of well-being*. New York: W. W. Norton & Co.

Stanley, S. A. (1994). *The process and development of empathy in educators: A phenomenological inquiry*. Unpublished Doctoral Dissertation, University of Victoria, Victoria, British Columbia.

Zwicky, J. (2004). *Robinson's crossing*. London: Brick Books.

NOTES ON CONTRIBUTORS

Lace Marie Brogden, Ph.D., is Assistant Professor of French education in minority language contexts in the Faculty of Education at the University of Regina, Canada. She began her professional life as a French Immersion teacher and then worked in curriculum for the Official Minority Language Office Branch of Saskatchewan's Ministry of Education. Her research interests include autoethnography, the negotiation of linguistic subjectivities in preservice and inservice teaching contexts, and the impact of architecture(s) on identity performance/production. Among her multiple, shifting identities, Lace is a mother, gardener and sometimes poet.

Douglas Brown is Assistant Professor in the Faculty of Education, University of Regina – Regina, Saskatchewan. Before joining the University of Regina he served at the University of Alberta as well as the University of Lethbridge. He has taught in the areas of educational foundations, social justice and multicultural education, and social studies education. His research focus centres on public policy interpretation, analysis, and the ethic of fairness as specifically applied to dimensions of student 'difference', mainstream educational discourse/curricula design, and inclusive education. He has an applied background in curricula analysis as well as involvement with the design and review of official curricula policy and products. Dr. Brown maintains a dedication to the foundational ethics of inclusive education and social justice and has contributed to a number of campaigns and organizations. He obtained his Ph.D. (international/intercultural education) from the Department of Educational Educational Policy Studies, University of Alberta.

Wendy Donawa is now an itinerant scholar, teaching in BC and Alberta after spending three decades in Barbados as teacher, artist, and museum curator (she designed and installed the Barbados Museum's children's gallery, *Yesterday's Children*). Her dissertation (University of Victoria, 2000) examines post-colonial narratives of women who suggest friendship as a source of identity and moral agency. She is at present co-authoring (with Leah Fowler) *Reading Canada*, a text for teaching Canadian literature in high schools. She lives in Victoria, dividing her time between writing, art, and year-round gardening on her condo balcony. Her poems have appeared in Caribbean and Canadian literary journals, and her poetry chapbook, *Sliding Towards Equinox* (Rubicon Press), will be published in 2009.

Leah C. Fowler is Associate Professor in the Faculty of Education at University of Lethbridge where she teaches undergraduate pre-service teachers and experienced graduate student educators. Her first book, *A Curriculum of Difficulty: Narrative Research in Education and the Practice of Teaching*, was published in 2006 by Peter Lang (New York). She is interested in generative responses to authentic challenges, especially by curriculum theorists such as Dwayne Huebner. One productive way she thinks about those challenges is by engaging qualitative research methodologies (especially interpretive inquiry, such as radical hermeneutics, narrative, and new research epistemologies like phenomenography and a/r/tography). Her research and teaching work centres around Narrative Inquiry, Difficulty in Teaching, Teacher Development (especially of experienced teachers), Curriculum Studies, Canadian Literature, and First Nations (Blackfoot) Teacher Education. Dr. Fowler has two new books being readied for publication: *The T' Ching: Mindful Teaching Amid Difficulty and Change,* and *Reading Canada: Teaching Canadian Fiction in Secondary Schools,* with co-author Dr. Wendy Donawa. As an old biologist and thinker, Dr. Fowler likes to kayak and garden. As a perennial writer, literature, music, Vipassana meditation, art, theatre, film, literature, walking, and gentle, sentient people contribute to her best consciousness.

Erika Hasebe-Ludt is Associate Professor of teacher education in the Faculty of Education at the University of Lethbridge. She teaches and researches in the areas of language and literacy, and curriculum studies. She received her degrees from the Freie Universität Berlin, Germany and the University of British Columbia, Canada. In addition to various articles in edited books and journals, she is the co-editor (with Wanda Hurren) of *Curriculum Intertext: Place/Language/Pedagogy*. She is interested in cosmopolitan and transnational concepts of education and autobiographical and other forms of life writing. Her current research study (with Carl Leggo and Cynthia Chambers and other researchers in British Columbia and Alberta) focuses on investigating life writing as one of the new literacies in Canadian cosmopolitan schooling contexts.

Carl Leggo is a poet and professor in the Department of Language and Literacy Education at the University of British Columbia where he teaches courses in English Education, writing, and narrative research. His poetry and fiction and scholarly essays have been published in many journals in North America and around the world. He is the author of three collections of poems: *Growing Up Perpendicular on the Side of a Hill, View from My Mother's House* (Killick Press, St. John's), and *Come-By-Chance* (Breakwater Books, St. John's), as well as a book about reading and teaching poetry: *Teaching to Wonder: Responding to Poetry in the Secondary Classroom* (Pacific Educational Press, Vancouver). Also, he is a co-editor (with Stephanie Springgay, Rita L. Irwin, and Peter Gouzouasis) of *Being with A/r/tography* (Sense Publishers, Rotterdam), and a co-editor (with Robert Kelly) of *Creative Expression, Creative Education* (Detselig Press, Calgary). He is currently completing a new book titled *Pedagogy of the Heart: Learning to Live Poetically*. He recently became a grandfather—an experience of intimate and ultimate poetic inspiration.

P. J. Lewis is a storyteller-teacher-researcher with a keen interest in story, narrative identity, and storytelling as teaching. He taught as a primary teacher for 18 years before joining the Faculty of Education at the University of Regina. He is

NOTES OF CONTRIBUTORS

an associate professor of Early Childhood Education working with pre-service and inservice teachers. In addition to co-editing this collection he also has various articles in journals and a recent book entitled, *How We Think, but not in School: A Storied Approach to Teaching* published with Sense Publishers.

Karen Meyer is Associate Professor in the Department of Curriculum and Pedagogy at the University of British Columbia. Her teaching and writing engage what she calls 'Living Inquiry', which focuses on awareness of daily life, its structure, content and movement, in order to understand how we, as individuals and communities, interpret and act in the world. Her work in this area has extended to inner-city teachers and young adolescents.

Barbara McNeil is Assistant Professor (Language and Literacy) in the Faculty of Education, University of Regina. Her research interests include student transience, literacy, children's and young adult literature, school librarianship, and second language acquisition.

James McNinch is Associate Professor and Dean of the Faculty of Education at the University of Regina. He started his teaching career teaching English and "typing" in the high school in Lac La Biche, Alberta. He is a past Director of the Saskatchewan Urban Native Teacher Education Programs of the Gabriel Dumont Institute. In 1994 the Saskatchewan School Trustee's Association published his study, *The Recruitment and Retention of Aboriginal Teachers in Saskatchewan Schools*. In 1996 he became Director of the University of Regina's first Teaching Development Centre. He has produced guides for faculty on First Nation and Métis students and on International Students. He also published in the contested field of the use and abuse of student evaluations of teaching. Last year he piloted the university's first graduate course on Teaching and Learning in Higher Education. Since 2003, he has taught an education foundations course on Schooling and Sexual Identities. He is the co-editor of and contributor to the 2004 anthology, *I Could Not Speak My Heart: Education and Social Justice for Gay and Lesbian Youth*. His current research involves interviews with Aboriginal youth who identify as GLBT, queer, questioning or two-spirited.

Valerie Mulholland's interest in the landscape as a site of curriculum can be attributed to the influence of Dr. Wanda Hurren, University of Victoria. Valerie has taught courses in curriculum, language and methods for over ten years at the University of Regina. Her research interests include autobiography in teacher education, language and power, and postcolonial theory in education.

Heather M. Ritenburg lives in Findlater, Saskatchewan, and is a doctoral student and sessional lecturer in the Faculty of Education (Arts Education) at the University of Regina. Her research interests build on 30 years working with children and the arts in public, private, municipal and educational settings, and include the arts as ways of knowing, the distinctive knowing in arts-based inquiries, and relationships in learning.

NOTES OF CONTRIBUTORS

David Geoffrey Smith, Ph.D., is Professor in the Department of Secondary Education at the University of Alberta. He teaches and researches in the areas of Globalization Studies, Curriculum Theory, Pedagogy, and Religious Education. Collections of his published articles can be found in *Pedagon: Interdisciplinary Essays in the Human Sciences, Pedagogy and Culture* (Peter Lang Publishers, 1999), and *Trying to Teach in a Season of Great Untruth: Globalization, Empire and the Crises of Pedagogy* (Sense Publishers, 2006).

Jennifer A. Tupper, Ph.D., is Associate Professor in the Faculty of Education at the University of Regina. She began teaching high school social studies in Edmonton before receiving her graduate degrees from the University of British Columbia and the University of Alberta. Her research interests include curricular spaces as sites of struggle and (dis)empowerment; treaty education as (un)usual narrative; challenging liberal democratic conceptions of universal citizenship; and the complexities of students' understandings of what it might mean to be a citizen. She has published in national and international journals as well as many edited collections of scholarly works. She is passionate about teaching and research, but especially about being a mother to her two beautiful girls, Ayla age 6 and Alise almost 1. They keep her smiling, laughing, and always mindful of the magic and meaningfulness of being.